LOGISTICS AND THE FAILURE OF THE BRITISH ARMY IN AMERICA
1775–1783

R. ARTHUR BOWLER

Logistics and the Failure
OF THE
British Army in America

1775–1783

PRINCETON UNIVERSITY PRESS

PRINCETON, NEW JERSEY

COPYRIGHT © 1975 BY PRINCETON UNIVERSITY PRESS

PUBLISHED BY PRINCETON UNIVERSITY PRESS, PRINCETON AND LONDON

ALL RIGHTS RESERVED

LIBRARY OF CONGRESS CATALOGING IN PUBLICATION DATA WILL
BE FOUND ON THE LAST PRINTED PAGE OF THIS BOOK

THIS BOOK HAS BEEN COMPOSED IN LINOTYPE BASKERVILLE

PRINTED IN THE UNITED STATES OF AMERICA
BY PRINCETON UNIVERSITY PRESS
PRINCETON, NEW JERSEY

For Winifred Margaret Bowler
and for
Max and Esther MacLaggan

PREFACE

THIS IS A STUDY OF THE LOGISTICAL PROBLEMS ENCOUNTERED by the British armies that fought in America during the War of American Independence, and of the effect these problems had on the course of the war. The term "logistics" was not in use in the English language in the eighteenth century and as late as 1929 meant no more than the moving and quartering of troops, the direct derivation from the French *logistique*. Not until the Second World War did the word achieve its more comprehensive meaning. Even so, modern definitions vary; for the purposes of this book that given in the *New Military and Naval Dictionary* (New York, 1951), is used: ". . . the planning and implementation of the production, procurement, storage, transportation, distribution and movement of personnel, supplies and equipment."

This is a specialized rather than a general study of British army logistics during the war. It is specialized first of all in that it deals only with the armies operating in the Thirteen Colonies and Canada and then only with logistical problems and their effect on operations. The other major aspects of army logistics during the war are dealt with in two other books carried out, as this one was, as doctoral theses under the direction of Professor I. R. Christie of University College, London. Norman Baker's *Government and Contractors: The British Treasury and War Supplies, 1774-1783* (London, 1971) deals with the procurement of supplies and equipment in Britain, David Syrett's *Shipping and the American War, 1775-1783* (London, 1970) with the problems of maintaining an adequate communications link between Britain and its armies in

America. The work of these two scholars has been used extensively in this book; for the full story of British army logistics the reader is referred to those studies as well as the present one.

This book has other limitations. First, while medical services are usually considered a part of logistics, no attempt has been made to deal with that subject in any comprehensive way. Some details related to health, such as the efforts to obtain fresh provisions to ward off the scurvy that inevitably came as a result of a continuous diet of salt rations, are necessarily included. But hospitals and pharmaceuticals, and the efficiency of the former and the efficacy of the latter, must be left to a specialist in medical history.

Source material has also imposed a limitation. Every historian is aware of the importance of personality when it comes to the commanders who initiate strategy and tactics, but it is often forgotten that personality also plays a part at other and lower levels of the army organization. The amount of material pertinent to this study that survived the vicissitudes of the damp basements and musty closets of British administrative departments until its value was recognized in the nineteenth century is truly amazing. Only the completeness of departmental records allowed the preparation of the continuous graph of the army's food situation given in Appendix I. But the logistical services of the army were run by men, and with a few minor exceptions we know nothing about them. They survive, for the most part, only in their official correspondence, with but an occasional private letter signed with a sobriquet or a first name to reveal private as well as public thoughts or even to give the lie to the apparent formality of the age. In armies as small as those operating in North America, with staff sections much smaller than would be the case with modern armies of the same size, personalities and their harmonies and conflicts must have played a considerable part in determining the course of events. Yet of this we know very little.

A note about passages quoted here from eighteenth-century manuscript sources is in order. Eighteenth-century writers did not feel bound by rules of punctuation and capitalization in the way later generations have. Sentences, particularly in manuscripts, end as often with dashes, semi-colons, and colons as with periods, and capitalized words are scattered without definite order. I have taken the liberty, in these two respects, of modernizing the passages quoted.

This book is the product of several years' work on two continents. During those years I contracted many debts that can never be repaid but must be acknowledged. First, I must thank Professor S. F. Wise of Carleton University, Ottawa. Without his example, help, and encouragement through undergraduate and graduate studies, I would never have got to the point of writing a work such as this. I am indebted also to Professor I. R. Christie of University College, London, who suggested this study at a most critical time for me and under whose direction it was carried out. Professor Norman Baker of the State University of New York at Buffalo and Professor David Syrett of Queen's College, New York, also have my sincere thanks. Their books, mentioned earlier, preceded mine, and their freely shared knowledge of the intricacies of British administration in the eighteenth century made my work easier. Dr. Richard Middleton of University College, Belfast, a student of army administration in the Seven Years' War, very kindly read my chapter on administrative organization and made a number of valuable suggestions. Professors Franklin Wickwire and Mary Wickwire of the University of Massachusetts, as well as sharing their extensive knowledge of Lord Cornwallis and his campaigns, provided moral support throughout the whole period of the preparation of the book. Insofar as this study is successful it is in part due to the kindness of these people, although, of course, they bear no responsibility for its failings.

I am also indebted to the staffs of the many libraries and

document repositories where I worked so long for their kindness, patience, and help, but I must particularly mention those of the Public Record Office, the British Museum, the W. L. Clements Library at Ann Arbor, Michigan, and the New-York Historical Society. Special thanks must also be extended to the Honourable Charles Strutt of Berwick Place, Hatfield Peverel, Essex, England, for opening his home and the papers of Francis Rush Clark to me, and to Mrs. Julia A. Thompson of New York City for permission to use the microfilm copies of the papers of Staats Morris Dyckman in the New-York Historical Society.

Finally, it must be pointed out that this book could never have been undertaken without the financial assistance provided by a McLaughlin Travelling Fellowship from Queen's University, Kingston, Ontario, a Canada Council Predoctoral Fellowship, and a research grant from the State University of New York at Buffalo.

Buffalo, N.Y.
1973

CONTENTS

xi

ABBREVIATIONS

Add. Mss.	British Museum, Additional Manuscripts
ADM	Admiralty Papers, Public Record Office
AO	Audit Office Papers, Public Record Office
BAHQP	British Army Headquarters Papers (microfilm, State University of New York at Buffalo. Originals in Public Record Office)
CP	Clinton Papers, W. L. Clements Library
HMC	Historical Manuscripts Commission
HSP	Historical Society of Pennsylvania
N-YHS	New-York Historical Society
PRO	Public Record Office
RAI	Royal Artillery Institution, Woolwich
SRO	Scottish Record Office
T	Treasury Papers, Public Record Office
WO	War Office Papers, Public Record Office

LOGISTICS AND THE FAILURE OF THE
BRITISH ARMY IN AMERICA
1775–1783

INTRODUCTION

WHEN ASKED BY GEORGE WASHINGTON TO TAKE UP THE POST
of quartermaster general for the American army, General
Nathaniel Greene at first demurred. "Who," he asked, "ever
heard of a Quarter Master in History as such?"[1] Greene
was an ambitious man and his point was well taken. In
the study of warfare, logistics and military administration
have been neglected stepchildren. Since human society began, minstrels and historians have told over and again the
exploits of men on the field of battle while condemning to
limbo by the process of neglect the more prosaic activities
of contractors, commissaries, quartermasters, subtlers, and
administrators generally. Victories and defeats are seen only
in terms of such factors as training, generalship, numerical
strength, and luck. Even the great Sir John Fortescue could
not cast this veil from his eyes.[2] Only in the present century,
when the full application of the industrial revolution to
warfare has resulted in the consumption of staggering
quantities of materiel and hence made it brutally clear that
sound logistics and intelligent administration can mean the
difference between victory and defeat, have historians come
to consider this aspect of war seriously. The result, although
much remains to be done, has been such impressive studies
as R. G. Albion's *Forests and Sea Power* (Cambridge, Mass.,
1926), R. Glover's *Peninsular Preparation* (Cambridge,
1963), R. E. Scouller's *The Armies of Queen Anne* (Oxford,

[1] M. F. Treacy, *Prelude to Yorktown* (Chapel Hill, N.C., 1963), 29.
[2] J. W. Fortescue, *A History of the British Army* (London, 1902).
Fortescue compresses all the administrative problems Britain faced
in the American war into a simple condemnation of "Germain with his
blindness to facts" (vol. III, 397).

3

1966), and J. A. Huston's *The Sinews of War* (Washington, 1966).

If the history of military administration generally has suffered from neglect, that of the British army during the American Revolution has been doubly cursed. While the American side of the war has undergone the minutest investigation from Lexington to the final evacuation of New York, the British side has been, with equal thoroughness, neglected. Only recently have such books as Piers Mackesy's *The War for America* (London, 1964), William Willcox's *Portrait of a General* (New York, 1964), and Franklin and Mary Wickwire's *Cornwallis* (Boston, 1970) begun adequately to probe the reasons for the British defeat. But despite these heartening trends one great myth about the war remains, that implicit in William Willcox's rhetorical question, "Why were the British such fools as to be defeated?"[3] This is the myth of the British "military machine" which remains despite the pioneering work of E. E. Curtis in his *Administration of the British Army during the American Revolution* (New York, 1926). The myth sets up the British army as the finest fighting force of its day, a war machine that normally rolled over the opposition. So set up it serves as a foil against which, on the one side, the astounding effects of liberty on the fighting qualities of the American yeomanry and the generalship of Washington and Greene can be extolled, and, on the other, the total inadequacy of Howe, Clinton, and Germain can be exposed.

It is the purpose of this work to investigate the idea of the invincible fighting machine. The premise on which it is based is that an army, to be an effective fighting force, must be adequately fed, clothed, housed, transported, and serviced generally. This is not, of course, to deny that the fighting qualities of either British or American soldiers had

[3] W. B. Willcox, "Why did the British lose the American Revolution" (*University of Michigan Alumnus Quarterly Review*, LXII, Summer 1956), 317.

any effect on the outcome of the war. Nor is it meant to supersede the conclusions of Mackesy respecting administrative and strategic confusion in Britain and the problems of war aims, or the conclusions of Willcox, the Wickwires, and others respecting the quality of British generalship. These were all critical factors in determining the outcome of the war. Rather, this book seeks to demonstrate that the fighting efficiency of an army is very often a function of its logistical efficiency and to point out where logistical and administrative problems in America affected the course of the war.

Although the word was not coined until recently, logistics has been an integral part of warfare since men first organized to do battle with each other. A mark of successful commanders has always been their ability to choose outstanding officers to administer logistics. In the Middle Ages the task, if not easy, was at least relatively simple; the feudal levy provided its own arms and the unlucky countryside through which it marched was ravaged to feed men and animals: logistics was basically the organization of marches. The introduction of firearms and professional soldiers changed things somewhat, but the real development of the field did not come until the late seventeenth century. That era, with its growing nationalism and general pattern of bureaucratic growth, saw the creation of the modern army. From collections of hired mercenary bands, armies became long-service professional corps, made up of various arms, whose officers were commissioned by the state. The command structure that still exists today came into being then. With the army the complete creature of the state, its logistics, in the interests of uniformity and efficiency, became also a state function. Further, the development of linear tactics acted at the same time to make logistics a more vital concern. To bring men to stand up in ordered ranks on the field of battle and deliver and receive volleys required long training in intricate formation movements and the instillation of stern discipline. It seldom took less than two years to transform a raw recruit into a competent soldier. Such a soldier, although little respected as a person, was a valuable investment. As such it was important that he be well clothed and armed, properly housed in time of peace, and when campaigning supplied with the paraphernalia of a reasonably healthful life in the open. For this same reason, as well also because of the eighteenth-century humanistic idea that civilians in war areas should not be left destitute by the passage of scavenging armies and to reduce soldiers' opportunities for desertion, it was desirable that the supplying of food and forage cease to be a matter of unit or individual enterprise.[4] All of these considerations, then, brought about the development of logistical organizations at least as complex as the military organizations they supported.

Nevertheless, it is tempting in these days of elephantine vehicles, nuclear artillery, airborne infantry, and moveable ports and airfields to think of eighteenth-century army logistics as simple and relatively unimportant. To do so is self-deception. Rommel's observation that before the fighting proper the battle is won or lost by quartermasters[5] is as applicable to the eighteenth century as to our own time. The needs of the eighteenth-century army were indeed few and small when compared to those of a modern army, but in relation to the facilities available to satisfy them and the ability of government to command and organize those facilities, they bulked as large as the needs of a modern army. Further, during the American Revolution Britain supported an unprecedented number of troops overseas—over 92,000 at one point, including those in the Floridas and the West Indies.[6] For the most part those troops had to be

---

[4] R. A. Preston, S. F. Wise, and H. O. Werner, *Men in Arms* (2d ed., New York, 1962), 129-146.

[5] Eric Robson, *The American Revolution in its Political and Military Aspects, 1763-1783* (New York, 1966), quoted on p. 102.

[6] Norman Baker, *Government and Contractors: The British Treasury and War Supplies, 1775-1783* (London, 1971), 4. This was the peak

not only equipped but also fed from Britain. And if the eighteenth-century commander did not have to think in terms of the bulk, variety, and complexity of material demanded by the modern army, neither does the twentieth-century commander have to face the incredible problems of supplying troops over a 3,000-mile supply line harried not merely by the enemy but also by the wind or the lack of it, nor those of preserving and stockpiling food in the era before the tin can.

In any case, the needs of the British armies that fought in America during the Revolution were by no means simple. Beginning with the basic uniform, the personal needs of the soldier ran through such predictable items as boots, shirts, stockings, leggings, and coats to the more esoteric weskit, shoebuckles, stocks, rollers, epaulettes, and sashes. The expected replacement period for most of these items was, even in times of peace, one year. And uniforms were just the beginning. The eighteenth-century commander, reluctant to subject his small and expensive army to the rigors of cold-weather campaigning, considered the winter as a period of rest and recuperation. In Europe an army could be provided for at this season by billeting the soldiers on the hapless civilians of numerous towns and cities, but this was not possible in thinly populated America. Hence barracks were usually necessary, equipped with beds and bedding, stoves, lanterns, and fireplace equipment, and supplied with coal, wood, and candles. For periods spent in the field an entirely different set of equipment was needed, including tents of various sizes, camp kettles, axes, haversacks, knapsacks, water bottles, and water decks. Again little was expected to survive for a second campaign. The cavalry, of course, required not only the above but a whole range of equipment for outfitting, controlling, and caring for their mounts and considerable special equipment for themselves.

---

year of 1780-1781. In 1776 supplies for about 60,000 were contracted for. The supplies were for British, German, and Provincial forces.

Then, both men and horses had to eat. In the eighteenth century the staples of the British soldier's diet were bread and meat and his daily ration one pound of the former and either one pound of beef or nine ounces of pork. In addition to these basics he was entitled also to a number of "small species" issued on a weekly basis. He received eight ounces of oatmeal and either butter or cheese and three pints of pease as well as an occasional issue of rice at the rate of one ounce a day.[7] Considerations of morale and of the health of an army in the field and operating in a cold climate led during the American Revolution to a number of special issues. Rum, previously considered as a reward for arduous duty, came to be a daily issue at the rate of a quart for each six men. It was apparently considered as a water purifier for its use was usually justified as being necessary for the health of the troops.[8] In the field the ration was mixed in each soldier's canteen of water under the supervision of sergeants. The ever-present threat of scurvy led to several special issues. For the winter of 1775-1776 some 468,750 gallons of porter were provided for the 12,000 men at Boston—almost a quart per day for each man from October through March.[9] Porter, however, was soon replaced by spruce beer brewed in America. Concocted of a fermented mixture of spruce essence (extracted by boiling spruce needles), molasses, and water, it was at first sold to regiments at the rate of 4/6 per barrel and later issued at the rate of three to four quarts per man per day. Sauerkraut and vinegar shipped from Britain and fresh vegetables grown in every available space within the army posts were also considered necessary to the soldier's health. The extent of the food requirements of the army on the American coast alone can be judged from quantities that passed through the hands of Commissary General Daniel Wier

---

[7] T 1/550, 405-406. At various times and places this varied in one or more items but it was the basic ration.

[8] Add. Mss. 38,343, 61-62, "Observations on the Extraordinaries."

[9] T 1/513, 140-149, Mure, Son & Atkinson to Howe, 25 Sept. 75.

from 27 May 1777 to 11 November 1781: 79,465,184 pounds of bread, flour, and rice; 10,711,820 pounds of salt beef and 38,202,081 pounds of salt pork as well as 3,093,952 pounds of fresh meat; 3,997,043 pounds of butter; 7,282,071 pounds of oatmeal; 427,452 bushels of pease; 176,672 gallons of molasses; 134,378 gallons of vinegar; and 2,865,782 gallons of rum.[10]

The diet of draft animals and cavalry horses made up in bulk what it lacked in variety. A working horse, depending on size, required up to twenty pounds of hay and nine of oats a day as well as green grazing in season. Thus the 4,000 or so horses that the armies on the average maintained from 1776 required annually some 14,000 tons of hay and 6,000 of oats.

Weapons, of course, were another whole area of supply; they began with the infantryman's Brown Bess. The soldier was also equipped with bayonet, scabbard, and cartridge box as well as cleaning equipment and cartridges. The cavalry required another set of equipment including carbines with their buckles, swivels and straps, pistols and holsters, and swords, scabbards, and sword belts. Artillery was another special field with a large range of requirements. Guns ranged from the light field pieces that accompanied infantry units to the incredibly heavy twenty-four and thirty-two pounders that loured from the embrasures of permanent fortifications, and each required its own handling and servicing equipment.

In addition to equipment the armies in America required a broad range of services, themselves complex and requiring a considerable range of skills and equipment. There had first to be organizations for the procurement and distribution of the equipment and supplies mentioned above. While most procurement was through contract with civilian firms in Britain, it had to be organized and there still remained the task of organizing ships, warehouses, docks,

---

[10] AO 3/224, "A General Account of provisions, Rum &c Received, Issued and Expended by Daniel Wier Esq. . . ."

purchasing agents, packers, coopers, shippers, clerks, and laborers by the hundred. Further, since some of the food and other supplies consumed by the armies in America was procured in America, a whole range of tradesmen from butchers to woodcutters were regularly employed there.

Transportation was one of the most important service requirements. This meant an establishment of thousands of horses, hundreds of wagons, and an armada of small ships. The wagon transport service, which controlled the bulk of the army's horse population, was responsible for the transportation of provisions, stores, and special equipment during land operations and for the normal transportation needs of the garrisons. Duties as mundane as the transportation of food and fuel between the various parts of the garrison complex at New York City, and as romantic as the carrying of dispatches and the moving of raiding parties, kept a fleet of small ships busy. The operation of this transportation service required not only the vehicles themselves and teamsters and sailors, but also support facilities and a whole cast of repair and maintenance men. Carpenters, wagon makers, wheelwrights, collar and harness makers, blacksmiths, and stable men crowded every major British base, and the army shipyard at New York City employed men in every trade concerned with ship building and ship maintenance.

Engineering services were also required on a grand scale. Primarily employed in the construction of the fortifications of varying complexity that sprouted like ugly mushrooms every time an army paused for more than a few days, the engineers nevertheless also carried on such regular chores as the erection of barracks and bridges and the maintenance of services in occupied cities.

The logistical needs of the army that fought in America, then, were not inconsiderable. Britain, of course, had long experience in the maintenance of overseas forces, most recently during the incredibly successful Seven Years' War (1756-1763) when she fielded forces in India, the Caribbean,

America, and Europe. During that war much of the organizational structure that was to last through the American war took form. The first task of this book will be to examine that organization and its development as the war progressed.

I

The Logistical Organization

THE PROVISION OF THE GOODS AND SERVICES REQUIRED BY THE British army in America during the American Revolution was a huge task, and one for which neither the army nor the British government was well prepared. The importance of the navy to the very existence of the nation had long since led to the development under the Lords Commissioners of the Admiralty of a permanent command structure and a complete logistical service, but the British army in the eighteenth century had developed very little above the regimental level. It was considered primarily a peacekeeping force rather than an instrument for making war, and was normally scattered throughout the kingdom in regimental or smaller units. No general staff as it is known today existed. Such central direction as the army received came from the cabinet, which set policy and determined strategy. When a situation requiring an army arose, an appropriate number of regiments were collected and a commander-in-chief and staff appointed. When the situation was resolved, the army and its staff were dispersed. The commander-in-chief received his instructions from the cabinet via the secretary of state in whose area of competence he was operating. If Britain itself was threatened, then a commander-in-chief for the home forces was appointed, as General Lord Amherst was in 1778 when the French entered the American war. He sat in the cabinet and participated in its decisions, but his military authority was confined to the home forces except insofar as he was also in charge of the War Office.

The War Office was the army's only permanent institution above the regimental level. Its concern, however, was little more than the administrative and financial affairs of the regiments. Its importance was indicated by the fact that except in periods where there was a commander-in-chief of the home forces, it came under the direction of a civilian politician without cabinet rank, the secretary at war.[1]

The problem with this organization—if it may be flattered with that name—was lack of continuity and professional direction. In each war the process of building up a general staff from officers who had not thought beyond the regimental level since the last war had to be repeated.[2] Further, the execution of strategic aims established by the cabinet was entrusted to a civilian, the secretary of state, who in turn directed the commander-in-chief in the field. The secretary of state might have had military experience, as did Germain, the American secretary during the greater part of the American war, but he did not have an organization behind him that was experienced in the direction of armies.

The logistical organization was equally undeveloped. Over time a number of government departments had acquired responsibility for providing material and services required by the army. The War Office had charge of medical supplies, uniforms, and camp equipment, a function it carried out for the regiments in peace as well as the armies in war. For the most part, however, it did nothing more than lay down standards of quality, design, and quantity, leaving the actual responsibility for furnishing the items to the commanders of regiments, who in turn worked through

[1] Piers Mackesy, *The War for America, 1775-1783* (London, 1964), 12-17.

[2] Most general officers held rank for a particular area of operations only: thus most of those who served in America held rank "in America only." Even those who did have permanent rank were not regularly employed in peacetime except insofar as they were also colonels of regiments, although on infrequent occasions they might be called together to sit on boards of general officers to consider specific military problems placed before them by the King or the War Office.

agents in London. In peace time, with the army living in barracks and seldom if ever engaged in field exercises of any kind, little beyond uniforms and personal equipment was required. This system of regimental responsibility was maintained even through 1774 and 1775 when an army that needed tents and field equipment of all kinds was assembled at Boston.[3] By the end of the latter year, the problems in ordering, collecting, and transporting these goods was beyond regimental control, and the War Office had to take over this task for all the regiments serving in America.[4]

The major responsibility for supplying the army, however, fell on the Treasury department. Even in the area of clothing, equipment, and medical supplies it was expected to look after the German and Provincial troops as the War Office looked after the regular British regiments. By far the Treasury's most onerous duty, though, was supplying food—a traditional responsibility that had never been very demanding until the Seven Years' War. The army was normally scattered about the British Isles in detachments each of which looked after its own feeding. Only on occasions when parts of the army were called together into encampments did the Treasury become involved and then only in supplying bread, although it also had to provide firewood and forage. In wartime, armies abroad were expected to find their own food locally, and the Treasury's responsibility was increased only insofar as encampments increased in frequency and usually included large numbers of militia. The conditions under which the armies serving in America had to operate during the Seven Years' War enormously increased the Treasury's task. The campaigns of that war took the army into remote areas of wilderness or of sparse population, where there was no possibility of

[3] BAHQP, 10,437, Howe Orderly Book, 13 Aug, 17 & 18 Nov 75; WO 36/3.

[4] T 1/514, 181-182, Barrington to Col. Roy, 14 Oct 75; T 29/46, 15 Aug 77.

obtaining supplies locally. Everything needed had to be collected in distant areas and transported to the army. The problems of organization on that scale finally forced the Treasury to become involved. For the first time it took up the task of contracting for provisions and ensuring their delivery. Although most of the food eventually came from the old settled parts of the Thirteen Colonies, for a time considerable quantities had to be shipped from Britain.[5] When the decision was made to maintain a permanent force in America after the war, the Treasury's responsibility remained. In the period from 1760 to 1775, however, a system worked out during the Seven Years' War prevailed. The Treasury negotiated contracts with London firms for supplying the troops in specific areas. These firms in turn usually subcontracted with American merchants who actually collected, delivered, and issued the rations.

The system worked well enough in peace time but collapsed entirely when, on the outbreak of fighting at Boston, Rebel organizations throughout the Thirteen Colonies began intercepting supplies destined for the army. Thus, from the spring of 1775, provisions contractors had to rely on British sources of supply. In the first year of the crisis the Treasury still called on the contractors to deliver the provisions to the army, but serious incursions on the supply fleets by Rebel privateers and a severe shortage of shipping led it reluctantly to take on this task itself in 1776. A collection and storage depot, where contractors made their deliveries, was established at Cork under the direction of a Treasury commissary, Robert Gordon. There provisions collected from all over the British Isles were received, inspected, and loaded into the victualling transports hired by the Treasury. Armed with cannon (supplied by the Ordnance Board and manned often by troop replacements for the army) to protect them from privateers, the victual-

[5] S. M. Pargellis, *Lord Loudoun in America* (New Haven, 1933), 67, 233.

lers were dispatched singly or in groups as they were loaded.[6] Although the Treasury regularly protested, with good reason, its own incompetence as a shipping agent,[7] this task remained with the department until 1779, when it was assumed by the Navy Board.

The organization of the supply of food, clothing, and personal and camp equipment was by far the major logistical task of the Treasury, but it was by no means the only one. In the period immediately before the war the barrack master's department at Boston ordered the various supplies it required through the Boston merchant firm of John and George Ewing. By the early fall of 1775, however, the London agents of this firm reported that they were unable to execute the orders placed with them, and the Treasury was forced to take up this responsibility also.[8] The demands of this department included iron cooking pots for each barrack room, axes, stoves, and fire iron sets, but the most burdensome requirement was for bedding, candles, and fuel. Beds, each of which accommodated two enlisted men, were supplied with a paillasse, two sheets, two blankets, and a rug. Although the main requisition for these items came early in the war—as in 1776, for instance, when 52,000 blankets were ordered[9]—replacements in the order of 10,000 rugs and blankets a year were required.[10] Fuel, except for some futile attempts to ship coal from England in the early years of the war, was obtained by the barrack department in America, but candles were another matter and each year some sixty-three tons were procured and shipped to the army.[11]

Numerous less demanding tasks also fell to the Treasury.

[6] Add. Mss. 38,343, "Observations on the Extraordinaries."

[7] The Treasury did not actually hire the ships itself. It employed Mure, Son & Atkinson to do this.

[8] T 27/31, 53-54, Robinson to Howe, 9 Sept 75.

[9] WO 1/890, "General abstract of the Ordinary and Extraordinary Camp Necessaries."

[10] T 64/110, 113, 273.

[11] T 64/108, 117; T 64/109, 103; BAHQP, 1,115.

When, for instance, General Howe requested a wagon train for the army, the request was passed on to that department. The Treasury turned to the Ordnance Office for the actual procurement of wagons, harness, and horses, but retained responsibility for the train,[12] appointing a superintendent, hiring drivers and conductors, and arranging transportation to America.[13]

Finally, in the list of logistical tasks assigned to the Treasury were those of supplying the army in America with the money it required and, in coordination with the War Office, contracting for medical supplies. Since this study is not concerned with the medical side of the army, except insofar as diet was a medical problem, the latter responsibility need not be discussed here. Money, however, was required for the procurement of a multitude of goods and services in America as well as for army pay, and the supply of this most necessary article remained a major responsibility of the Treasury. To fulfill this responsibility the Treasury contracted with the London firm of Harley and Drummond. Prior to 1775 virtually all the money that the army in North America required could be obtained by the sale in America of bills drawn on London. When informed by the deputy paymaster in America that cash was required, the commander-in-chief requested an appropriate amount from Harley and Drummond, informing the Treasury at the same time. Harley and Drummond then applied to the Paymaster in London, who issued them with a draft on the Bank of England. At this point Harley and Drummond then directed their agents in North America to sell bills drawn on them, and the cash thus raised was turned over to the deputy paymaster. Although slow, the system worked smoothly and, indeed, to some profit since the chronic imbalance of trade between America and Britain meant that there was usually a premium on London bills in America. Only on rare occasions, when specie ran short in the colo-

12 T 29/45, 19 Jan 76.
13 T 64/106, 45; T 1/537, 137-138.

nies and London bills sold at a discount, was it necessary to send out cash. On those occasions Harley and Drummond were responsible for the more difficult task of collecting the necessary specie. The Treasury then arranged for its transportation to America on board a warship. With the war, the situation rapidly reversed itself. The suspension of trade drastically reduced the normal inflow of specie into the colonies and what was there, especially in the British-held enclaves, quickly drained out to pay for food and other necessities, or went into private hordes to serve as hedges against the economic perils of war. Further, beyond the British enclaves a decree of Congress forbade Americans accepting British army bills.[14] In this situation the discount on government bills could and did rise to fifteen percent and higher and at times it was impossible to sell them at all.[15] To bring the exchange rate down and keep it down required the continuous infusion of large quantities of specie. In the first year of the war alone, from June 1775 to June 1776, over half a million pounds in specie was shipped to the army and the amount increased in later years. From 1770 to 1783, the period of their contract, Harley and Drummond supplied the army with £17,002,598-4-2 in specie and bills, all but a small part of it during the war period.[16]

The Board of Ordnance, of course, also played a vital part in army logistics. It was responsible for supplying not only arms and ammunition for the whole army but also all of the clothing and equipment needs of the engineers and the artillery, both of which came under its control. The needs of these two arms included not only such obvious items as artillery pieces and all the equipment needed to service and transport them but also such items as axes, pick-axes, shovels, mobile forges, and shoes for artillery horses.

[14] CO 5/92, 231, Gage to Dartmouth, 24 July 75.

[15] T 64/106, 14-16, Robinson to Howe, 1 Oct 76, Clinton to [Eden] 10 Jan 79.

[16] Baker, *Government and Contractors*, 176.

The last of the government departments with a major involvement in army logistics was the Navy Board. From the very beginning of the war, this division of the Admiralty supplied, on demand, transports to carry troops, camp equipment, clothing, horses, quartermaster's stores, and a variety of other items to the army in America.[17] In March 1779 it also took over from the Treasury the much more onerous responsibility of organizing the shipment of food and forage to the army.[18] It was expected at first that the Board could limit its task to the procurement of ships and the organization of convoys, leaving the reception and inspection of provisions to the Treasury. This division of authority, however, proved to be unworkable. Robert Gordon, the Treasury commissary at Cork, and Lieutenant Stephen Harris, the Navy Board representative there, soon came to loggerheads, with the result that the whole organization was turned over to the Board.[19] A short time later, as a measure to relieve the long-standing problem of congestion at Cork, a second victualling depot was established at Cowes on the Isle of Wight. Cork continued to be the center for shipments to the army on the American seaboard while Cowes handled provisions for Canada, the West Indies, and West Florida.[20]

This transfer of authority from the Treasury to the Navy Board was judicious. The Navy Board had long experience in the handling of provisions and the organization of shipping, while the Treasury, despite three years at this task, still had much to learn. It also made sense to eliminate competition in the hiring of shipping and to call the experience of the navy to the service of the army. Further, France came into the war in 1778, and with the French navy rather than just American privateers to contend with, it was clear that the safety of victuallers could no longer be assured by arming them with a few pieces of ordnance.

---

[17] D. Syrett, *Shipping and the American War, 1775-1783* (London, 1970), 181.

[18] *Ibid.*, 135-139.   [19] *Ibid.*, 140-142.   [20] *Ibid.*, 143.

Convoys guarded by the Royal Navy had become necessary and the navy was the obvious agency to organize them. The new system went through some serious teething problems, so serious that Germain was led at one point to request that the Treasury resume its old responsibilities,[21] but these were overcome, and by the middle of 1781 the troubles that had plagued supply from Britain since the beginning of the war virtually came to an end.

But the procurement of supplies and their transportation to America was only one aspect of army logistics. Not only had there to be a distribution organization with the army but also facilities for procurement since some supplies could be obtained only in America. Further, logistics involves services as well as supplies and hence service departments. The basic organization of the logistical services with the army was a holdover from the Seven Years' War. Under normal circumstances the army that served in America during that war would have been returned to England and resolved into its regimental components, and its staff and service organization dismissed. However, the decision to maintain a force in America after 1763 was, in administrative terms at least, a decision to maintain an army in being. Although the staff and services that thus persisted were small, as befitted the size of the force, they became the basis of the logistical service of the Revolutionary War period. At the heart of the service were four extensive departments: quartermaster, commissary, barrack master, and engineer.

The senior department was that headed by the quartermaster general. It would be misleading, however, to equate the quartermaster general of the twentieth century with the man who held the appointment of the same name in a British army of the eighteenth century; there are distinct similarities in their functions but even more striking differences. The quartermaster general of today is the chief supply officer of the army, while the eighteenth century offi-

21 T 27/33, 203-204, Robinson to Knox, 3 Aug 80.

cer had a dichotomous role. On the one hand he was an administrative officer, responsible for the field equipment and transportation of the army. On the other hand, however, he was also a command officer, often the most trusted member of the commander-in-chief's "family." In this role he usually had charge of a division in battle, and was responsible for intelligence, the organization of the movements of the army, and the selection and laying out of campsites. This dichotomy came out of the development of the office. The quartermaster general first appears in a British army organization in 1689, combining the functions of the two earlier offices of scoutmaster general and provost marshal general, and shortly thereafter also took on the responsibility for intelligence and army movements.[22] Not surprisingly these duties led in turn to direct responsibility for field and transportation equipment, and a quartermaster general's department with a hierarchy of personnel, and storehouses, stables, repair shops, and accounting offices gradually came into being. By the mid-eighteenth century, with armies more and more encumbered with equipment, supplies, and vehicles, it had become impossible for a QMG personally to fill both his command and administrative roles. The latter thus came in practice to be almost completely exercised by one or more deputies. Indeed, by the time of the American Revolution the quartermaster general had become the prototype of the chief of staff. He retained the responsibility for the QMG department (and hence the pay and prerogatives of office) but exercised little more than a vague supervisory function in it. Brigadier General Sir William Erskine, who served for almost three years as QMG to Howe and Clinton, was one of the new breed. Although he was appointed to the office in September 1776, his command duties kept him so busy that he did not take over the department accounts or even attempt to familiarize himself with the administrative side of his

[22] R. W. Scouller, *The Armies of Queen Anne* (Oxford, 1966), 62.

duties until early 1777.[23] Even when formally installed in the administrative side of his office though, Erskine spent very little time at the department headquarters at New York. He went on the Pennsylvania campaign in 1777-1778 and on his return commanded several small expeditions, such as that against Danforth, Connecticut, in 1778. During the winter of 1778-1779 he commanded a large detachment based at the east end of Long Island. The heavy duties of his office having impaired his health, Erskine returned to England in September 1779[24] and was replaced temporarily by Major Lord William Cathcart, who held the office until the end of March 1780. Erskine's permanent replacement was Brigadier General William Dalrymple, colonel of the 14th Regiment, of Boston Massacre fame. Although Dalrymple had little opportunity to demonstrate his talents in the field, he nevertheless spent little time in the administrative side of his duties either. Clinton sent him to England in the fall of 1780 to persuade Germain to remove Admiral Arbuthnot from the naval command in North America, a task that occupied almost a year.[25] Then in the early months of 1782 he led a British team in negotiations with the Americans for the exchange of prisoners.

Perhaps nothing better demonstrates the dual nature of the quartermaster general's office than the history of the department in America. Formed during the Seven Years' War, it continued in existence after 1763 to serve the force remaining in North America. With the end of the war, however, the command functions of the department ceased and only the administrative remained, and the senior officer in the department until 1775 was the deputy quartermaster general. The holder of that office in 1775 was Major (later Lieutenant Colonel) William Shirreff, and although Howe professed himself satisfied with Shirreff's perform-

23 Add. Mss. 21,680, Hutcheson to Haldimand, 5 Jan 77.

24 B. A. Uhlendorf (ed. & trans.), *The Revolution in America* (New Brunswick, N.J., 1959), 269.

25 W. B. Willcox, *Portrait of a General* (New York, 1964), 355.

ance, he nevertheless appointed Erskine as quartermaster general in September 1776 because ". . . for an active campaign in the field where operations will be more extensive, it may require an officer of more experience in the higher duties of that department. . . ."[26]

But while the "higher duties" of the department demanded skills and experience that Shirreff did not possess, the administrative functions that the deputy quartermaster general performed were nevertheless extensive and demanding. With the commencement of war the QMG department became the largest service department in the army, the extent of whose functions may in part be judged by its expenditures. Even as late as 1774 the total expenses in the department, which at that time included Canada, over a six-month period were only £6,000.[27] From mid-1775 to mid-1782, however, total expenses exclusive of Canada were £1,939,460, an average of £137,109 in each six-month period.[28]

A wide variety of tasks fell to the QMG department. It was responsible for the ordering, issuing, and care and maintenance of the camp and field equipment of the army and, for the first year of the war, supplied forage for the army's horses. A departmental account book covering the period 1777-1782 indicates that the department also undertook to provide a number of city services at New York and Philadelphia, including the maintenance of roads, dykes, bridges, lights, and fire engines and that it managed a number of large gardens that provided fresh vegetables for the army.[29]

The most extensive duty of the QMG department, how-

[26] CO 5/92, 321, Howe to Dartmouth, 26 Nov 75.

[27] T 64/101, 34-39; AO 1/336/1344, Accounts of Lt. Col. William Shirreff.

[28] These figures are drawn from the accounts of the various QMGs and DQMGs in the Audit Office Records. Quartermasters were responsible for the distribution of batt, baggage, and forage money and this appears in their accounts. It is not included in the total given above.

[29] N-YHS, British QMG Account Book, 1777-1782.

ever, was that of providing land transport. At the beginning of the war, the army obtained the horses and wagons it needed by hiring them (or impressing them if the situation warranted) from civilians on an as-needed basis. This policy continued through 1776 despite the arrival in that year of the wagon train dispatched from England by the Treasury. The horses in that train suffered the fate of most livestock submitted to an Atlantic crossing at that time. Of the 845 horses embarked in England in June 1776, only 478 survived to land in New York on October 29, and they were in such poor condition that 165 more died before the end of the following February.[30] Of the wagons, few seem to have seen any service. They were, it was claimed, too heavy for American conditions.[31]

The casual hiring policy came under severe test during the American attack on Trenton and Princeton in December 1776. As usual, most of the wagons employed during the previous campaign had been dismissed when the army moved into winter quarters and in the confused and dangerous situation following the American attack it proved impossible to reassemble them; great quantities of stores and equipment and even a number of wounded men had to be abandoned for want of transportation.[32] Thus in the spring of 1777 Howe ordered the QMG to establish a more dependable wagon service.[33] The new system set up by Erskine still involved hired wagons and drivers, but they were under a continuing contract, and to provide flexibility the quartermaster supplied provisions for both men and beasts. Maintenance of horses and wagons was the respon-

[30] WO 60/32, "Return of Horses embarked June 1776 at Portsmouth for America." Of the remaining horses, 213 died or were captured before the end of 1777.

[31] New-York Historical Society, *Collections*, 1916, "Minute Book of a Board of General Officers of the British Army in New York, 1781," 74-76.

[32] Uhlendorf, 41; W. S. Stryker, *The Battles of Trenton and Princeton* (New York, 1898), 399-400.

[33] N-YHS, "Board of General Officers," 72, 74-76.

sibility of the owners, but it was provided, nevertheless, that they would be "assisted by the artificers of the QMG department when not otherwise employed." In practice the department seems to have done all the maintenance.[34] No particular size for the train was established, but, rather, Howe specified that it should always be adequate to the task of supplying an army operating in the field for three weeks. This was presumably just a minimum, for the actual number of horses and wagons on the QMG establishment at New York varied from a low of 523 wagons and 1,515 horses in early 1779 to a high of 1,376 and 3,111 respectively in the third quarter of 1777, averaging about 730 wagons and 2,100 horses.[35] These vehicles, of course, did not stand idle between campaigns; the army in quarters was like a city, constantly in need of transportation. Vehicles were assigned to each regiment for general use and to the various headquarters units and hospitals. But by far the largest number were employed by the commissary, barrackmaster, engineer, and, to a lesser extent, the quartermaster department itself in the performance of their various duties.

Operating on the sea coast, the army also required water transportation for a multitude of tasks ranging from the delivery of dispatches to the collecting and distribution of forage and firewood. This too was provided in the first part of the war by the quartermaster, who hired all vessels and allocated them to the various departments as required. In January 1777, to reduce the burden on the quartermaster general's department, the commander-in-chief appointed a superintendent of vessels, Captain Henry Chads, charged with hiring, inspection, and allocation.[36] With the capture of Charleston, another official, Captain George Gayton, was

[34] T 64/112, 81-84, Winthrop & Kemble to Sir William Erskine, 18 April 1777. For further on the transport service and hiring contracts see Ch. v.

[35] *Journal of the House of Commons*, vol. XXXVIII, 1109.

[36] *Ibid.*, 1068. Chads was also the Navy Board's principal agent for transports in America (Syrett, 51-52).

appointed for the south. The number of vessels employed from time to time varied, but the strength given in returns at the end of 1778 is a good median. At that time the quartermaster, commissary, and barrack departments had between them 120 vessels totalling close to 10,000 tons.[37] Few figures exist for South Carolina, but a return of January 1782 lists 30 vessels totalling 1,424 tons.[38]

But even when it no longer had charge of hiring, the quartermaster general's department was still very much in the shipping business. It was responsible for a fleet of over one hundred batteaux, scows, and rowboats owned by the army and used for transport in the New York area. It also kept on hire, apart from the vessels supplied by Captain Chads, half a dozen armed sloops and brigs for the protection of local transports, as well as a number of dispatch boats.[39] Many of these vessels were built in the QMG shipyard. The department got into that business in 1776 when it had to provide transportation for 6,000 men and fifty guns for the move from Staten Island to Long Island.[40]

To carry out the services assigned to it, the QMG department employed at New York alone some 1,100 people, exclusive of wagon drivers and sailors, and a further 230 in the South. The DQMGs and ADQMGs were invariably army officers detached for the period of their appointments from their regiments or corps; they received ten shillings and five shillings per day respectively beyond their regular pay as compensation. With the exception of New York, where the extent of the department demanded two, there was usually one DQMG at each major army base and an assistant at each minor one. There were, however, at the greatest extent, only sixteen such officers in the army com-

[37] CP, 1 Dec 78, 13 Jan 79.

[38] CP, 30 Jan 82, "Return of Vessels Employed in His Majesty's Service . . . Charlestown. . . ."

[39] CP, "Return of Vessels in the QMG Department," 1 Dec 78; Mackenzie Papers, "List of Armed Vessels and Dispatch Boats," 1 Apr 81.

[40] Add. Mss. 21,680, Hutcheson to Haldimand, 8 Aug 76.

manded by Howe and Clinton.[41] The remainder of the department—the people who staffed the warehouses, shipyards, and wagon depots—were civilians. Although the majority of the staff were unskilled laborers, a number were tradesmen. For instance, the 225 civilians employed by the department in South Carolina included one storekeeper, two clerks, two wagon masters, nineteen wagon conductors, fifteen ship's carpenters, eighteen regular carpenters, six blacksmiths, four collarmakers, sixteen batteauxmen, and a farrier.[42]

The commissary general's office was the second army logistical department in size. This department stood out from the others in that it was staffed entirely by civilians, a situation made necessary by the requirement that a commissary have a considerable knowledge of trade and trade practices, and the social code that required that an officer and a gentleman despise such knowledge.[43]

The office of commissary general was, in the eighteenth century, one of the oldest in the British army staff. Although the term "commissary" means, properly, anyone to whom a duty is given by commission—hence commissary of horse, commissary of accounts, etc.—by the seventeenth century at the latest the term "commissary" by itself had

[41] Mackenzie Papers, "Quartermaster General's Department," 1 Jan 82.

[42] CP, "Return of . . . Quarter Master General's Department in South Carolina," 1 June 80.

[43] Of the inferior social status of a commissary there can be little doubt. Lord Percy resigned from his command in 1777 because he believed that Howe had preferred the word of a commissary over his (see p. 69, and Col. Watson of the 3d Regiment of Guards, when he was refused extra rations by the commissary department, wrote in a seething letter to Clinton that "an officer unless he had done something he is ashamed of, ill brooks an insult from a commissary" (CP, Watson to Clinton, 14 July 81). Even thirty years later Wellington noted that "the prejudices of society against a commissary almost prevent him from receiving the common respect due to the character of a gentleman" (quoted in R. Glover, *Peninsular Preparation* [Cambridge, 1963], 256).

come to mean a person attached to the army and concerned with the supplying of food. The commissary general, although not a military officer, was nevertheless an important member of the commander-in-chief's staff, appointed for the duration of the existence of the particular field unit. Until the American wars the commissary general's responsibility in terms of food seems to have been limited to supplying bread, although he also provided fuel, forage, and transportation for the army in the field. These items were sometimes obtained by contract with local merchants in the areas of operations and merely distributed by the commissaries, but more often the department seems to have done the actual collecting and not infrequently also commandeered mills to turn the grain into flour and operated bake ovens to make bread. The remaining dietary needs of the army were purchased by the soldiers themselves from the hordes of subtlers who followed inevitably in the wake of armies.[44] This was the system followed by armies that campaigned in Europe during the Seven Years' War.

The situation in America during the same war, however, led to the virtual elimination of the commissary general's office. The army was operating in areas of wilderness or at best sparse population, and food had to come from the more populous areas of the colonies or from Britain itself. To supply the army the Treasury turned to civilian contractors, who collected the provisions and delivered them to storehouses either on the seaboard or in the interior. There agents issued them to the army quartermasters. The other tasks that normally fell to the commissary general— the provision of transportation, fuel, and forage—were taken over by the quartermaster general and the barrackmaster general. There was a commissary holding a War Office commission (and a commissary department), but, significantly, his title was just that, not commissary general, and his only function was to ensure that provisions con-

[44] Scrouller, 215-235; Havilland LeMesurier, "A System for the British Commissariat" (1796), printed as an appendix to Glover, 267-305.

tractors fulfilled their contracts in terms of quantity, quality, and time of delivery.[45]

The Revolutionary War saw the revival of the office of commissary general in America. The first step came in early 1776, after a number of contractors' provisions ships en route to Boston were intercepted by American privateers. The immediate result of the captures was a sharp increase in shipping insurance rates and a request from General Howe that supply ships be armed in the future. The contractors, however, protested that they could afford neither the new insurance rates nor the cost of arming their ships and the Treasury was thus forced to take over the task of shipping itself. This in turn forced considerable reorganization and expansion within the Treasury. First, a receiving and shipping depot was established at Cork, Ireland, under Robert Gordon. There supplies were received from the contractors, inspected, and shipped out to America on Treasury victuallers. Secondly, an agency was needed in America to receive, store, and issue the provisions, functions previously carried out by contractors' agents. The duties of this agency went far beyond those of the old commissary so a new commission was issued.[46] The man appointed to the task was Daniel Chamier, the incumbent commissary; he was given, initially, three deputies and three assistants. But, clearly, this was not seen as a permanent situation. It was expected that once the army left Boston and established control over a considerable area of the colonies it would be able to feed itself in the manner of armies operating in Europe. Hence, Chamier was also appointed to the post of commissary general, receiving commissions from the War Office and the Treasury. The War

[45] Pargellis, 293. The original appointee was Robert Leake, who held office until 1774. His successor was Daniel Chamier. Chamier's commission from the War Office referred to him only as "Commissary of Stores and Provisions for all our forces employed or to be employed in North America" (WO 25/32, Commission Books, 7 Feb 74).

[46] T 64/106, 26-28, Robinson to Howe, 12 Apr 76.

Office commission, under which he received three pounds per day, authorized him "to inspect the buying and delivering of stores, provisions & forage for the use of the army." The Treasury commission, worth two pounds per day, instructed him ". . . to procure and provide forage, provisions, bread, waggons and waggon horses, wood, straw, and all other necessaries and conveniences commonly called contingencies for the use of the army, to make such contracts and agreements as should be necessary, and to take care that the same be faithfully performed, and that the supplies provided be faithfully distributed to the army."[47] Both Daniel Wier, who succeeded Chamier as commissary general on 23 May 1777, and Brook Watson, who succeeded Wier on 27 May 1782, held identical commissions.[48] As it turned out, until 1782 the provision of transportation for the army remained with the QMG and of fuel with the BMG, and the army departments generally handled their own contingency purchases and funds.

Nevertheless, the task that remained with the commissary general was extensive. Throughout the war the commissary with the main army fed on the average 35,000 men and 4,000 horses, who consumed every day some thirty-seven tons of food and thirty-eight of hay and oats. Since control of an area of the colonies large enough to supply this food was never achieved, most of it had to come from Britain. Hence one of the commissary general's main tasks was that of reception, storage, and distribution. To store supplies the department employed forty warehouses and a number of ships at New York City alone.[49] The staffing of

[47] PRO 30/8/187, 110, Brook Watson to Pitt, 4 June 89.

[48] Although their commissions are dated 1 Feb 1777 and 14 March 1782 respectively, the dates above are those on which they actually took over the department (WO 25/33, 36; AO 1/494/100; AO 1/495/104). Wier died in office on 12 November 1781 and until Watson's arrival the department was managed in the north by Peter Paumier and in the south by John Morrison, the senior deputy commissaries.

[49] WO 60/33. This is the average of several lists in this box from the

these and of the issuing depots scattered throughout the garrison areas employed most of the clerks and a good part of the twenty coopers and 300-odd laborers in the department's employ. Most of the provisions were issued in bulk quantities to regimental quartermasters, but there were enough refugees, headquarters people, and detached personnel about to make necessary several stores that issued on a small scale.

Equally demanding was the task of procuring supplies locally. The commissary department was not only responsible for ensuring a regular supply of fresh provisions for the troops and hay for the army's horses, but, on those occasions when shipments from Britain were delayed, it was on the skill of the department in ferreting out civilian stocks of food on which the very existence of the army depended. A part of these needs could be met from those areas under British control. For this task the department maintained cattle and forage offices employing almost one hundred people.[50] But a considerable part came also from secret trading with, and foraging expeditions into, hostile areas.

From 1777 the commissariat was also responsible for contracting for the rum that the army guzzled at the extraordinary rate of over 500,000 gallons a year,[51] and for providing spruce beer. Procured at first from civilian suppliers, the beer was later produced in commissariat breweries, one of which, in New York City, employed eleven men and turned out 4,233 gallons every two days.[52]

In all, the commissary general's department usually em-

---

wartime period. Another enumeration dated 24 April 1783 lists seventy-two warehouses, wharves, barns, sheds, and cellars.

[50] WO 60/33, "Return of persons Employed in the Commissary General's Department at New York and Posts Dependant, 22 May 1782."

[51] T 29/46, 22; T 64/108, 51. The consumption for 36,000 men for one year is given as 550,000 gallons.

[52] HSP, Wier Letter Book, Wier to Robinson, 20 May 77, "State of the King's Brewery. . . ."

ployed over 500 men, exclusive of twenty-eight deputy and assistant commissaries.[53] It also had on hire fifty ships on the average, ranging from sixteen to one hundred and sixty tons.[54] In addition to providing work for a large part of the quartermaster general's wagon train when the army was in quarters, the department usually hired a number of wagons on its own.[55]

The provision of quarters for troops not actually campaigning in the field during the war was the responsibility of another separate department, that of the barrackmaster general. In Britain, barracks were the province of the Board of Ordnance. Just why that department did not undertake the same responsibility in North America is not clear, except insofar as that it was generally reluctant to undertake administrative responsibilities outside Britain.[56] The first barrackmaster general for America was commissioned in 1765, the appointment being made necessary by the Quartering Act of that year, which made it illegal to billet soldiers in private houses.[57] Although the Act also required the Colonies to support the troops on station, and this help sometimes came in the form of providing barracks, there was nevertheless a considerable gap between the needs of

[53] T 64/114, 58-61, Wier to Robinson, 22 May 78.

[54] CP, "Return of Vessels. . . ," 1 Dec 78.

[55] Although the QMG department provided most of the wagons required by the departments, each also hired a few on its own. The total expenditure by these other departments was £25,000 a year, which would hire 210 four-horse wagons ("*Board of General Officers*," 17-23). The QMG supplied the artillery with wagons until 1777 when that department purchased its own train (RAI, Ms. 7, 33-34).

[56] The Board was probably responsible for the construction and maintenance of barracks through the Engineers, as it was for fortifications. In Britain, however, the Board also provided furniture, bedding, fuel and lighting (E. E. Curtis, *The Organization of the British Army in the American Revolution* [New York, 1926], 40; Scouller, 167).

[57] C. M. Clode, *The Military Forces of the Crown* (London, 1869), vol. I, 229.

the army and the help given.[58] A notation in General Haldimand's accounts for the first quarter of 1774, beside a warrant for expenses in the BMG department, gives some idea of the area in which the department operated. The warrant was for "expenses incurred for supplying the barracks at the several garrisons in North America, with fuel, candles, officers' lodgings, and bedding—repairs of barracks furniture, & sundry contingent expenses. . . ."[59]

With the approach of war and the buildup of forces in Boston, the duties of the BMG became both more difficult and more extensive. The department came to employ directly as many as 250 men and indirectly perhaps twice that number as sailors in the thirty ships in the department's permanent employ and as woodcutters.[60] The BMG was responsible not only for the care of permanent barracks, the procurement of barrack supplies, and the issuing and receiving of barrack furniture and bedding as the troops moved into "permanent" quarters in the fall and out again in the spring, but also for the identification and allotment of buildings suitable for barracks and other military uses in the various cities and towns occupied by the army. It was, of course, neither possible nor desirable to house all the troops in permanent buildings; no American city—particularly New York, a third destroyed by the fire of 1776—could have accommodated the army even if the continuing possibility of American attack had not dictated the maintenance of a defense perimeter manned by the largest part of the army. Thus most of the army lived in tents during the warm months and moved to huts constructed of sod and timber for the winter. These huts, variously described as warm, snug, and preferable to living in a

---

[58] J. Shy, *Toward Lexington* (Princeton, 1965), 250-258.

[59] T 64/101, 4-11.

[60] WO 60/33, "Return of Persons Employed. . . ," 25 May 82; CP, "Return of Vessels. . . ," 1 Dec 78; T 1/574, "Vessels Employed by the Services in South Carolina," 14 June 82.

house, and as dirty, dark, and unhealthful, were built by the troops themselves.[61] Once built, the huts came under the administration of the barrackmaster, who also supplied them with furniture and stoves.[62]

But the most demanding task of the BMG department was not the provision of quarters. It was, rather, heating them. Although attempts were made several times to procure coal for this purpose, they met only moderate success, and wood was the main fuel used. Wood was issued on the basis of rooms (or huts), and the size of the ration and the number of weeks per year it was issued depended on the climate. In New York and Philadelphia the ration was one half a cord per week for twenty-six weeks. The allotment of rooms depended on rank and in a regiment descended from two rooms for the colonel, through one half a room for a subaltern, to one room for each twelve enlisted men. A full regiment of 612 men plus officers thus occupied seventy-three rooms and required 949 cords of wood to get it through the winter. For the winter of 1778-1779, with an estimated 40,000 men occupying 4,900 rooms, the BMG computed the army's need at 70,000 cords of wood. The estimate, of course, included the requirements of the army staff, which were not inconsiderable; a lieutenant general rated five rooms and the rate fell off one room per rank for the other general ranks. Senior department heads rated

[61] Uhlendorf, 231-233, 237; J. C. Buettner, *Narrative of Johann Carl Buettner in the American Revolution* (New York, n.d.), 45.

[62] These huts, interestingly enough, were "barracks" in the original meaning of the term. An English Military Dictionary of 1702 defines a barrack as: "A hut like a little Cottage, for soldiers to lie in Camp. . . . These are made, either when the soldiers have not tents, or when the Army lies long in a Place in bad Weather, because they keep out the cold, heat, or rain better than tents, and are otherwise more commodious. They are generally made by fixing four strong forked Poles in the ground, and laying four others across them; then they build the Walls and Wattles, or sods, or such as the Place affords. The Top is either thatch'd, if there be straw to spare, or covered with Planks, or sometimes with Turf." (Quoted in Scouller, 166.)

two rooms, their deputies one, and assistants one half.[63]

The BMG also supplied candles. Each room received one pound of candles per week, the enlisted men getting dipped candles that ran ten to the pound, the officers more expensive molded candles.

The barrackmaster general, unlike the quartermaster general and the commissary general, was appointed by the commander-in-chief in America and received his commission from him.[64] Colonel James Robertson, the first BMG, was appointed in 1765 and held office until the spring of 1776, when a directive from the King barring regimental commanders from the post forced his resignation.[65] Robertson's replacement, appointed by Howe, was Lt. Colonel George Clerk of the 43d Regiment. Clerk held the position until ill health forced his resignation in July 1780. To succeed him Clinton appointed Major George Crosbie of the Royal Fusiliers, a member of his military "family." Crosbie retained the office until the final evacuation of the British army.

In the logistical organization of the army in Britain, the Ordnance Board played a considerable part. One historian has summed it up as follows: "It had charge of arms, ammunition, ordnance, tents, bedding, wagons, the erection of barracks, fortifications, hospitals and magazines. It provided military prisons, regulated the inspection of arms and accoutrements, was charged with the repair of the Royal Observatory at Greenwich and the preparation of maps for military purposes."[66] In North America, however, many of these duties were performed by the army departments discussed above. The Ordnance Board was involved in army logistics only via its two military arms, the Royal Artillery and the Engineers. The Royal Artillery, besides being totally responsible for the artillery, was charged with ordering

[63] T 64/108, 117, "Calculation of Fewel and Candles for 40,000 Men During the 26 Winter Weeks," 20 Mar 77; Mackenzie Papers, "Proportion of Fuel and Candles at New York, 1780."
[64] T 64/112, 67-68.   [65] WO 4/273, 71-72.   [66] Curtis, 40.

all the small arms, ammunition, and powder required for the whole army as well as for maintaining repair facilities and magazines for them. The logistical relationship of this arm to the rest of the army reflected the great independence of the Ordnance Board. In many important ways it looked after itself, depending on the general army services for food and quarters but little else. Its specialized equipment came, naturally, from the Ordnance Board, but so also did the tents, camp equipment, and clothing that the rest of the army obtained through the quartermaster general.[67] From 1778 on, also, it maintained its own independent wagon and shipping services, employing in that year 603 horses and ten vessels.[68] To feed its horses it was often a competitor with the commissary general's department for forage and in the field seems often to have organized its own foraging expeditions.[69] Its accounts were also entirely separate from the rest of the army; it maintained its own military chest and its accounts were not, as were those of the other departments, subject to the approval of the commander-in-chief.[70]

The Department of Engineers was something of an oddity even in an army full of eighteenth-century eccentricities. The engineers were not a corps but rather a professional service organized by the Ordnance Board. In the whole service in 1775 there were only forty-seven people from the chief engineer and colonel down to practitioners and ensigns.[71] In peace time the engineers were employed in the construction of permanent military facilities in all parts of the empire. In wartime, assigned to the armies in the field, they planned and built defensive works and, re-

---

[67] RAI, Ms. 7, 40, 59-60, 146.   [68] *Ibid.*, 74-75, 150-151.

[69] *Ibid.*, 69; Ms. 57, 195.

[70] It should not be assumed, however, that the Artillery was virtually an independent command. The chief artillery officer in America was clearly subordinate to the commander-in-chief and even had to seek his approval before reducing the size of the artillery wagon train. RAI, Ms. 7, 150-151.

[71] Curtis, 40.

versing the process, advised the commander-in-chief on the best approaches when laying siege to enemy works. To carry out their tasks in the field, the engineers organized departments staffed by civilian tradesmen and laborers. Unlike the artillery, however, these departments came entirely under the orders of the commander-in-chief. Their expenses were met out of the military chest and their transportation needs from the common facilities provided by the QMG. The number of men employed by the department depended on the scale of its activities. In the fall of 1778, for example, there were only 258 on the department payroll, while a year later when the defenses of New York were being strengthened, there were 921.[72] These figures, however, do not necessarily represent the total manpower employed, for it was common practice for the department to use soldiers in its construction work. For this "extra" duty—a revealing commentary itself on the concept of duty and privileges in eighteenth-century society—the soldiers received an extra sixpence and a second ration of rum for each day's work.[73] Also, infantry regiments were regularly given the task of constructing fascines, mats of woven branches used by the engineers for shoring up the sides of earth works.

The army departments thus far discussed—those of the quartermaster general, the commissary general, the barrackmaster general, and the artillery and engineers—between them provided most of the logistical support the army required in America. But since virtually all this support involved very large expenditures in America, two officers concerned with money and its accounting should also be mentioned. The deputy paymaster general can be dismissed quickly, for he was little more than the custodian of the army's cash box, the military chest. With one hand he received cash supplied by the Treasury's money contractors, and with the other he dispensed it as directed by warrants from the commander-in-chief. His most significant duty was

[72] T 64/114, 93-94, 219. [73] Uhlendorf, 273.

that of reporting to the Treasury and the commander-in-chief as to the state of the army's cash reserves. There was little change in the duties of the paymaster from war to peace except, of course, in the amount of money that went through his hands.

Of much greater significance were the offices concerned with the auditing of accounts. In the prewar period and the first year of the war, the responsibility for checking on expenditures rested in two places: with the commander-in-chief in America personally and with the Audit Office in London. Department heads or their deputies who were authorized as public accountants presented the commander-in-chief, as the occasion demanded, with accounts for goods and services already supplied. If the commander was satisfied that the expenditures were authorized and reasonable, he issued a warrant directing the deputy paymaster to turn over the appropriate amount of cash to the accountant. The second check was made by the Audit Office in London when the accountant surrendered his commission. This, however, was merely a mechanical check in which clerks re-added figures to check for accuracy and matched stated expenditures with receipts.[74]

In a period of stringent economy, as the interwar period was, the idea of requiring the commander-in-chief to approve all expenditures and to certify all accounts was perhaps reasonable; under wartime conditions it was impossible. In wartime expenses were not only huge but often impossible to predict, and in many cases payments for goods and services could not be put off until a warrant could be drawn.[75] General Gage, thoroughly conditioned by his years of peacetime service, attempted to keep the old system going as long as he remained in command, but when Howe took over, it very rapidly broke down. Two basic factors

[74] *Journal of the House of Commons*, vol. xxxviii, 1,066-1,067. The first pages of the Seventh Report of the Commissioners of Public Accounts outline the system of accounting in America.

[75] T 1/517, Carleton to Colin Drummond, Sept 75; T 64/101, 73.

were involved in the breakdown. First, in response to the conditions noted above, Howe turned more and more to the issuing of temporary warrants. These authorized the deputy paymaster to issue to the department head involved a specific sum for "expenses in the department." Later, when the department turned in an approved accounting of the expenditure of the money, the temporary warrant was converted into a final warrant. By 1777 Howe was issuing temporary warrants for as much as £40,000 at a time.[76]

The second factor involved in the breakdown of the old system was the load on the commander-in-chief. He, obviously, could not both run a war and personally supervise all expenditures and check all departmental accounts. As a result, few of the required quarterly accountings of expenditures were turned in during 1775 and 1776.[77] To rectify this situation the Treasury appointed, in early 1777, a comptroller of commissaries accounts to examine, audit, and certify all the extraordinary accounts of the army in America.[78] The first appointee was Daniel Chamier, transferred from the post of commissary general, but he died in November 1778 without ever taking up his duties.[79] To replace him Clinton, then the commander-in-chief, recommended Major Duncan Drummond, an artillery officer and latterly one of his aides de camp. Drummond's commission was virtually the same as Chamier's but gave him the broader title of commissary of accounts. Although his commission was dated 15 February 1779, Drummond did not in fact begin to act in his office until early in 1781.[80] Army

---

[76] T 64/108, 29-31; T 64/106, 29-44; AO 1/494/100; AO 1/494/99.

[77] *Ibid.*

[78] T 64/118, 65.

[79] There are, however, final warrants for Howe's whole period as commander-in-chief. Presumably the checking of accounts, if it was done at all, was carried out without the aid of a specialist. (T 64/108, 9-17, 58-66, 79-83, 93-100, 117-123; T 64/109, 3-20.)

[80] BAHQP, 2,964; CP, Drummond to Robinson, 30 Mar 81. There are no final warrants for Clinton's period as commander-in-chief until 1782.

accounts, then, to the great detriment of the British tax-payer, were without adequate supervision for the greater part of the war.

Of the mechanism for the control and use of the army, Piers Mackesy has written, with considerable restraint, ". . . it was in need of great reforms."[81] The same may be said of the organization for the logistical support of the army. As with strategy, major logistical decisions were made by the cabinet. On receiving the King's approval, they were executed by the appropriate secretary of state, who, in logistical matters, then directed the cooperation of the various executive departments of government—Treasury, War Office, etc. As with most organizations, the system and its component parts had flaws and failings, but in the past they had not stood in the way of success. The conditions of the American war, however, threw up new problems and posed old ones on a new scale. The logistical problems of an army of up to 65,000 operating thousands of miles from its supply base are enormous. No European government had faced such a task since Roman times. That the British government was able to undertake the task and carry it out as well as it did under the social, political, and economic conditions of the time is itself a tribute to its efficiency in the eighteenth century. Yet it was not efficient enough. The problems of the American war accentuated the flaws and failings in the system, and before they were recognized and corrected they had contributed significantly to the failure of the British army in America. In the following chapters the problems and failings and their effects on operations are examined.

[81] Mackesy, 14.

II

AMERICA AS A SOURCE OF SUPPLY

WHEN THE BRITISH GOVERNMENT DECIDED IN 1774 THAT A show of force was necessary to maintain order in the American colonies and to enforce the restrictive measures voted by Parliament against Massachusetts, there is no indication that problems in supplying the troops were anticipated. It was assumed that the 3,000 soldiers in Boston in late 1774, and even the additional 6,000 ordered out in the same year, could be supplied through existing procedures. The confidence in, or at least the failure to question, the capacity of the existing supply procedures to provide for the increased force in America was not without reason. America was a bountiful land that once before, during the Seven Years' War, supplied large armies. There had been at that time some problems of organization that were blamed for the failure of Governor Shirley's expedition against Niagara and William Johnson's against Ticonderoga,[1] but these were solved under Lords Loudoun and Amherst in 1757 and 1758. The basic organization they established survived with the troops who remained in America after 1763. But what was basically a police action in 1774 became war in 1775, and a whole new set of logistical problems developed.

The first indication that the old supply procedures could not be counted on came in late March of 1775 when the firm of Nesbitt, Drummond, and Franks, the prime contractors for supplying food for the troops in America, warned the Treasury that the colonies might not "suffer provisions to be shipped for the troops at Boston."[2] The

[1] Pargellis, 67.   [2] T 27/31, 106, Grey Cooper to Gage, 30 Mar 75.

warning was well founded; within days of the clash at Lexington and Concord the gathering Minutemen ended all trade between Boston and the Massachusetts countryside. As word of the resort to arms was carried post haste up and down the coast, supplies from the other colonies were also cut off. The messenger from the Rebel army galloped into New York on April 23, and on the same day the Whig faction there seized and unloaded a sloop about to sail with provisions for the army at Boston.[3] By May 10 the news had reached Charleston, and a week later Gage had to report to the Treasury that "all the ports from whence our supply usually came have refused suffering any provisions or necessary whatever to be shipped for the King's use." He requested that the contractors be directed to ship provisions from Britain.[4]

London began to act in this direction even before Gage's letter arrived. Appearing before the Treasury Board on June 13, Nesbitt, Drummond, and Franks reported that, anticipating problems, they had already directed subcontractors in Ireland to procure and ship 2,000 barrels of flour and 1,000 of pork, quantities the Board immediately ordered increased by 6,000 and 4,000 barrels respectively. But the problem was not seen as serious, for at a meeting two weeks later the contractors reported that by their information the food already at Boston, along with some surplus supplies redirected from Quebec, would last 10,000 men until September 9. The further supplies already ordered would carry the same numbers through until March 1776.[5] At the end of July, the Board, in a mood of caution—the news of Bunker Hill having been received in the interim—ordered that everything necessary to provide for 10,000 men until July 1776 be sent out and set the first week in October as the deadline for the sailing of the sup-

[3] C. Ward, *The War of the Revolution* (New York, 1952), I, 52.

[4] T 64/101, 72, Gage to Grey Cooper, 19 May 75.

[5] T 29/44, 13 and 28 June 75.

ply ships.[6] Then, content with its efforts, the Board proceeded on a more than usually extended summer recess.

The view from Boston, however, was somewhat less satisfactory. Contractors were supposed to maintain a six-month reserve of food with the army at all times, but already on March 24 they were a month and a half short of this requirement in meat and almost four months in bread, the basic items of the military diet. Two months later, the number of troops drawing rations having increased from 4,650 to 5,960, the situation was no better. Gage's initiative in obtaining two cargoes from Quebec and some surplus provisions from the garrison at Halifax brought reserves up to 130 days in early June, but thereafter, with those sources exhausted and the army growing rapidly in strength, the situation steadily worsened. Early in October, after two months during which the army existed on the food stocks of troop transports and naval vessels and often had less than thirty days' supplies on hand, five contractors' ships from England and Ireland arrived. To the immense dismay of all, however, most of the 5,200 barrels of flour on board proved to be rotten. When the next group of twelve ships arrived in late December, they were sorely needed.[7] In the next three months only six ships arrived,[8] and the timing of the evacuation of Boston was influenced as much by the fact that there were only two months' bread and one month's meat in the storehouses as by tactical and strategic considerations.[9]

The failure of the contractors drove Gage, and Howe when he became commander-in-chief, to exert every effort to find supplies in North America. They had little success. Their first resort was to the wide-ranging navy. In this first year of the Revolution—particularly before the tenth of

[6] *Ibid.*, 21 and 27 July 75.

[7] T 64/108, 23-25, "Memorandum of Failure on the Part of the Contractors for Victualling His Majesty's Troops at Boston," 17 Jan 76.

[8] T 1/519, "List of Ships sent to America."

[9] CP, Howe to Clinton, 21 Mar 76.

September, when the Association agreement on nonexportation came into effect—a curious sort of half-war existed up and down the coast of America. As usual, British warships put into American harbors and river mouths, where they depended upon the inhabitants for pleasant variations from the monotony of their seagoing salt fare. It was in their own interest, then, for the sailors to maintain good relations with the ports. On their part, the inhabitants, anxious to maintain their trade with the West Indies and elsewhere until the Association cut it off, had no desire to provoke the British captains into blockading the ports. Thus local committees and provincial congresses who praised the Rebel actions at Boston, at the same time—and despite the occasional protests of shocked patriots—sanctioned the continued intercourse between the shore and the British navy. This uneasy truce became almost a game when the naval commanders received orders to find and collect supplies for the army.[10] For the Americans the game was to keep the British ships stocked without providing anything extra; for the navy it was to procure provisions for the army without jeopardizing its own supplies.[11]

But the game had a strong tendency to fundamental violence. Disputes between Captain Barclay and the town of Portsmouth, and Captain Vandeput and New York, not infrequently ended in gun fire, and when, early in October, the town of Bristol, Connecticut, refused the demand of Captain Wallace for a large number of sheep and cattle, he commenced a bombardment that quickly brought the town to agree to supply a part of his demands.[12] Even more serious engagements were not at all infrequent. In June a Loy-

[10] ADM 1/485 Admiral Graves to Captains Vandeput, Wallace, and Barclay.

[11] Alan French, *The First Year of the American Revolution* (Boston and New York, 1934), 359.

[12] Peter Force, *American Archives* (Washington, 1837-1853), 4:3:259-262, 4:3:990-991.

alist named Ichabod Jones, with a small party from Boston, sailed into the harbor of Machias seeking lumber. His force was attacked and decimated by local Patriots. And earlier, in April, when H.M.S. *Falcon* under Captain Linzee attempted to seize sheep and cattle at Buzzard's Bay, two American ships commandeered for the purpose of carrying stock and manned with British sailors were forcibly retaken by the Americans and their crews imprisoned.[13]

Other attempts to find provisions, while more subtle, were no more successful. For instance, shortly after the Rebel embargo on shipments to Boston commenced, Loyalist merchants in various ports in the colonies began to increase their food shipments to the West Indies and elsewhere. Patriot committees, however, soon realized that a suspiciously high proportion of these ships were intercepted by the Royal Navy and taken to Boston, and this ingenious source of supply dried up.[14] Indeed, the only really successful provisioning foray at this stage of the war took place in late July when a small fleet of transports and armed ships slipped out of Boston and descended a short time later on the eastern end of Long Island. There, with the aid of local Loyalists, 1,900 sheep and a hundred-odd cattle were commandeered.[15] Although much was made of this success, 2,000 animals could not long feed an army that grew during July and August from 6,000 to 11,000. The development of an American privateer navy and British naval weakness in American waters at this time combined to end such operations very shortly after they began.[16]

This period of the war also proved that no secure dependence for food could be placed on the two settled prov-

13 French, 170, 360.

14 Force, 4:2:956-957; CO 5/92, 467, Gage to Dartmouth, 24 July 75; T 64/108, 23-25.

15 Add. Mss. 21,680, Hutcheson to Haldimand, Boston, 19 Aug 75; CO 5/92, 232, Gage to Dartmouth, 24 July 75.

16 French, Chs. XXIII and XXIV.

inces that did not enter into the rebellion: Nova Scotia and Quebec. Immediately after Boston was cut off from the surrounding countryside, the deputy quartermaster general, Colonel Sherriff, engaged the firm of Scott and Day, of Boston and Halifax, to supply the army with provisions, forage, and livestock from Nova Scotia. The exact quantities of various supplies that Scott and Day provided cannot be ascertained, but their accounts with the army from the fifth of June 1775, when they made their first delivery, to March 1776 amounted to only £7,285.[17] A large part of this was for hay but even if it had all gone for provisions, at the going rate of sixpence halfpenny (New York currency) per ration it could have fed the army for only three weeks. Even this, however, so reduced the supply of provisions in Nova Scotia that when the army arrived in Halifax from Boston a considerable dispersion of units was necessary to find food for both horses and men. On April 12, Howe wrote to Clinton that "in a very few days we shall be reduced to fish-flour and potatoes."[18]

Quebec proved to be an equally weak reed. Gage appealed for supplies to Guy Carleton, governor and military commander in Quebec, as early as May 1775, expecting that province to be most useful as a source of flour.[19] The accounts of the deputy quartermaster general in Canada, however, indicate, that in the period from July to November of 1775 he was able to collect and ship only some 2,600 bushels of wheat, 400 sheep, and 200 bullocks, along with several thousand bushels of oats—less than two weeks' supply for the army, providing the wheat could be ground to flour.[20] In any case, Quebec soon had its own troubles with Arnold and Montgomery. When they were cleared up, the considerable army stationed in Canada more than took care

17 T 1/571, 151-153, 167-168, 226-227, 247-248; T 1/568, 86-94.
18 CP, 12 Apr 76.
19 T 64/101, 72, Gage to Grey Cooper, 19 May 75.
20 AO 3/120 Account of Major Thomas Gamble.

of any surplus that province produced for the remainder of the war.[21]

The failures in 1775 did not end all hope of feeding the army from America, although the Treasury did, in early 1776, come to the reluctant conclusion that for the time being at least all the food required by the army would have to be sent from Britain. With the move to New York in the summer of 1776 and the subsequent domination of large parts of New Jersey, Long Island, and Rhode Island, the hope of provisioning the army from North America revived. Although the supply of food on Staten Island, where the army first landed, was limited, once the move was made to Long Island and then to the mainland in August and September of 1776, the countryside began to deliver up its abundance. Large supplies of foodstuffs were captured with the Rebel magazines at New York and Forts Lee and Washington and further quantities confiscated from the establishments of known or suspected Rebels—into which category abandoned farms were placed.[22] More important, though, as defeat succeeded defeat for the Rebels and the area of British control extended, the inhabitants, perhaps because they were Loyalists but more probably because they wished to avoid a ruinous levy, began to volunteer to bring in food and forage for the army.[23] By mid-October prices of various commodities had been set for the guidance of local commanders and the army warned against "molesting the inhabitants."[24] In December, when local supplies had already carried the army through two periods when stocks of salt provisions from Britain fell to dangerously low lev-

[21] The supply situation of the army in Canada is treated separately in Ch. VI.

[22] For example Commissary General Chamier reported that 2,000 barrels of flour were captured at Fort Lee as well as quantities of pork, bread, rum, gin and molasses. (T 64/108, 18-19, Chamier to Robinson, 30 Nov 76.)

[23] Stryker, 343, Thomas Gamble to Colonel von Donop, 24 Dec 76.

[24] RAI, Ms. 8, "Orderly Book of Sir William Howe," 12 Oct 76.

els, Howe ordered local commanders to take and submit inventories of food and forage in their areas, and the commissary department began to salt down meat for future use.[25] Clearly the hope was that the campaign of 1777 would not depend on supplies from Britain.[26]

Washington's brilliant Christmas counterattack ended the British control of New Jersey and with it all these bright dreams. Supplies of fresh food dwindled and prices went up. Daniel Wier, the new commissary general, reported shortly after he took over in May that although he was prepared to pay the exorbitant price of tenpence a pound for fresh beef he could not obtain enough to supply even the hospitals.[27]

The experience at Philadelphia a year later repeated that at New York. The army fed well on a profusion of locally procured food for over a month, again at a time when salt provisions from Europe were running low, and glowing reports from Wier led the Treasury once again cautiously to hope that there could be "some dependence on America for the support of His Majesty's troops."[28] Within several months, however, local supplies virtually dried up and for the second time in a year Wier had to dash the hopes of the Treasury that the enormous expense of shipping food from Europe could be reduced. "We have," he wrote in December, "by no means a reasonable prospect of obtaining supplies of any kind or in any degree from this country."[29] And, despite persistent appeals by the Treasury year after year, that verdict remained.

Throughout the remainder of the war the army did on occasion sustain itself from North America. In the late sum-

[25] Stryker, 317, Howe to von Donop, 13 Dec 76.

[26] Dartmouth Papers, D1778/II/1708, Searle to Dartmouth, 25 Sept 78.

[27] HSP, Wier Letter Book, Wier to Robinson, 20 May 77.

[28] T 64/119, 4-5, Robinson to Wier, 29 Oct 77.

[29] T 64/114, 20-22, 4 Mar 78.

mer of 1778, for instance, when reserves of salt provisions were down to some forty days, Major General Grey took an expedition to Martha's Vineyard and returned triumphant with 10,000 sheep and 300 head of cattle.[30] In the latter months of that same year, only the most strenuous exertions in obtaining food locally allowed the army to remain at New York.[31] But these instances more than anything proved the repeated assertions of Chamier and Wier that no dependence could be had on North America for supplies. Grey's success was due to the isolation of his target, strength, surprise, and the use of the sea. These elements were not easy to bring into combination, as so many unsuccessful raids up and down the coast testified, even if the British were willing to so use major portions of their strength. And, for all its apparent success, Grey's expedition kept the army in meat for no more than two weeks. Similarly, the strenuous activities of the fall of 1778 did no more than keep the army together. For all the exertions there were still only four day's provisions in the storehouses when the British fleet arrived in New York harbor in January 1779.

The most interesting part of this record of failure, however, was surely the continuing hope that the situation would improve. The experience of 1775 at Boston did not discourage hope for 1776 at New York, nor the winter of 1776 at New York and Burgoyne's disastrous campaign in 1777 the hope for better things for the army at Philadelphia. Although Wier, during the occupation of Philadelphia, came to the unequivocal conclusion that no dependence for supplies could ever be placed on America, the Treasury could and did persist in its dreams. Nor was it alone. The reason for this continued and, from hindsight, unwarranted optimism lay in the conception of the rebel-

[30] Sir Henry Clinton, *The American Rebellion* (ed. W. B. Willcox, New Haven, 1954), 49.

[31] T 64/114, 107-108, Wier to Robinson, 21 Dec 78.

lion held by many Britons. Convinced that Britain had developed the perfect form of government, a "balanced" government that achieved at the same time both order and freedom, and that the colonies shared in this perfection, they could only believe that the trouble in America was the work of a demagogic minority that had climbed to power by misrepresentation and maintained itself there by force. It followed from this belief that the task of the British army was not to conquer but to free. Given the chance, the people would throw off the delusions that gripped them and return to loyalty. Germain, writing in 1779 to Clinton to applaud the commander's decision to make more use of Loyalists, went on: "I am convinced our utmost efforts will fail of their effects if we cannot find means to engage the people of America in support of a cause, which is equally their own and ours; and when their enemies are driven away or subdued, induce them to employ their own force to protect themselves, in the enjoyment of the blessing of that constitution to which they shall have been restored."[32]

"Deluded" was the word constantly used to describe the Americans. Although the first few years of the war convinced most that the northern colonies were so sunk in delusion as to be totally damned, it was still believed that the South could be redeemed. Nothing indicates this better than the proclamation issued by Clinton and Arbuthnot on the fall of Charleston in 1780: "His Majesty having been pleased by his letters patent, under the great seal of Great Britain, to appoint us to be his commissioners, to restore the blessing of peace and liberty to the several colonies in rebellion in America, we do hereby make public his most gracious intentions, and in obedience to his commands, do declare to such of his deluded subjects as have been perverted from their duty by the factious arts of self-interested and ambitious men, that they will be received with mercy and foregiveness, if they immediately return to their allegiance, and a due obedience to those laws and that govern-

[32] BAHQP, 2,170, 5 Aug 79.

ment which they formerly boasted was their best birthright and noblest inheritance. . . ."[33]

While Clinton was nevertheless inclined to be cautious, even expressing the fear that the British raids into the Chesapeake area in 1780 and 1781 would lead to Loyalist uprisings that could not be supported and hence were doomed, Cornwallis was much more confident. His confidence led him to repeat the most fundamental mistakes of the early part of the war. He attempted to control South Carolina with a series of small, relatively weak posts. When this control was threatened by Rebel guerrillas and General Nathaniel Greene's army, he determined to move into North Carolina and destroy Greene's forces.[34] Sure that the people of that state would rise up to his support, he cut his lines of communications with his bases in South Carolina and even destroyed his supply train to increase the mobility of his army. Two months on the march proved how few Loyalists there were in North Carolina or, at least, how few were convinced enough of a British victory to risk their all to support Cornwallis. When Greene was finally brought to battle at Guilford Court House, Cornwallis' army was hungry, ragged, barefoot, and alone.[35] Greene was driven from the field of battle but Cornwallis was too weak to pursue the disorganized Americans. He was forced instead to turn to the British base at the mouth of the Cape

[33] Lt. Col. Banestre Tarleton, *A History of the Campaigns of 1780 and 1781 in the Southern Provinces of North America* (London, 1787), 74. Another example of the same sort of thinking can be found in a letter of Gage to Dartmouth of 25 June 75 (Dartmouth Papers, D1778/II/1334). Bernard Bailyn in his *Origins of American Politics* (New York, 1968) and his *Ideological Origins of the American Revolution* (Cambridge, Mass., 1967) discusses the whole problem of the ideological background of the war.

[34] Franklin Wickwire and Mary Wickwire, *Cornwallis: The American Adventure* (Boston, 1970), 250.

[35] Roger Lamb, *Original and Authentic Journal of Occurrences During the Late American War* (Dublin, 1809), 348, 357, 381; PRO 30/11/76, 28-29, Cornwallis to Germain, 17 Mar 81.

Fear River to rest and refit.[36] While he did so, Greene, quickly reorganized, refitted, and reinforced, slipped back into South Carolina to begin the reduction of British control there.

It is to the credit of the Treasury that, despite its consuming desire to reduce the costs of the war and its continuous appeals to the commanders in America and the commissary general to reduce the dependence of the army on Britain, it very quickly faced up to the fact that, at least in the short run, the army would have to be fed from Britain. Despite the pain of the extravagance, it seldom consciously skimped on that responsibility. But there were areas of supply, the most important of which was fresh food, in which the army was necessarily left to its own resources. Flour, salt beef and pork, butter, cheese, and dried pease could all be supplied from Britain but fresh food, which could come only from America, was indispensable also. In part it was required to combat scurvy, the grim companion, as every sailor knew and every soldier soon learned, of a continuous diet of salt provisions. But had it been for this purpose alone the sauerkraut, porter, and vinegar sent from Britain and the spruce beer brewed in America[37] would have done almost as well as fresh food.

---

[36] PRO 30/11/85, 18, Cornwallis to Rawdon, 2 Apr 81. In January of 1781, Cornwallis, anticipating a need for supplies while in North Carolina back country, ordered a small force under Major Craig of the 82d Regt. established at Wilmington, at the mouth of the Cape Fear River. Craig's job was to set up a supply depot and establish communications with Cross Creek at the fall line on the Cape Fear River, where he was to meet Cornwallis with provisions, supplies, and reinforcements. It was anticipated that the North Carolina Loyalists would assist in opening and maintaining the communications between Wilmington and Cross Creek. Although Craig easily took Wilmington, he found himself hemmed in by Rebel militia and unable to command the countryside around the town, much less a hundred-odd miles of river. Since his supplies could not come to him, Cornwalls had to break contact with Greene and move to them. (PRO 30/11/109, 1-2; /5, 33, 79-80; /85, 18.)

[37] The ration of sauerkraut was two pounds a week and of vinegar a pint.

More importantly, it was necessary to maintain morale and hence reduce the desertion that inevitably accompanied low morale. Eighteenth-century food preservation techniques were far from perfect. Deterioration usually set in quite quickly and could proceed a considerable way before the food was declared "unfit for his Majesty's troops."[38] Even in the American army, where soldiers were presumably motivated by patriotism, periods of short or bad rations were invariably accompanied by desertions or at least a reluctance to renew short-term enlistments. In the British army and its hired German corps, where patriotism was a minimal factor and the soldiers on long-term enlistments, the tendency to desertion at such periods was even greater. In the early winter of 1778-1779, for instance, when the army was approaching its logistical nadir and bad oatmeal was substituted for bread, one German officer reported that "the Yagers deserted in large numbers on account of bad camp . . . and poor rations. . . ."[39]

Thus for reasons of the health of the men and the army, it was imperative that a supply of fresh food be maintained. In the first year of the war the Treasury undertook this task also, instructing the contractors to provide everything the army might require. The firm of Mure, Son & Atkinson proceeded with tremendous vigor and foresight to do just that. Besides the usual beef, pork, bread, pease, and oatmeal, they loaded on board the thirty-six ships dispatched for Boston in October and November of 1775 some 500 tons of potatoes, sixty of onions, fifty of parsnips, forty of carrots, and twenty of raisins, as well as 4,000 sheep and hogs and 468,750 gallons of porter.[40] The army was to have an easy winter and be ready early in the spring to take the offensive. Considerable care attended all this. The contrac-

[38] The quality of the salt provisions from Britain is discussed in Ch. III.

[39] "Lt. John Charles Philip von Kraft, Journal, 1776, 1784" (New-York Historical Society, *Collections*, 1882), 90.

[40] T 1/513, "List of Victualling Transports Bound to Boston. . . ."

tors noted that they had gone to great trouble to determine the best method of storing potatoes, and they were loaded very gently into the ships "so as not to bruise them." Onions were packed in hampers for the same reason, and as the several tons of sauerkraut being shipped would not have completed the fermentation process, each cask was fitted with a spring-loaded pressure relief valve.[41] Finally, in recognition of the perils of shipping livestock, a premium of two shillings and sixpence was promised to the masters of the transports for each animal delivered alive.

The fate of this fine example of British capacity and ingenuity had all the proportions of a Greek tragedy. Nemesis struck in the form of the most violent autumnal storms in years. A number of ships turned back or were driven back to England before reaching the American littoral. The remainder spent days and weeks impotently beating up and down the American coast waiting for a break in the weather, and fifteen, damaged or worn out, finally gave up and bore off to the safe harbor of Antigua. American privateers took their toll also so that in the end only thirteen ships straggled into Boston. The disappointment was compounded when it was found that only seventeen of the 200 tons of potatoes on board were useable: the remainder, along with almost all of the 328 bushels of onions, were "much grown and rotten owing to the heat." Of the 550 sheep and 290 hogs on board the ships but sixty of the former and eighty-eight of the latter survived. Only the preserved food—the sauerkraut, porter, and vinegar—survived intact. Or the ships that went to Antigua, a few joined the army in the summer, but none of their fresh provisions, live or otherwise, survived.[42] Instead of four months of rest and good health, the army spent four months on short rations plagued by the diseases accompanying an ill-balanced diet.[43]

[41] T 64/106, 20-26, Mure, Son & Atkinson to Howe, 25 Sept 75.

[42] T 64/108, 18-19, 38-39.

[43] The numerous diaries of officers stationed at Boston over the winter all attest to this, as does Clinton in his *American Rebellion* (23).

The failure of this venture, plus, of course, the hope that the army once out of Boston could fend for itself, virtually ended the efforts to supply fresh food from Britain. Only one more attempt, and that of cattle alone, was made. On the basis that the first failure might have resulted from hurry, bad weather, and the season of the year, the Treasury in 1776 let out a contract with Anthony Merry, a London merchant, to ship cattle from the port of Milford in Wales for the use of the army. Merry's efforts, although they cost the government nearly £17,000, were not significantly more successful than those of Mure, Son & Atkinson. Perhaps their main achievement was to supply the army with a number of ships adapted to the transport of live cattle for use in foraging raids such as that of General Grey.[44]

A second area in which the army had to remain dependent on North American supplies was that of animal fodder. Until World War II the horse was as much a part of war as the soldier and just slightly less necessary. In the winter of 1775-1776, Howe, planning for the coming campaign, estimated that he would need a minimum of 3,662 horses,[45] and in the following years there were seldom fewer than that with the army, including cavalry and artillery horses. Many factors, apart from the size of the cavalry and artillery detachments, governed the extent of the requirement for horses. Of primary importance was the provisions train that accompanied the army in the field. No eighteenth-century commander raised in the European tradition would think of taking the field without such a train. The alternative to carrying the food needed by the army was living off the land, and the rationalist and gentlemanly concept of war in that century frowned on such conduct as barbarous since it left innocent civilian populations to starve and

[44] BAHQP, 22, North to Howe, 25 June 76; T 1/525, 340, "Account of Anthony Merry."

[45] T 64/108, 12, Howe to Robinson, 1 Dec 75. A second estimate in the same letter was for 4,738 horses, if the army were equipped with pack horses instead of wagons.

opened the way to looting. More important, however, was the effect on the army itself. Armies of the period tended to be small and expensive to the point that even victories attended by considerable losses were unacceptable. Aware of the problems of health and morale that accompanied poor and short rations, few commanders willingly trusted the feeding of their armies to the chance that sufficient food could be obtained along the line of march. Further, soldiers were usually long-term enlistees from the outcast orders of society. Indifferent to causes and used to their comforts, they often did not take well to the hardships of war.[46] Shortages of food, or even the prospect of shortages, was a motive for desertion and foraging expeditions, wide ranging and in small parties, provided the opportunity for those so inclined. In the winters of 1775-1776 and 1778-1779, when supplies from England failed and rations were cut, a steady stream of desertions ensued,[47] and when Cornwallis burned his supplies and wagon train before setting out in pursuit of Greene in January of 1781, over 250 men chose to desert rather than face the hardships involved in living off the land.[48] Understandably, then, commanders reluctantly took the field without bringing with them virtually all the provisions their force required; the result was a provisions train of considerable proportions. An army of 20,000 consumed in one day thirty-three tons of food.[49] Since the stand-

[46] Although the analysis therein is confirmed by my own research, the arguments in this paragraph are derived from several secondary sources: Preston *et al.*, Ch. 9; Mackesy, 78; French, Ch. VIII.

[47] Anderson, 70; N-YHS, "von Kraft Journal," 70.

[48] Ward, vol. 2, 765.

[49] Although the normal ration was a pound each of bread and meat per man per day plus "small species," the diet was reduced to bread and meat alone when in the field and the ration increased to as much as a pound and a half of each.

[50] G. Tylden, *Horses and Saddlery* (London, 1965), 179. Tylden gives a load of 800 pounds for the two-horse cart which was also extensively used by the army.

ard four-horse wagon could carry about a ton,[50] an army of that size proceeding on a campaign of more than three or four days duration—the limit at which soldiers were expected to carry their own rations—required at least thirty-three wagons and 132 horses for each day beyond that.[51]

But provisions were by no means the only items that required transportation. For reasons identical to those which influenced his thinking on food, no eighteenth-century commander would think of taking the field for any length of time without bringing with him all the paraphernalia of life in the open: tents, axes, kettles, blankets, and so on. And if the soldiers' comforts were looked to, why not then the officers' also? Indeed, drawn from the self-indulgent aristocracy and gentry class, the officers were seldom prepared to give up even the smallest comforts. The reluctance of Burgoyne's officers to part with their personal baggage during the campaign of 1777 is justly infamous and most assuredly figured in the defeat of that army.[52] Even so, probably few of them campaigned with quite the oppulence of Lt. Col. William Harcourt, who, on the eve of his departure for America, wrote to his father in respect to his personal equippage: "Your last offer relative to the plate affords me no small satisfaction; not that I mean to avail myself of it in its full extent, but because it ensures me your approbation of the order I had already given relative to that matter. The fact is the tureens would be of small service, as the circular one in which the plates are packed is quite sufficient for that purpose; with regard to the additional dozen of plates, I might perhaps have been induced to trespass so far upon your indulgence, but that the things

[51] The number required would obviously vary with the distance from and ease of communications with the supply base. Few commanders, however, cared to risk even the possibility of their supply lines being cut. Howe's estimate of his horse requirements stated specifically that "the magazine for this army should be carried by water and not more than twenty miles distance from it."

[52] See Ch. VI.

are already finished and packed; the deep dish and lamp will be extremely useful. . . ."[53]

While some might not expect to take their comforts beyond the winter cantonments, such was not the feeling of Lt. William Hale of the 45th Regiment who, shortly after the army had landed at the head of the Chesapeake in 1777, wrote to his father that "for this week past we have lived like beasts, no plates, no dishes, no tablecloth. . . ."[54] It is not surprising, then, that even the twelve wagons and fifty-eight horses allotted in Howe's estimate for regimental baggage (ten horses only being for the transport of soldiers' tents) were, when headquarters equipment, ammunitions, and other accoutrements were added on, often insufficient and officers who could afford it procured extras.

Nor did the numbering of horses end there. The general and staff officers alone were allotted 342 horses, and although the medical service usually made do with empty provisions' wagons for ambulances, other special branches could not be so easily satisfied. Blacksmiths, carpenters, harnessmakers, and other tradesmen with their mobile workshops always accompanied the army, and Cornwallis' experience in losing Washington across the Delaware River in 1776 for want of boats or a bridge resulted in the formation of a bridging unit that required 118 horses for the transport of its equipment.[55]

Finally, horses were required to carry the food for other horses. Although at times the daily ration went as low as fourteen pounds of hay and seven of oats, the ideal feed for a large working horse was twenty of hay and nine of oats. If all this had to be carried with the army, a campaign of a week's duration would require two horses pulling fodder for each three engaged in more military tasks. Not surpris-

[53] E. W. Harcourt (ed.), *The Harcourt Papers* (Oxford, 1880), vol. XL, 167.

[54] W. H. Wilkins, *Some British Soldiers in America* (London, 1914), 277.

[55] CP, Report on Pontoons by Capt. Robert Fenwick, 3 Mar 79.

ingly, most commanders opted to put off the opening of the campaign year in the spring until at least hay, or a green substitute, was available in the field—a decision that brought down a great deal of unjust criticism on Howe by contemporaries and historians.[56] By an arrangement that the forage horses would carry just oats, the proportion was reduced from two in five to one in eight for a week-long expedition.

The problem of feeding horses came up almost as soon as the problem of feeding the soldiers. Dismayed by the difficulties of finding fodder for the less than 500 horses the army had at Boston, even when drawing on Nova Scotia, Howe requested in his outline of the campaign of 1776 that both hay and oats be sent out from Britain. While hay, he pointed out, was available on Rhode Island and Long and Staten Islands, its procurement would be difficult if the inhabitants were "inimical." And while oats could be procured from Canada, transportation problems would be no worse and quality better if they were sent from Ireland.[57] The Treasury was less than enthusiastic about the idea. Nevertheless, aware that Canada was then in American hands, as Howe had not been when he wrote, it was conceded that oats could and would be sent from Britain. A quarter of a million bushels, sufficient for 3,000 horses for a year, were ordered out. Hay was another matter. The bulk of the article and a shortage of shipping made its provision impossible; Howe was provided with a number of hay presses and politely told that he would have to find his own supplies.[58]

There were two other areas of logistics, somewhat less spectacular but nonetheless important, in which the British found themselves dependent on America: horses and fuel. As mentioned, Howe, in his list of requirements for the

[56] HMC, Stopford-Sackville Mss., Howe to Germain, 19 Apr 78.

[57] T 64/108, 7, Remarks [by Howe on the forthcoming campaign] 27 Nov 75.

[58] T 64/106, 29-44, Robinson to Howe, 1 May 76.

campaign of 1776, specified a need for 3,662 horses and, for reasons basically the same as those governing his request for hay, asked that they be supplied from Britain. While Lord George Germain considered the scale of the request impossible and suggested that the army would have to depend more on "water carriage" a smaller wagon train was ordered out.[59] The loss in transit of 532 of the 856 horses in the train, at sixteen guineas each, was more than the Treasury could accept and thereafter dependence had to be on America.[60]

The problem of fuel began even before the cool weather set in at Boston in the fall of 1775, and as with all its needs the army's requirements for this commodity were on a grand scale. Even in warm weather, cooking, baking, washing, and a myriad of other tasks consumed large quantities of fuel. Once it became necessary to heat living quarters, the army became a devourer of forests. The force at New York alone consumed in the neighborhood of 70,000 cords a year.[61]

Because of easy access to the forests of North America, the acquisition of wood on the scale required by the army was relatively simple. For an army cut off from those forests, as was that at Boston, the search for fuel became a destructive force. The burning of Charlestown, begun during the battle of Bunker Hill, was completed in watch fires of the army the following winter. The old North Church, the steeple of the West Church, wharves, ships in the least unsound, dozens of buildings, and fencing by the mile were broken up and burned to keep the army warm during the winter of 1775-1776, as were the Liberty Tree and a good

59 Dartmouth Papers, D1778/II/1646, Germain to Howe, 5 Jan 76. See also p. 24.

60 T 64/108, 74-75, Howe to Robinson, 2 Dec 76. Thirty-one of ninety-eight cavalry remounts on the same convoy also died.

61 T 64/108, 117, "Calculation of Fewel and Candles for 40,000 Men during the 26 Winter Weeks," New York, 20 Mar 77; Mackenzie Papers, "Proportion of fuel and Candles allowed at New York, 1780."

part of the other shade trees of old Boston. Even so many still went cold, and the clandestine dismantling of fences and buildings reached such a pace that Howe finally ordered the immediate hanging of anyone caught in such an act.[62]

There was an alternative to wood, however: coal, substituted for wood at the rate of one-third of a chaldron (12 bushels) per cord. The sources of coal were two, Britain and the old French mines of Cape Breton, and both were called on to some extent. Reports of the fuel shortage at Boston led the Treasury, as early as the summer of 1775, to order 3,000 chaldrons shipped to the army.[63] But the idea was never completely to the liking of the Treasury for reasons both of the cost of coal and shipping, and because of the perennial shortage of shipping. Although it was suggested that the coal could come as ballast on victuallers, this turned out to be impractical as ships' masters already used barrels of wet provisions for that purpose. It was with distinct relief, then, that the department received a letter from Howe in the early fall of 1776 informing it that the fuel situation had improved immensely with the move to New York and that further supplies from Britain would not be necessary. Howe must have changed his mind shortly thereafter, though, for the Treasury again negotiated contracts for coal in 1777 and 1778. There is no record of contracts after that date.[64]

The Treasury was never happy with the task of shipping coal, however, feeling that it was an unnecessary burden on its facilities. For that reason it suggested very early in the war that the army attempt to reopen the old French mines at Spanish River on Cape Breton Island.[65] The idea seems to have occurred simultaneously to the army, and during

[62] T. S. Anderson, *The Command of the Howe Brothers During the American Revolution* (New York, 1936), 91; Ward, 113-115.

[63] T 27/31, 116-117, Robinson to Anthony Bacon, 23 Sept. 75.

[64] See Baker, 241-254, for a comprehensive account of coal contracts.

[65] T 29/44, 26 July 75; T 64/106, 11, Robinson to Howe, 14 Sept 75.

1775 a contract was concluded with William Knutton of Boston to supply the army from that source.[66] Knutton's experience was not a happy one. Nor was that of the various successive detachments of the Nova Scotia volunteers and regular army units who took over the mines from 1776 on. Technical problems as well as gas and water seepage plagued the operation, and although each new unit on the site began with high hopes of production in the thousands of chaldrons—it was this optimism along with the initial abundance of wood in New York that led to Howe's confident renunciation of supplies from Britain—they were never realized. Further, the mines required protection from American and French privateers as did the ships that were sent to transport the coal. In the end the mines did little more than supply the garrison at Halifax and the main army at New York remained dependent on wood obtained locally.[67]

The first year of the war, then, demonstrated, if it did not prove, that a dependence on North America for the supplies the army needed would be at best precarious. But at the same time it became equally clear that transportation problems, shortage of shipping, and cost nevertheless made it unavoidable that the army should be dependent on North America for a number of vital needs. Although neither of these revelations was accepted easily, and although there were periods when it seemed that the situation might change, the succeeding years confirmed them. The adjustment to this situation, the necessity of filling these needs, became an important determinant of British strategy.

The first major strategic decision made for basically logistical reasons was to evacuate Boston. Burgoyne recognized the problems of conducting a war in New England very

[66] T 29/48, 9 June 79; T 64/112, 121-122, General Clinton's Accounts.
[67] T 64/108, 29-44, 50, 103-105; HMC, Dartmouth Mss., 408, 416, BAHQP, 596, 1,193, 1,237, 2,007; T 1/534, 177-178; T 1/525, 216.

shortly after his arrival in Boston in May 1775. Although he felt that topography would turn any campaign in New England into a series of Bunker Hills, the main emphasis of an analysis be sent to Lord Rochford was logistics. The enemy, he was sure, would sweep the country clean of food ahead of a British army and even if that army had a complete supply train, which it did not, the nature of the country would render communications between the army and its supply base precarious in the extreme.[68] It took the problems of the summer of 1775 to bring Gage to the same point, but in one of his last letters as commander-in-chief he recommended the evacuation of Boston. "It appears to me," he wrote to Dartmouth on October 1, "most necessary for the prosecution of the war to be in possession of some province where you can be secured, and from whence draw supplies of provisions and forage, and that New York seems to be the most proper to answer these purposes."[69] Gage's successor, General Howe, and his deputy, General Clinton, agreed with this analysis and, but for the want of necessary shipping, the evacuation might have been carried out in November.[70]

Logistical considerations figured largely, also, in the choice of New York as the new base for army operations. Not only was it a port and in a position to command the Hudson River and thus split the rebellious colonies in two, but, equally important, the area around it was believed to be the home of many "friends of government" and thus a good source of the supplies the army would need.[71]

Although there were problems, New York seemed at first

[68] E. B. DeFonblanque, *Political and Military Episodes . . . from the Life and Correspondence of the Rt. Hon. John Burgoyne . . .* (London, 1876), 142.

[69] CO 5/92, 291. Gage's thoughts were moving in this direction even earlier; see CO 5/92, 260, 20 Aug 75 and also letters of 12 June and 24 July, also in CO 92/5.

[70] CO 5/92, 641, Howe to Dartmouth, 26 Nov 75; CP, Clinton to Harvey, June 75.

[71] See note 69 above.

to be the answer to all the army's logistical needs. The wagon train sent from England did not arrive in time for the opening of the campaign, but it made little difference. Once the move was made to Long Island, horses and wagons—plundered, purchased, or hired—became available in such abundance that not only was every regimental need fulfilled but many officers acquired several for their own use.[72] Food, although slow in coming in at first, was sufficient to provide everyone with a day or two of fresh rations each week. By the middle of December, with New Jersey in British hands, food became available in such abundance that beginnings were made on a stockpile for the campaign of 1777.[73]

Only in the article of forage was there any great problem. That problem, however, became a part of a major strategic decision. Staten Island, as could be expected, produced very little forage. But of Long Island greater things were expected. For reasons that are not entirely clear (possibly, though, involving American diligence in burning supplies)[74] it did not live up to its expectations. By early fall, rations for army horses had to be cut to fourteen pounds of hay and ten pounds of oats for the cavalry and eight and ten pounds respectively for wagon animals, and the commissary general urgently dispatched ships to Quebec and Halifax in search of supplies.[75] The situation was not helped by the late arrival of the oats promised from Britain and for a time the horses were fed on oatmeal meant for the navy and a shipload of captured bran.[76] It was this problem which, as much as anything else, seems to have been behind Howe's much criticized decision to

[72] Uhlendorf, 45, Baurmeister to von Jungkenn, 24 Sept 76.

[73] *Supra*, pp. 47-48.

[74] This is indicated in T 64/118, 36-40, Chamier to Robinson, 31 Mar 77.

[75] Frederick Mackenzie, *Diary of Frederick Mackenzie* (Harvard University Press, 1930), 64; T 64/118, 11, Chamier to Robinson, 24 Sept 76.

[76] T 64/118, 13-14, Chamier to Robinson, 9 Nov 76; T 64/118, 18-19, Chamier to Robinson, 30 Nov 76.

take Rhode Island in 1776 instead of waiting until the following year as expected by some.[77] Rhode Island had long been seen as a major source of not only forage but provisions of all sorts for the army, and it is not surprising that Howe, although motivated also by a desire to provide a secure winter anchorage for his brother's fleet, chose to take it at this time.[78] The problem of forage, of course, was apparently solved, just before Clinton's expedition for Rhode Island departed, by Cornwallis' victories in New Jersey. But at the time it was ordered, in early November, the forage shortage was at its height and Howe had no intention of proceeding farther into New Jersey that winter than New Brunswick.[79] With the expedition already mounted, why not allow it to proceed: the navy would have its anchorage and the army could stockpile hay and oats for the forthcoming campaign?

At the point of December 24, 1776, then, the war seemed finally to be going well for Britain. A base area including lower New York and most of New Jersey had been established, capable of supplying most of the food needs of the army, a port taken through which the remaining needs could be supplied from Britain, and harbors and anchorages for the navy secured. The war could proceed in 1777 according to European pattern. This ideal situation was shattered with painful suddenness on December 25 when Washington attacked and destroyed the British post at Trenton, New Jersey. Howe learned what Clinton had suspected all along: while the American army might not be able to stand up to European regulars in a comparatively evenly matched battle, it was nevertheless dangerous. Any attempt to hold territory with relatively weak and unsup-

[77] Mackenzie, 94-95.

[78] Dartmouth Papers D1778/11/1448, Jo. Irving to Sir George Collier, 20 Aug 75; T 1/514, "Remarks of General Howe," 27 Nov 75; HMC, Stopford-Sackville Mss., Howe to Germain, 12 May 76; Clinton, *American Rebellion*, 56, n.34.

[79] CO 5/94, 31-36, Howe to Germain, 20 Dec 76.

ported detachments was to invite repetitions of the Trenton disaster.[80] Henceforth the army would have to be restricted to an area that could be protected by highly developed, interlocking defensive works, basically an area comprising Manhattan Island and the tip of Long Island, with toeholds across the Hudson and East Rivers. For the area abandoned by the British, the remainder of the winter of 1776-1777 proved that Rebel loyalties (or fear of Rebel reprisals) dominated and no secure dependence could be placed on it for supplies. British control extended only when and for as long as British forces moved out in strength from their fortifications. This in turn meant that the basic dependence for food had to be on Britain, and fortified ports, the termini of the support line from Britain, became the *sine qua non* of the British presence in the colonies. New York City, thus, instead of being the collection point of a supply area, became a supply depot. Although there was hope that Pennsylvania would prove more loyal than New Jersey, Howe remembered the lesson of Trenton when he established his army at Philadelphia, and the building of a tight ring of fortifications around that city occupied a large part of the army during the fall and winter of 1777.[81] Only for a period well short of a year, in South Carolina while Cornwallis learned the same lesson, did the British ever again seek to control completely any considerable area of the Thirteen Colonies.[82]

But, as pointed out, there could be no complete dependence on Britain either. Fresh food, forage, fuel, and transport had to be obtained in America and therein lay the basis of a whole neglected phase of the war. The military histories of the American Revolution have by and large concentrated on the great set-piece battles such as Bunker Hill, Long Island, White Plains, and Brandywine Creek.

[80] Willcox, *Portrait of a General*, 120.

[81] "The Montressor Journals" (New-York Historical Society, *Collections*, 1881), 459-494.

[82] For details of this see the last part of this chapter.

They have neglected, or failed to see as a whole, a deadly and vitally important battle that went on continuously as a result of the British logistical dependence on North America. This battle, although foreshadowed at Boston, really began when Washington's winter campaign of 1776-1777 drove the British out of New Jersey. It is not suggested that the attack on Trenton and Princeton was inspired by logistical insights on Washington's part; indeed, it is best seen as a desperate measure, breaking all military traditions, to revive Rebel morale. Nevertheless, Washington was well aware of the British logistical position. In 1775 he had instituted a privateer service—the beginnings of the American navy—to harass the ships supplying Boston[83] and specifically ordered his spies in the British bases to report regularly on the supply situation.[84] It is not surprising, then, that he was thinking on similar lines in 1777. His army, too weak and too ill-supplied to press the successes of Trenton and Princeton, was still adequate, nevertheless, to attempt the equally vital task of denying the British the resources of New Jersey. As he could deny them forage and horses, so he could paralyze their land operations; as he could deny them fresh food, so he could increase discontent and sickness.[85]

The remainder of the winter of 1776-1777 set a pattern that was followed in the environs of almost every British base for the remainder of the war. The need for hay, fresh provisions, fuel, and horses drove the British to regular foraging expeditions into the countryside. The Rebels in turn sought to deny to the British everything possible, removing what they could and harassing the foraging parties at every turn.[86] Large covering parties became necessary to

[83] For the details of the institution of the privateer navy and its effects see Ch. III.

[84] C. Ford, *A Peculiar Service* (Boston, 1965), 193.

[85] D. H. Freeman, *George Washington* (New York, 1952), vol. 4, 283-284.

[86] *Ibid.*

protect the foragers and a kind of warfare resulted that was more like Lexington and Concord than Long Island or Brandywine, and with the same advantage to the Americans—the opportunity to use the tactic of strike-and-run and harassment from cover of fence or forest, the option of melting into the countryside when British covering forces became too strong, and, most of all, the possibility of using militia and raw regulars in the kind of warfare in which they proved themselves highly competent. Captain Stuart, writing to his father Lord Bute, felt that this type of warfare was a positive advantage to the American army: "The Rebel soldiers, from being accustomed to peril in the skirmishes, begin to have more confidence, and their officers seldom meet with our foraging parties, but they try every ruse to entrap them, and, tho' they do not always succeed, yet the following the people as they return, and the wounding and killing many of our rearguards, gives them the notion of victory, and habituates them to the profession."[87]

For the British, foraging became a constant of the war. It demanded an inordinate effort, unwelcome to soldiers used to the formalities of European warfare—one of whom described it as "a dirty kind of *tiraillerie*"[88]—and was expensive in men and equipment. The story of the winter of 1776-1777 is well told in the diaries of two officers stationed in New Jersey, Captain Archibald Robertson of the Engineers and Captain John Peebles of the 42d Regiment.[89] The frequency of the foraging operations that engaged their units alone is astonishing; six in each of January and

[87] E. Stuart Wortley (ed.), *A Prime Minister to His Son* (London, 1925), 20 Mar 77.

[88] Sir James Murray, *Letters from America* (ed. E. Robson, Manchester, 1951), 38-39, Murray to his sister, 25 Feb 77.

[89] H. M. Lydenberg (ed.), *Archibald Robertson . . . Diary and Sketches in America, 1762-80* (New York, 1930); SRO, GD 21/492, "Journal of Captain John Peebles of the 42d or Royal Highland Regiment during the War of Independence."

February and ten in March. The size of the expeditions was never small, and the covering force involved seldom less than 500 men and more often 2,000 or more. Occasionally the forage could be gathered and the cattle driven in without incident, but more often the days were a series of short, sharp clashes, with casualties ranging from a few to as many as seventy-five. One officer remarked that the struggle for forage "kept the army the whole winter in perpetual harassment, and upon a modest computation has lost us more men than the last campaign."[90]

Yet, despite all the effort, results were meagre. Fresh provisions procured were never more than enough for the hospitals and often not even that. The forage shortage so agitated the normally placid Howe that it led to a break with one of the few able and daring generals under his command, Lt. Gen. Lord Percy. Percy commanded at Newport, Rhode Island, having taken over from Clinton shortly after Newport fell to the British. When the disaster in New Jersey cut off forage from that source, Howe turned to Percy for some of the 15,000 tons of hay he had been told was available in Rhode Island. Percy's response was disappointing. A commissary department survey, he reported, indicated that there were no more than 1,440 tons of hay on Newport Island and 800 tons of that were absolutely necessary for the maintenance of the civilian livestock. Swallowing his disappointment, Howe ordered most of the remainder shipped to New York at once. When only 100 tons were forthcoming and an ill-informed letter from the deputy commissary general on Rhode Island, Major John Morrison, indicated that Percy intended to keep the remainder for the use of his own forces, Howe's disappointment turned to anger. In fact, Percy's reluctance was based on difficulties in collecting the hay and some well-founded doubts as to

[90] Wortley, 101-102, Stuart to Bute, 29 Mar 77. For similar comments see, Alnwick Castle Mss. LI, Robert Mackenzie to Percy, 4 Feb 77, and quote in Anderson, 236.

the accuracy of the commissary survey, but before this could be explained, Howe issued a mild reproof. However unjustified, the reproof was understandable in view of Howe's situation and anyone else might have borne it patiently. Percy, however, was of the blood of Hotspur, and the thought that his honor and position could be undermined by the word of a commissary so angered him that he requested and was shortly afterwards granted leave to return to Britain.[91]

The campaign in Pennsylvania in 1777-1778 was remarkably similar to that of the previous year. Although Washington attempted to sweep the countryside bare in front of the British army, there was not time enough for effective measures, and the battles and defeats at Brandywine and Germantown turned his attention to more fundamental matters. Thus in the first two months after the landings at Head of Elk, the army fed almost every other day on fresh provisions from the well-developed farms of eastern Pennsylvania, long providers of food for the less well-endowed areas of the colonies. The abundance of the food, and the ease with which it was secured, led both Daniel Wier, the new commissary general installed in office just before the campaign began, and the Treasury cautiously to hope again that dependence on Britain could be reduced. The forage situation seemed equally bright. Wier reported late in October that 1,800 tons of hay had been collected, with prospects of enough more easily available to see the army through the winter.[92] But the hope was premature. Defeated in pitched battle, Washington turned his forces to the harassing tactic of the previous winter. Even the stubborn defense of Fort Mifflin and Red Bank was a part of this strategy, for so long as they blocked the sea approaches of Philadelphia the British were compelled to forage for most of their needs, wearing out men and equipment and

[91] All of the letters pertinent to this incident, dated between 21 Jan and 23 Mar 77 are in Alnwick Castle Mss., vol. LI.

[92] HSP, Wier Letter Book, Wier to [Robinson], 25 Oct 77.

giving the Americans the opportunity to engage in the type of fighting for which they were as yet still best suited.[93]

This strategy was again impressive in its results. Despite the victories of Brandywine and Germantown, the British once again found themselves in possession of no more territory than they could protect by developed fortifications. The early success of the army in collecting food and forage from the countryside did in fact see the army through until Fort Mifflin and Red Bank were finally taken on November 22 and supplies from England could come up the river. But as Washington turned his forces to harassment so the unchallenged access to the countryside that the British enjoyed in the first few weeks of the campaign ended. As early as September 27 it became highly dangerous for small parties to stray far from the main British encampments[94] and by mid-October Howe was forced to draw his lines tight and absolutely forbid soldiers to go beyond them.[95] At the end of November, Wier, his own fond hopes dashed, wrote to destroy those of the Treasury: "The whole country around us is possessed by the enemy. . . . We can expect no supplies or assistance from this country but must place our whole dependence on what we receive from the other side of the water. It is with the greatest difficulty and at the hazard of mens lives that we are even able to obtain fresh provisions sufficient for our hospitals as we cannot with safety go an hundred yards beyond our lines without a large escort. . . ."[96]

By December the old routine of foraging with large covering parties got underway again when on the seventh of that month Cornwallis took a force of 4,000 into the field

[93] Freeman, 499.

[94] Major André, for instance, reported the wounding of four men and two officers near the camp on 27 September which somewhat surprises him as "Washington was supposed to be beyond Perkiomy Creek" (Major John André, *Major André's Journal* [Tarryton, 1930], 53).

[95] RAI, Howe Orderly Book, 16 Oct 77.

[96] HSP, Wier Letter Book, Wier to Robinson, 29 Nov 77.

for five days, returning with 800 sheep and cattle.[97] Two weeks later Howe took the best part of his force out for almost a week, with the dual purpose of foraging and tempting Washington to battle. Washington, however, wisely decided to fight on his own terms, and for the remainder of the winter the British had to field battalion-sized detachments two or three times a week to cover foraging and wood-cutting parties. Engagements with the enemy on these expeditions were fewer than in the previous year but sufficient nevertheless to prevent the British from dropping their guard. Even so, the shortage of forage finally led Howe to send some of his horses to winter on Long Island, and to import hay from Rhode Island to feed the remainder.[98]

The winter of 1777-1778 also saw the inauguration of another bitter phase of the war. In an attempt to obtain food for both the army and the civilian population Howe reopened the public market in Philadelphia and by handbills advertised the desire of the army to purchase food brought there. The weakness of the American army, which prevented a Boston-type blockade of the city, and the offer of hard money brought in a steady stream of farmers from farther and farther afield and at one point in January prices, which had been impossible a few weeks earlier, came down to a range accessible to an officer's pocketbook.[99] American reaction to this trade was a Congressional edict forbidding persons living more than six miles from Philadelphia any contact with that city and, far more important, the dispatch of military detachments to intercept and turn back the farm wagons.[100] Bitterness, or perhaps lack of military strength, led the intercepting parties to use the weapon of terror against the traders. Reports soon spread of people

[97] Murray, 171.

[98] Parker Papers, PA9-65; RAI, Howe Orderly Book; SRO, Peebles Diary, vols. 4-5; N-YHS, "Montressor Journals"; Uhlendorf, 149.

[99] Uhlendorf, 149-150.

[100] Ibid., 164; SRO, Peebles Diary, 26 Feb 78.

being branded on the forehead with the letters "WH," "Howe's mark as they call it," or even hanged for attempting to trade with the British.[101] The prices General Baurmeister so admired earlier rapidly inflated, and expeditions to protect the "market people" were added to the duties of the British army.

This illicit trade with the British, carried on often by otherwise "patriotic" Americans, became, in fact, a continuing feature of the whole war. Despite harsh penalties for those caught, the traders were spurred on by the opportunity of obtaining scarce "hard money" instead of Congressional paper and equally scarce industrial products from Britain. The actual value of the trade is impossible to estimate. British commissary accounts seldom indicate the source of local purchases and, in any case, a large part of the trade was probably private, supplying the public markets in New York City and elsewhere. One aspect of this trade, called by Lossing "London Trading," was carried out by small boats "from almost every inlet from New London to Shrewsbury . . ." with either British vessels or posts and towns on Long, Staten, New York, and Rhode Islands.[102] It was to combat this trade, in large part, that the Rebels outfitted whaleboats very early in the war to patrol the waters between the mainland and the British-controlled islands. From this beginning whaleboat warfare developed into a daring and continuous harassment of the

[101] This practice is reported in a number of places: Parker Papers, 920 PAR, PA9-66, 67, 70; N-YHS, "Montressor Journals," 8 June 78; Uhlendorf, 157.

[102] J. Lossing, *The Pictorial Field Book of the Revolution* (New York, 1850-1852), vol. II, 851. Other products were also in demand, particularly salt. A letter from the office of the commander of New York of November 1779 discusses the trade moving through the British post at Morrisania and particularly the question of how much salt those bringing in cattle should be allowed to take back with them. (New-York Historical Society, *Collections*, 1875, "Correspondence of Major General James Pattison, 1779-1780," 279, Stephen Payne to Captain Nesbitt, 12 Nov 79.)

British communications and sources of supply.[103] When France entered the war and a good part of the British navy had to turn to duties elsewhere in the world, the number of these raiders increased, and the threat they posed became more serious. As early as 1779 Clinton expressed his fear for the safety even of victualling ships coming into American waters unprotected by strong naval forces.[104] In 1781 not only was it unsafe to venture into Long Island Sound as far as Lloyd's Neck, but ships were taken in New York Bay itself as far up as Governor's Island.[105]

Nor was this sort of operation confined entirely to the sea. Military prudence and the British navy made it unwise for the Americans to contest directly for the control of the various British-held islands. Indeed, one can imagine nothing more dear to the heart of the British commanders in North America than the vision of a major American force isolated on Long Island. But at the same time it was in the American interest to ensure that the British were not permitted peacefully to exploit the resources of their islands, particularly Long Island, the biggest and most productive. Whaleboats were the instrument of this policy also and throughout the war raids aimed at carrying off grain, cattle, forage, and even Loyalists and the occasional unwary British detachment were mounted across the Sound.[106] So daring did these raids become, and so persistent, that Baroness Riedesel, who could see the lights of New York from the bedroom window of her husband's headquarters

---

[103] M. M. Boatner, *Encyclopedia of the American Revolution* (New York, 1966), articles "London Trading," "Whaleboat Warfare," "Adam Hyler."

[104] Clinton, *American Rebellion*, 126-127.

[105] Mackenzie, 507, 528.

[106] Uhlendorf, 197; CP, Richard Floyd to Daniel Jones, 12 June 79; W. O. Raymond (ed.), *The Winslow Papers* (St. John, N.B., 1901), 19; A. Searle, *The American Journal of Ambrose Searle* (San Marino, 1940), 135; Mackenzie, 528.

on Long Island, feared every night that she would be the victim of one of them.[107]

The records that exist pertaining to the fresh food supply of the main army at New York for the remainder of the war are considerably less detailed than those for the period from 1775 to 1778. Nevertheless it is quite clear that a high level of foraging activity was a continuing necessity and at times, such as during d'Estaing's blockade in the summer of 1778 and in the ensuing winter when supplies from Britain failed, they became virtually the sole support of the army. It is also clear that as the war dragged on, the areas within easy reach of the posts at New York became less and less productive as both British and Americans foraged through them, taking what they could and often destroying what was left. General Baurmeister reported in the fall of 1778 that an expedition to the Mamaroneck area produced only fifty tons of hay and that the population was destitute.[108] Although there were occasional windfalls—such as the capture of a Rebel army herd of 1,000 cattle and sheep in June of 1779[109]—the average British soldier had to be in the hospital to enjoy more than occasional relief from his salt diet.

The forage situation was no better. Every summer and fall at New York the commissary department struggled to collect enough hay to see the army through the winter and allow it an early start on the spring campaign. Every winter saw a crisis in feeding the army's horses and in several years the ration of hay had to be cut and an extra portion of the oats shipped from England supplied instead.[110] With the movement of the British forces from Florida into Georgia

[107] M. L. Brown, *Baroness von Riedesel and the American Revolution* (Chapel Hill, N.C., 1965), 109.

[108] Uhlendorf, 218.   [109] *Ibid.*, 280.

[110] T 64/114, 74-76, Wier to Robinson, 5 Sept 78; Mackenzie, 427; T 64/114, 161, Wier to Robinson, 10 Apr 79; *Ibid.*, 183, Wier to Robinson, 24 July 79; CP, L.J.A. von Wurmb to André, 13 Sept 80; SRO, Peebles Diary, 5 July 80.

in 1779 a supply of rough rice for use as forage began to come into New York and at times was a valuable supplement to the dwindling forage supplies there.[111] It could never, of course, substitute completely for hay in the diet of horses and, in any case, supplies were so small and irregular, especially after operations began in South Carolina, that no dependence could be placed on it. So bad did the situation look in the summer of 1779 that the formation of Rawdon's cavalry legion was delayed because there was no assurance that the extra two hundred horses involved could be fed.[112] The problem became even more acute after the abandonment of Rhode Island later that same year. For, despite the experience of the winter of 1776-1777, that province proved in later years to be a considerable supplier of the army's hay needs.[113] The bad winters usually saw a plea by the commissary general to reduce the number of horses on the army establishment, and this placed the commander-in-chief in a serious dilemma. Reducing the establishment would solve the hay problem, but it would also mean a delay at the beginning of each campaign while transport was collected. Perhaps more important, the very act of collecting would advertise to the enemy that a campaign was imminent. Clinton invariably opted to maintain his transport service intact, which meant frantic efforts to find forage and often a delay in the spring while the horses recuperated from the hardships of the winter.[114]

The procurement of horses never seemed to be a great problem for the army, perhaps because the commandeering of all the hay and oats except that essential to the farmers made feeding them by anyone not on the army ration pro-

[111] T 64/114, 458, Wier to Robinson, 3 Apr 79.

[112] N-YHS, Wier Letter Book, Wier to Rawdon, 11 Aug 79.

[113] T 64/114, 215-219, Wier to Robinson, 11 Nov 79; CP, Robertson to Clinton, 29 May 80; T 27/33, Robinson to Clinton, 30 May 81.

[114] T 64/114, 33, Wier to Robinson, 25 May 78; Mackenzie, 427; CP, Delancey to Robertson, 27 Dec 80.

hibitively expensive. But fuel was an entirely different matter. The rate at which wood was consumed by the army in winter rapidly exhausted the limited timber stands in the areas safely held by British troops. By 1777 the detachment at Newport had run through its available supply and began the practice of sending ships and cutters to neighboring islands and to Long Island. Involving several ships and one hundred or more men, these expeditions soon became almost weekly events.[115] Even with this effort it was often necessary to cut the regular ration by a third. At one point the detachment was driven to cutting very poor peat and attempting to find coal mines on Newport Island.[116] At New York, with its much greater local resources, the problem of fuel did not come to a head until 1779. In that year, a combination of events brought near disaster to the army. By 1779 wood was no longer available in the immediate area of the city and had to be brought from a considerable distance, feasible only when water transport was available. But that year also combined a mild shortage of shipping with a drastic increase in the number of Rebel whaleboats and privateers. The Rebels found both wood cutters and their shipping easy prey. There was thus already a shortage of fuel when the coldest winter in memory set in. New York Bay froze over and all shipping came to a standstill. The price of wood soared to over £5 a cord and coal to £12 a chaldron but even at those prices very little was available. By the time the cold eased, New York had been completely stripped of trees and bushes, and a considerable number of older ships had disappeared from the harbor. Even with these measures, the army ration had to be cut by a third and then by a half.[117]

The activities of the Rebels against woodcutters and wood ships led, in New York, to the formation of a Loyalist

[115] Mackenzie, 171-437.   [116] *Ibid.*, 237, 245, 399.
[117] Wortley, 165, Fred. Smyth to Stuart, 25 Mar 80; N-YHS, "Pattison Correspondence," 305, 336, 340.

refugee woodcutting brigade under the command of Major Abraham Cuyler.[118] Cuyler's force cut wood in such outlying areas as Bergen Neck and Lloyd's Neck and was armed and built forts to protect itself from Rebel raids. Even with this protection, however, the brigade was forced to withdraw from Lloyd's Neck in 1781 because of the intensity of Rebel activity.[119] Although it did yeoman service from the time of its formation and grew to a strength of over 400 men, the price of a cord of good hardwood in New York City seldom fell below £4.

To obtain the supplies that could not be brought from Britain but were nevertheless vital to the army, the British were forced into a kind of warfare in which the discipline of the regular European troops was of little advantage and the initiative and sharpshooting of the American forces at a premium. There is no way accurately to determine the cost of this *petite guerre* to Britain, but it is clear that it must be measured in terms of the diversion of troops from the main task of the war, of time and worry, and of men and equipment worn out, as well as in terms of dead and wounded. It was a diversion of very scarce men and materials from the main task of destroying Washington's army and it no doubt contributed to that inertia on the part of British commanders which many historians have found so inexplicable.

There was another area, also, in which the British need to wrest some of their supplies from the colonies was a factor of considerable importance in the war. Although certainly not to the extent that most Britons believed, this was nevertheless in part a war for men's minds. How men think, how they determine their loyalties, can depend very much on how they are treated. Certainly British policy was attuned to this problem. The belief that the rebellion was the work of a demagogic, self-seeking minority that had

[118] CP, Abraham Cuyler to André, 21 June 80; CP, Gen. Robertson to Captain Thomas Ward, 22 Oct 81.
[119] Mackenzie, 528, 23 May 81.

succeeded in deluding the majority dictated a policy of leniency towards all but the Rebel leaders—hence the frequency with which captured American soldiers, particularly militia, were pardoned and paroled.[120] In the area of logistics this belief dictated a policy of respect for civilian property: the goods of known Rebels were subject to confiscation, but the property of others was to be respected as provided by British law at least as far as the exigencies of war would allow. While the needs of the army might at times require the commandeering of food, forage, and transportation, it was to be paid for at fair and established prices, and as soon as possible a return to the system of voluntary supply was to take place.[121] It meant, too, that the demands of the service should never leave the people destitute, a policy that was, of course, reinforced by the eighteenth-century concept of limited war mentioned earlier. Hence the anomaly of Howe, in urgent need of forage to maintain his transportation system at New York in the winter of 1776, acceding to Percy's analysis of the hay reserves on Newport Island, which left most of the available supply for the use of the inhabitants. Hence also the anger of a Hessian soldier who wrote home that ". . . at the King's express command the troops must treat these folk most handsomely—though we hear they are all rebels—and cannot demand even a grain of salt . . . without paying for it."[122]

But while this policy of moderation could be and generally was enforced in the areas within the firm control of the British army, it was somewhat less than effective in other places. The propensity of the regular private soldier

[120] As, for example, were those captured at Charleston.

[121] Stryker, 343; T 64/119, 4-5, Wier to Robinson, 29 Oct 77; BAHQP, 1,233, Proclamation by Clinton, 13 June 78; BAHQP, 5,460, Memorandum from Lord Cornwallis.

[122] R. W. Pettengill (ed. & trans.), *Letters from America* (Port Washington, N.Y., 1964), 164, letter from a Hessian soldier to his brother, 24 June 77.

was to take as his own everything that opportunity placed in his way, to plunder without bothering to ask on which side his victim's sympathies lay. While the army was campaigning and while it was engaged in the never-ending task of foraging, this propensity was, at the very least, difficult to restrain. Nothing indicated this better than the repeated orders against pillaging found in the general orders of the army and the equally numerous records of soldiers sentenced to death for that crime.[123] This pillaging can, in some respects, be understood if not condoned. A regular soldier, British, American, or German, underpaid, poorly fed and housed, his life continually in peril, found it easy to convince himself that he had a "right" to some of the good things that surrounded the safe and prosperous civilian. And a British or German soldier on a foraging expedition who had just been shot at from behind a fence or tree by an irregular, non-uniformed enemy no doubt found it even easier, as did the Hessian quoted above, to convince himself that all Americans were rebels and deserving of punishment. Whatever the motivation of the plunderer, though, the reaction of his victim was likely to be the same: a decided lack of sympathy for the cause and the army in which his oppressor fought.

The British need to forage and the pillaging to which it gave rise was undoubtedly a considerable factor in alienating otherwise neutral or even sympathetic Americans. Indeed, one British officer attributed the reverses of the winter of 1776-1777 to this cause.[124] But it must be pointed out that this alienation can also be blamed on unthinking official policy and unscrupulous British commissaries. Until 1780 regiments were, by order of the commander-in-chief, paid one dollar a head for enemy cattle rounded up during a campaign and turned over to the commissary department.

[123] For example, SRO, Peebles Diary, 26 Aug & 8 Sept 76, vol. 4, 14 Dec & 22 Dec 77; Uhlendorf, 95, 185; Add. Mss. 21,680, Hutcheson to Haldimand, 16 Feb 77.

[124] Add. Mss. 21,680, Hutcheson to Haldimand, 16 Feb 77.

That there was any real attempt to differentiate between "enemy" and "friendly" cattle is seriously to be doubted. Similarly, commissaries who looked on their positions as an opportunity to build private fortunes had ample opportunity to do so if their scruples were sufficiently pliable. Entrusted with cash or the authority to issue vouchers and backed up by soldiers, they could, and apparently often did, pay less than authorized or nothing at all for goods obtained from the country people while charging government the full allowance.[125]

The need to find some of its supplies in America, then, was a distinct impediment to the success of the British army. Since it could control only the very limited areas it could occupy in force, most of its needs had to be met from areas where basic control rested with the enemy. There the foraging expeditions were exposed to the *petite guerre*—guerrilla warfare—at which the Rebels were most adept. Further, foraging had a strong tendency to alienate the very people the army needed to bring to its side to win. The British were fighting in an area where the population had a strong tendency to take up arms to defend itself, and a man alienated was a potential enemy soldier. With, even at its greatest extent, only 55,000 men and half a continent to subdue, the army did not need to extend the list of its enemies.

So far this chapter has dealt with the problems resulting from the inability of the British army to control an area of the colonies sufficiently large to provide the supplies it needed. But there were some areas that, although inadequate to the whole supply, did remain for shorter or longer periods securely in British hands. Manhattan Island, for instance, was securely within the British lines from 1776 on and at that time was chiefly devoted to agriculture, as was

125 For a more extensive discussion of profiteering by commissaries and others, see Ch. v.

Staten Island. Similarly, Long Island, basically within British control throughout the war although harassed by American raiding groups, and Rhode Island, held from 1776 to 1779, were among the most highly developed parts of the colonies. Other areas, notably New Jersey, South Carolina, and part of Pennsylvania, were held briefly but in the belief that they would remain in British hands. How effectively were these areas organized to supply at least some of the needs of the army?

As in so many other things, the British record in this respect was somewhat mixed. Mure, Son & Atkinson pointed out that even the narrow confines of Boston in winter need not be totally barren and included in the wide assortment of supplies sent out in the fall of 1775 a large quantity of mustard and cress seeds. These seeds, they noted, could be grown indoors on shallow trays of earth or even on wet blankets and when harvested at the height of several inches would provide the basis of green salads.[126] In the following year, with the army at New York and considerably more space available to it, they began the practice of sending out garden vegetable seeds, and from the spring of 1777 individual units at both New York and Rhode Island were encouraged to plant gardens for their own use.[127] At New York City the quartermaster's department became engaged in this task also, expropriating Vauxhall and Ranelagh Gardens, Bowling Green, and Governor's Island for the purpose. In 1777 the department expended £521 for gardeners and laborers for the project and in the following year £858 although much of the latter was wasted when Admiral Gambier turned a herd of navy sheep, cows, and hogs loose on the maturing crop on Governor's Island.[128]

---

[126] T 1/513, 140-149, Mure, Son & Atkinson to Howe, 25 Sept 75.
[127] WO 36/2, 34-35, 30 Apr 77; T 64/108, 103-105, Howe to Robinson, 5 Apr 77.
[128] CP, "Abstract of Disbursement . . . for Raising Vegetables. . . ," 7 Mar 79.

The gardens were probably of considerable benefit to the health of the army, despite the depredations of admirals and hungry soldiers. But they also represented only a small portion of the possibilities of the British-held area. Just what the productive capacity of that area was is difficult if not impossible to determine accurately, but one instance of the war indicates that it was not as high as might be thought. In December of 1778 shortages of both food and forage at New York combined with transportation difficulties determined Clinton to send a contingent of 2,500 men under General Sir William Erskine to subsist on the eastern portion of Long Island, where a good crop of hay, oats, and wheat was reported. With them went all the cavalry and a good part of the other horses of the army. The move, it was hoped, would not merely relieve supply problems at New York but keep the horses in shape for an early spring campaign.[129]

For the first month or so Erskine's expedition seems to have subsisted well, but by early March the venture began to sour. The surplus of the area was quickly used up and shortage took the place of the expected abundance, with the inevitable effect on men and horses. On the 9th of March Erskine had to report that his cavalry horses were "scarcely fit for the common patroles" while only a small portion of the wagon horses were fit for duty. Oat supplies were gone completely, and the consequent necessity of larger rations of hay brought that item into short supply also.[130] Instead of relieving the demand at New York, Erskine's detachment remained a burden on it, and when two ships with oats and provisions for the expedition were captured by privateers and others delayed by lack of convoy, the whole detachment seemed in danger.[131] Throughout April Erskine's force wandered about the east end of

[129] CP, "Intelligence . . . 3 October 1778"; Erskine to Clinton, 9 Mar 79.

[130] *Ibid.*

[131] CP, Draft of letter to Drummond, n.d. but before 1 Apr 79.

Long Island like a band of mendicants, finding here and there a few days' subsistence. Unable to return to New York because the situation was no better there, they could only fix their eyes on the new crops expected to be useable by May.[132] Instead of preserving his cavalry and wagon train and having them ready for operations early in 1779, they were, Clinton despaired, rendered totally *hors de combat*, "a most cruel circumstance."[133]

It can be argued, of course, that Erskine's experience is not a good indication of the capacity of the colonies to support an army. It is true, as pointed out earlier, that small Rebel expeditions from across Long Island Sound were regularly at work on the Island, burning or buying surplus produce, depending on the loyalties of the individual farmer, and at one point one of Erskine's foraging wagon trains was attacked by such a party. Yet, Rebel experience speaks to the contrary. In the winter of 1779-1780, while covering the British forces at New York, Washington was forced to disperse his cavalry over five states—from Durham, Connecticut, to Winchester, Virginia—in order to obtain adequate forage.[134]

But while the capacity of the land held by the British to support the army was not all that could be wished, it is equally true that the best use was not being made of it. When the army moved into an area—as it did into Long Island, southern New York, New Jersey, and Rhode Island in 1776, and eastern Pennsylvania in 1777—large quantities of food, forage, and livestock became available both as a part of the normal surplus of a settled area and in the contents of farms abandoned by committed Rebels or those just fleeing the tide of war. It could be expected that any army in the logistical position of the British would attempt to reap the first fruits of occupation and to restore the area to maximum production. Until at least 1780, however, the

[132] CP, Erskine to Clinton, 10 Apr, 12 Apr, 16 Apr 79.
[133] CP, Clinton to Drummond, 10 Mar 79.
[134] Freeman, vol. 5, 87.

record is one of waste and disorganization. In September of 1776, for example, General Baurmeister reported that the southern part of Long Island was being systematically stripped of horses by the army, and he himself had procured three at ridiculous prices.[135] Two weeks later, when the army moved into New Jersey, Ambrose Searle, while rejoicing over the acquisition of hay and fodder to feed the newly acquired horses, deplored the lack of organization that allowed the country to be stripped "and the corn ha[u]led away in the straw only for the purposes of litter and beds for the camp."[136]

The problem was not that the potential of the land was not recognized but, rather, that no efficient organization was set up to exploit it. There were, of course, orders against plundering and wanton destruction, requiring that all captured food and other equipment be turned over to the commissary department.[137] But they were hardly in themselves sufficient in the face of hungry and unthinking troops whose officers, even those of Baurmeister's rank, were not themselves disinclined to accept some of the profit of the situation. Something more efficient was required, but apart from an order directing the payment of one dollar per head to units turning over captured enemy cattle to the commissary department, nothing was done. Even this payment did not produce much in the way of results unless cattle were in ample supply. As Major André pointed out in a report to Clinton in 1779, "3 dollars which a regiment receives in lieu of three bullocks was no compensation to 500 men for the loss of a good dinner." André also pointed out the effect of this haphazard system on morale:

". . . some soldiers being casually gorged with fresh meat by a waste which deprives many more of the same advantage cannot be considered at large as being for the benefit of the soldiers.

[135] Uhlendorf, 45.   [136] Searle, 119.
[137] BAHQP, 449 and 1,809, Proclamations by General Howe, 20 Mar 77, 8 Mar 79; von Kraft, 60; SRO, Peebles Diary, 1 Dec 76, 13 Dec 77.

"I have passed in front of a brigade and seen at the fires of a licentious regiment the greatest profusion of meat and poultry, whilst on their flanks other corps were living on salt provisions and inflicting a very severe punishment on such as had presumed to transgress orders.

"If there could exist an argument in favour of relaxation of discipline on the part of the officer or of mutiny on the part of the soldiers they would quote the above contrast."[138]

This situation apparently did not unduly bother Sir William Howe, perhaps because he optimistically expected an early end to the war. Sir Henry Clinton, however, was somewhat less sanguine about an easy and favorable termination of the conflict and hence more sensitive to the problem of food, morale, and public good will. Whether or not he commissioned André's report, he most certainly acted upon it when early in 1780 he undertook operations in South Carolina. On February 12, very shortly after the arrival of the army in the environs of Charleston, Clinton issued a general order establishing the office of commissary of captures and appointing three joint commissaries.[139] The commissaries, assisted by a considerable body of deputies and other subordinates, were to be entirely responsible during campaigns for procurement in the countryside, whether purchases from Loyalists or confiscations from Rebels. They were to accompany forward troops and to be present on foraging expeditions to keep account of everything collected, which would include not only livestock and foodstuffs but also Rebel-owned slaves and cash crops such as

138 CP, "Major André: On Plundering with proposed regulations," filed at end of 1779.

139 The only copy of these orders is in the "Letters and Papers relating to the activities of Major George Hay . . ." in the Scottish Record Office (King's Remembrancer's Office, Letters and Papers), dated 13 Feb 80. The appointees there are given as Captain James Moncrief, Major George Hay, and C. S. Stone. In the audit office accounts (AO 1/192/514), however, the names are given as Moncrief, Hay, and James Fraser.

tobacco and indigo. In the case of the slaves and horses, the commissaries of captures were responsible for assigning them to the various army departments on the orders of the commander-in-chief. The indigo and some of the tobacco they were responsible for selling. The remainder they were either to issue directly to the troops, keeping strict records, or turn over to the commissary general's department for the same purpose. The commissary general in turn was required to make over to the commissaries of captures the money normally taken from the soldier's pay for rations provided by the government. The money thus accumulated was, after the payment of the expenses of the new office, to be put into a "charitable fund in favour of the soldiers at the close of the campaign."

Thus, the resources of the countryside would be utilized rationally and profits of war, such as they were, distributed equitably. The government would also benefit by the saving to it of the difference between the cost of salt rations, including the enormous expense of transportation from Britain, and the fourpence halfpenny normally deducted from the soldier's pay for rations. A further strategic benefit would occur since the commissaries of captures, while empowered to confiscate Rebel property, were also strictly enjoined to issue receipts for the full value of material collected from "friends of government." The receipts, to be honored later at the commissary office at headquarters, acted, to a degree, as surety for the future conduct of the individuals involved.

There is no doubt that the office of commissary of captures was in large measure successful. By August of 1780 over half a million rations of fresh meat and almost 20,000 rations of other species had been issued by the commissary of captures department, a figure that, according to Clinton rose to over 1,000,000 by July of 1782.[140] Several hundred horses and the labor of as many slaves as well as consider-

---

[140] SRO, King's Remembrancer's Office, Letters and Papers, America, Commissary of Captures, 1780-1792; Clinton, *American Rebellion*, 177.

able amounts of forage were also provided for the army. And if the benefits of the "benevolent funds" never did appear, at least the troops did get an equitable distribution of fresh food.[141]

But the success of the office must also be kept in proportion. Its efforts were involved only when the army was campaigning—the first commission ended, for instance, with the surrender of Charleston—and the million rations of fresh meat boasted of by Clinton would feed an army of 30,000 for little more than a month. Much more important in concept if not in execution was an attempt by Cornwallis, after he assumed command in the South, to return to efficient operation under crown management the confiscated estates of American Rebels.

Throughout the war large numbers of farms were abandoned by committed Rebels in the face of advancing British forces. These farms, usually looted of everything of value including trees, were often left idle or at best partitioned among Loyalist refugees, who, without equipment or capital, could do little more than eke out a living for them-

[141] The distribution of the money ran into two problems. First, the legal right of the army to sell enemy property was not at all clear, a problem that arose also in the sharing with the navy of the spoils of Charleston. Secondly, large numbers of receipts issued by the commissaries of captures for material commandeered from Loyalists and other non-rebels remained outstanding at the termination of the commissaries' appointments. Hay and Fraser, who remained in possession of the profits of the department, refused to disperse them until they were guaranteed immunity from claims arising from the legality of the sales and for payment of outstanding receipts. They maintained this position and retained the money as late as 1792 (SRO, Hay Mss.). Clinton does not come out of this at all well, according to Hay. He records that Clinton, just before he left South Carolina to return to New York, was requested to take full responsibility for all the actions of the commissary of captures department, but when informed of the legal position that would put him in, "washed his hands of the whole affair." He was able to do this because the controversial actions of the commissaries were carried out on the basis of a clause in their instructions that was not in their commissions.

selves.[142] Perhaps the failure to bring these farms back into
efficient production in the North can be blamed on the fact
that the amount of land involved was relatively small, but
certainly this was not the case in the South. After the campaign of 1779 and 1780, virtually all of settled South Carolina and Georgia came under British control, and the army
found itself the custodian of numerous large Rebel estates.
When left to himself in South Carolina, Cornwallis determined to make use of these estates to feed at least that part
of his army stationed inland from Charleston. To carry out
this purpose he created a new office, that of commissary of
sequestered estates, and appointed John Cruden, a southern
Loyalist, as first commissary. Cruden's commission, dated
16 September 1780, was a long and complicated document
as was the public proclamation that announced his appointment, but in brief it empowered him to take into his cus-
tody and use for the benefit of the army "the estate and
property, real and personal" of all known Rebels in South
Carolina. In part his task overlapped that of the commissary of captures in that he was to allocate the captured
property for the use of the army and ensure that proper
credit was given for it. But generally, whereas the commissary of captures moved with the army, the commissary of
sequestered estates operated in what would now be called
the pacified areas. His main task, however, was to bring the
estates back into efficient operation.

Cruden's office was a very typical eighteenth-century compromise between the public and the private. Although his
commission came from the commander-in-chief and the
initial funding from the military chest, the department
operated like a private business. Negro slave labor, lumber,
and firewood were supplied to the various army departments under contract at competitive prices. Food and forage, although not contracted, were also competitively
priced. Out of the gross income of the department Cruden

[142] New York Public Library, Papers of Chief Justice William Smith,
vol. VI, 9 July 79.

was allowed a commission equal to that "heretofore allowed to the merchants by the custom and useage of Charleston in the transaction of business of like nature. . . ," but out of which he was to pay the personnel expenses of the department. The remainder, after operating expenses, was to be turned back to the military chest.[143]

Cornwallis' innovation had a most propitious beginning. Cruden took over some one hundred plantations and 4,000 slaves, the immediate products of which, along with the products of the commissary of captures department, made the army based in the interior of South Carolina and Georgia independent of the ports of Savannah and Charleston except for military stores, rum, and salt. And perhaps the department might have gone on to produce the £60,000 a year[144] profit so hopefully predicted by Cruden, but the logic of the war intervened. The fall of Charleston, Tarleton's victory at Waxhaws, and the rout of Gates at Camden all gave the impression that Georgia and South Carolina at least could be completely pacified and controlled. The posts established by Cornwallis at such places as Ebenezer, Augusta, Ninety-Six, and Camden were to effect this. The success of Cruden's venture obviously depended on the success of the pacification. But just as obviously the maintenance of "tranquility and submission" was not easy. Francis Marion and Thomas Sumpter—the "Swamp Fox" and the "Carolina Gamecock"—began to raise their partisan forces in the early summer of 1780 and their activities very quickly reduced the area of secure British control to the rectangle bounded by the Savannah River on one side and the Santee on the other, and from the sea to Wynnesborough.[145] Not even the disastrous defeat of Gates at Camden on August 20 really deterred these groups. By the end of October their activities made it impossible for the British

[143] For Cruden's commission see T 1/571, 337-340 and PRO 30/4/7, 22-24; for the public proclamation see Tarleton, 186-189.

[144] Tarleton, 86.

[145] PRO 30/11/3, 297-299, Rawdon to Clinton, 20 Oct 80.

to use the Santee River to transport material from the coast to the troops in the interior, a serious situation since Cornwallis was desperately short of wagons and horses. Also, grain supplies and vital mills on the Broad River were threatened.[146] In November even the land route to Camden, Wynnesborough, and Ninety-Six through Monk's Corners was menaced.[147] By December Cornwallis had to report that Rebel raids were being made even in the Charleston area. When Cornwallis moved the major part of his army against North Carolina, in part to destroy the supply base of the partisan groups, the deterioration became even more rapid. By May even the communications between the various British posts could not be guaranteed.[148] And as military control collapsed so did Cruden's enterprise, his estates being prime targets for the Rebel raiders. By the middle of 1781 his department was reduced to several estates in the environs of Charleston that did little more than feed the slaves still under his control. When in the spring of 1782 Cruden surrendered his commission, his accounts showed a net loss of about £17,000, largely due to capital investments in the estates that there had not been time to recoup.[149] It is ironical that this most imaginative attempt to utilize the resources of North America to supply the army should have resulted in probably as great a benefit to the Rebels, whose estates were restored and improved, as it did to the British army.

[146] PRO 30/11/3, 333, Rawdon to Balfour, 31 Oct 80, and 337, Rawdon to Major Wemyss, 31 Oct 80.

[147] PRO 30/11/4, 9-10, Balfour to Rawdon, 1 Nov 80, and 42-44, Balfour to Cornwallis, 5 Nov 80.

[148] CP, Balfour to Clinton, 6 May 81.

[149] PRO 30/11/10, "Report of a Board Assembled at Charleston. . . ," Feb 82.

III

BRITAIN AS A SOURCE OF SUPPLY:

The Problem of Food

An army might well be described as an organization for conspicuous consumption: it produces nothing, yet to operate effectively requires immense quantities of stores. The most basic of its requirements is food, and the result of the situation described in the previous chapter was that virtually all of the food required by the British army in America had to be supplied from Britain. The task of supplying it, while not easy, was certainly within the technical competence of the nation. There was no question of the ability of the country to produce a surplus sufficient to feed the army and the technology of food preservation was crude but adequate. Beef and pork, properly prepared, well salted, packed in sound barrels, and stored in reasonably cool surroundings, could be expected to remain good for up to two years. Flour, although still so crudely milled that the oily wheat germ was often broken, could nevertheless be expected to last at least as long if properly kiln dried and packed. Oatmeal, butter, and cheese could also be preserved, as well as pease and cabbage, the pease dried and the cabbage in the guise of sauerkraut. As with flour and meat, though, the period for which these items remained edible depended on the care taken in preparation and on good storage conditions. To collect the food the government could turn to a number of business men in the city of London who had experience in organizing large-scale supply. Transportation to America was probably the most formidable problem. An army of 35,000 with 4,000 horses consumed every day some thirty tons of food and sixteen of oats, in a year 13,500 tons of food and 5,840 of oats.[1] The ships available to carry these provisions did not average more than 220 tons burthen each and were clumsy affairs, slow under the best conditions and almost helpless in the face of contrary winds. With delays for loading, unloading, repairs, and waiting for convoy they could not be expected, as it proved, to make more than two crossings of the Atlantic in a year. Nevertheless, the task was not impossible, for even under those conditions the supply of the army required only the constant employment of about one hundred ships and for the world's greatest trading nation that should not have been too much of a burden.[2]

But despite the technical competence of the nation, from 1775 through to the middle of 1781 the British forces in America suffered persistent and sometimes acute shortages. That is not to say that the soldiers starved—far from it. By eighteenth-century standards they were probably well fed most of the time and only on rare occasions were established rations cut. Almost never was the main body of British soldiers reduced to the conditions the American army endured during the winter of 1777. The shortages that occurred were of reserves of food but they were none the less important for that. If the army's role had been merely to occupy a few ports then it could have got along with a minimum of reserves. But that was not its role. Both Howe and Clinton realized that if the rebellion was to be put down the Rebel army had to be destroyed and its strongholds reduced. To do that campaigns had to be mounted and since the campaigning armies had to depend on food from Britain rather than local supplies, and since the sup-

---

[1] T 64/201, 14, Robinson to Navy Board, 13 Mar 79.

[2] Only the actual ship loadings for food for 1776, 1777, and 1778 can be accurately ascertained. In 1775, 105 ships were dispatched but they were often grossly underloaded and many were well under 200 tons burthen. In 1777 sixty-three food ships were dispatched and in 1778 sixty-one. (T 64/118, 13-14, Chamier to Robinson, 9 Nov 76; T 1/549, 107.)

ply route was three thousand hazardous miles long, both generals insisted on having provisions for a campaign on hand before beginning it: a campaign that stalled for lack of food would at best be frustrating, at worst a disaster. Thus both generals in their turn recommended that sufficient provisions be shipped from Britain to ensure that there would always be a six month's reserve on hand for the army in America. When France entered the war and her navy became a threat to the Atlantic supply line Clinton sought a doubling of the reserve.[3]

Even when no operations were in the offing a reserve sufficient for at least two months was necessary if the army's position and, indeed, the army itself were not to be jeopardized. For when reserves fell to that level the commander-in-chief had to think of evacuation. To move the army with all its equipment and support personnel and the Loyalists who depended on it for protection required shipping resources far larger than the army ever had on hand. Even when Boston was evacuated in 1776, a move planned months in advance, many ships in the fleet used in the move had to make two trips between that city and Halifax. Only about 15,000 people were evacuated from Boston but there were seldom less than 50,000 who would have to leave New York. Thus the decision to evacuate had to be made when there were still provisions to feed the army during the time ships were collected and made several trips to distant ports; if it were held off for too long, evacuation would become impossible.

The need for reserves of food, then, was vital, and the government in Britain was regularly informed of it. Yet it was seldom met. The war in America lasted, effectively, for seventy-nine months—from the battles at Lexington and Concord in April 1775 to Cornwallis' surrender in October 1781—yet for no more than twenty-three of those months

[3] T 1/518, Howe to Treasury, 1 Dec 75; Add. Mss., 34,416, 153-159, "Notes of S[ir] H[enry] Clinton Relative to the Campaign of 1778."; T 64/114, 117-120, Wier to Robinson, 9 Jan 79.

did the army have the minimum six month's reserve desired by its commanders. During twenty-eight months, supplies were at a three to six month's level and for eight months were sufficient for no more than two to three months. During a further eleven months reserves fell to a paralyzing thirty to sixty day's and at least once in each year, except 1777, for a total of five months, the army had less than thirty day's provisions on hand.[4] An understanding of the reasons why these shortages occurred and the effect they had on operations is obviously vital to an understanding of the war.

As pointed out in the previous chapter, the activities of Rebels throughout the Thirteen Colonies in stopping provisions' shipments meant that the army in America came to depend on supplies from Britain almost as soon as the war began. Provisions' shortages commenced at the same time. In the summer and early fall of 1775, while the Treasury slowly became aware of the situation in North America and arranged to do something about it, the army went through a series of crises. By late fall, however, provisions from Britain started to arrive and, had all the Treasury's arrangements succeeded, the army would have spent a comfortable winter at Boston and been ready to begin operations as early in the spring of 1776 as weather permitted. But as the army found out in 1775 that it must depend on Britain for supplies, so it also discovered some of the problems of that dependence. The first was that provisions' ships were vulnerable to the weather and to the enemy. The most serious blow to the army was the devastation by autumnal storms of the great provisions' fleet assembled by Mure, Son & Atkinson,[5] but almost equally important were the activities of American armed vessels that between October 1775 and March of the following year captured at least nine victuallers carrying provisions from Britain to the army at

---

[4] These, of course, were not continuous periods. The graph in Appendix I gives the army's food reserves throughout the whole war.
[5] *Supra*, 53-54.

Boston.[6] Some of the American ships involved were privateers who had begun to operate against the ships attempting to supply Gage from Nova Scotia as early as July 1775.
But the British position at Boston was so precarious, and
the supply ships, being as yet unarmed, so vulnerable that
Washington took it upon himself to exploit the situation
further. Although desperately short of cannon, shot, and
powder for the army he nevertheless outfitted the schooner
Hannah as a commerce raider and sent her out to harass
the British supply lines. She was followed by ten other raiders and from September 1775 to September 1776 this small
fleet brought in twenty-three British vessels. Seven of these
were provisions' ships from Britain and two invaluable
ordnance stores' ships; four were troop ships and one carried clothing for the army. Of the remainder, seven carried
provisions, wood, and stores from Nova Scotia and one was
bringing rum from Antigua.[7] The total number of vessels
taken in this period by privateers and Washington's navy
is not clear, but one report by a British quartermaster in
April 1776 gave the figure of forty-five vessels of all sorts
bound for Boston and taken into Salem, Marblehead, and
Cape Ann alone.[8]

These losses persuaded the Treasury in 1776 to take over
the task, previously left to the contractors, of shipping provisions to the army, and to arm most of the vessels employed. This move reduced losses dramatically: only three
victuallers were taken during the remainder of 1776, five
in 1777, and one in 1778, the last only after it went

[6] The reports of these captures are scattered throughout American
and British sources and are often incomplete in such vital details as
ships' names and cargoes. Further, complete lists of the sailings from
Britain are not available. There might have been as many as twelve
but three of the reports are probably repetitions and I have chosen to
ignore them.

[7] The story of this fleet is told in W. B. Clark, *George Washington's
Navy* (Baton Rouge, 1960), Clark appends a list (229-236) of the prizes
taken.

[8] Add. Mss. 21,680, Hutcheson to Haldimand, 24 Apr 76.

aground. In 1776 two oats' ships were lost and in 1777 a coal ship and a transport carrying clothing were taken as well as eight oats' ships, although four of the latter were retaken. In 1779, when the Navy Board took over the task of shipping provisions, the system was changed again. Believing that the French navy was now the greatest threat to shipping, the Navy Board disarmed the victuallers and dispatched them instead in convoys guarded by warships of the Royal Navy. By coincidence rather than because the new system was defective, 1779 was also one of the worst years of the war for army shipping. In May seven ships of a fleet sailing from New York to Georgia were taken by American frigates and in October another fleet going to the South, along with its escort H.M.S. *Experiment* was lost when it fell in with Admiral d'Estaing's fleet. In December a single victualler that had strayed from its convoy was taken by a French frigate and in January 1780 three transports, a fourteen-gun brig, and two armed sloops carrying clothing and stores were taken by the American frigates *Providence* and *Ranger* off Tybee.[9]

Although American naval operations, particularly by privateers, increased significantly during the last three years of the war[10] very few major British ships were lost. There were many minor American conquests that were significant not so much in terms of ships or materials lost but in their effect on General Clinton. The expansion of the war, the consequent reduction of British naval strength in American waters, and the abandonment of Rhode Island and its naval base gave a wider scope of action to American naval vessels, privateers, and whaleboats than they had had since 1775.

[9] Alnwick Castle Mss., IL, 20 Oct 79; T 64/120, 17-20, Paumier to Robinson, 4 Nov 78; N-YHS, "Pattison Correspondence," 52; G. W. Allen, *A Naval History of the American Revolution* (New York, 1962), vol. II, 492.

[10] Allen, 716-717, states that Congress issued 441 letters of marque from 1776 to 1779, and 1,234 over the next three years. Most privateers, however, probably chose the British Isles, the West Indies, or the Grand Banks for their hunting grounds.

Two dispatch packets were captured in these years and numerous small boats. The Americans virtually controlled Long Island Sound and raided regularly within sight of the various garrisons around New York. At one point a vessel taking a relief guard to the Sandy Hook lighthouse was taken and ships as large as victuallers were taken inside the Hook. Seldom well stocked with provisions during these years, Clinton found his greatest fear was that the American vessels or the French fleet, which began to appear regularly on the coast in 1778, would take one of his supply convoys and leave his army with no choice but starvation or surrender. No such disaster occurred but Clinton never ceased to worry and the worry affected his capacity for action.[11]

Another provisioning problem that began in the first year of the war, but by no means ended there, was that of substandard provisions. That some provisions should arrive in America in a less than satisfactory state was, of course, to be expected: food preservation techniques were adequate but long, rough, damp sea voyages put them to a severe test. Further, during the first years of the war at least, the demand of the army was unexpected and delivery times short; under such circumstances quality control was almost bound to slip. No doubt, also, there were occasional mistakes in warehousing that resulted in packages being left in store far beyond their possible shelf-life. However, the quantity of provisions, particularly dry provisions such as bread, flour, and peas, which when landed in America proved to be inedible, was well beyond any acceptable limits. The first instance of this problem occurred in the fall of 1775 and involved five cargoes of flour, totalling almost one and a half million pounds, delivered at Boston. Of 6,995 barrels, 4,956 were condemned outright, for being "musty, sower . . . unfit for use." Nine hundred and sixty-six barrels were declared fit only for immediate use, and

[11] CP, Clinton to Eden, 2 July 79; Mackenzie, 507, 515, 528; for an examination of the effect on Clinton see *infra*, 122-24, 131, 136.

but 1,069 were found to be "sound, sweet and good."[12] Thus the army got forty-seven days' bread for 12,000 men from a fleet that was supposed to provide for the same number for five and a half months.

Although the Treasury carefully investigated the failure of the flour delivered in 1775 and drew assurances from the contractors of better quality and a stricter inspection in the future,[13] deliveries in later years often proved equally defective. This was especially true of bread. In planning the supplies for the 1776 campaign the Treasury decided that hard biscuits of the kind used by the Royal Navy should be substituted for most of the flour. The "bread," as it was called, was poor fare as a steady diet but ideal for campaign rations and would relieve the army of the task of setting up bakeries immediately it established itself at New York. The idea was good in theory but poor in execution. The navy claimed that the bread, if properly made and packed, would remain good for two years, but that delivered to the army seldom came even close to that standard. From 1776, when the first deliveries were made, until 1777, when the army finally established adequate bakeries of its own, it drew the complaints of commissaries and soldiers alike. Of the first delivery of 379,512 pounds, 285,984 pounds were condemned by Commissary General Chamier as being "indifferent in quality," "mouldy in the heart," short of weight, and often packed in bags "so thin and rotten they would scarce bear removing from the vessels in which they came without much waste."[14] The best that was said of the bread was that old rotten pieces were mixed in with the new; the worst was unprintable. One officer of the Queen's

12 T 64/101, 106, Gage to Robinson, 10 Oct 75; T 64/108, 4, Howe to Robinson, 1 Dec 75.

13 T 64/106, 29-44, Robinson to Howe, 1 May 76. Ironically, the bad flour of 1775 came originally from America. It had been shipped to Britain and there purchased by the contractors.

14 T 64/118, 5, 7-8, 10, Chamier to Robinson, 7 July, 11 Aug, 4 Sept 76; T 29/45, 14 Aug 76.

Rangers with twenty-two years' maritime experience swore that the bread that came to his unit could only have been the sweepings of a naval purser's store, and William Butler, a commissary of fifteen years' experience, believed that even the bread that was sound had been made out of a mixture of pea, potato, and oat meals, with "a very little flour."[15]

By terms of the contract all provisions that were in any way substandard on arrival in America should have been returned to the contractors for replacement, but the army was seldom so well stocked with provisions that it could afford to do this. More often the bread was needed for immediate issue and the commissaries were forced to sort through the sacks, discarding the obviously bad and hoping for the best with the remainder. Deputy Commissary Peter Paumier, who had charge of the dry provisions for the army, reported that forty percent of the bread delivered was discarded in the sorting.[16] Even then, complaints did not cease. Sir William Erskine appeared in the middle of January at the commissary general's stores in Amboy with a convoy of wagons bearing a message from Lord Cornwallis and demanding flour. "Your bread is so damned bad Lord Cornwallis says his men shall not eat it," Erskine reported.[17]

The other dry provisions continued to give problems too. At the same time as he made his first complaints about the bread, Chamier also noted that the barrels and casks in which flour and peas were packed were "so slight that they would not admit of being removed far by land carriage."[18] Shortly afterwards, the question of the qual-

[15] T 64/108, 135, 143.

[16] T 64/108, 142. In all, 4,639,104 pounds of bread were sent out. If Paumier's estimate that 40 percent of it was bad was correct, then 1,855,640 pounds were thrown away: enough for 20,000 men for three months.

[17] *Ibid.*, 146.

[18] T 64/118, 7-8, Chamier to Robinson, 11 Aug 76. In the prewar years America was a major source of barrel staves, and Chamier admitted that a shortage of staves was probably a part of the problem. He arranged the shipment of some staves on victuallers returning to Cork

ity of the flour came up again. In part the problem at this time was one of stowage. On one occasion inspectors reported that almost one hundred barrels of flour on one ship had been severely damaged because of the failure to provide dunnage between the flour and coal used as ballast. As the ship rocked and swayed across the Atlantic, the flour barrels had worked their way into the coal and picked up moisture. On another occasion, barrels of butter were stacked on top of flour. When some of the barrels of flour began to heat up, the butter melted and soaked through into the flour.[19] But quality was the great problem. Chamier reported to Howe that the flour received in the fall of 1776 was "coarse—dead—and otherwise deficient. . . ." Of the flour on one ship a board of inspectors reported that it was "very old flour of different sorts and very inferior qualities, & in general musty & rotten. . . ."[20] Deliveries in 1777 were no better. Robert Gordon, the Treasury agent at Cork, warned the Treasury in late 1776 that because of a shortage of first-quality flour on the market the first fleet carrying provisions for 1777 would not sail on time unless the contractors were allowed to substitute second-quality flour in their deliveries. Since the only difference between first- and second-quality flour was supposed to be the coarseness of the grind the Treasury agreed to the substitution and informed the commissary general in America of it. Wier was less sanguine about the change, and instructed Paumier to "be particular in your examination of it . . . as I know great liberties are taken with those indulgences." His fears were well founded. Paumier wrote of this shipment that it was "of a very inferior second sort, old, musty, and sour." He also found that the oatmeal in the same shipment was

---

but, nevertheless, the contractors were still driven at one stage to request that they be allowed to deliver flour in deal chests rather than barrels.

[19] T 64/118, 54; HSP, Wier Letter Book, Wier to Robinson, 25 Oct 77.

[20] CP, Chamier to Clinton, 12 July 77; T 64/118, 54.

no better and that pease casks were still bad.[21] Although the contractors were supposed to return to first-quality flour after the initial shipment of 1777, as far as the army was concerned the situation did not change at all. Letters from Paumier on 28 August, 28 September, and 9 October, following the arrival of convoys, again reported bad provisions. In the final letter he wrote: " 'Tis impossible to conceive the badness of the flour in general which they have sent out this year, not above one ship in a fleet, whose flour is good for any thing scarcely; almost the whole old, musty, and sour; the oatmeal in general in the same state."[22]

Another failing in the provisions came to light in 1777 also: deficiencies in the invoiced weights of cargoes. In early November Paumier informed Wier that although the wet provisions being received were of good quality, the barrels were almost invariably short of weight. A check of the cargoes of four ships, he reported, revealed that barrels of beef supposed to contain 210 pounds of meat were generally fifteen to twenty pounds short and barrels of pork supposed to contain 208 pounds, eight to ten pounds short.[23] Similar deficiencies in cargoes of flour ranging as high as five and six percent were found. For flour alone in 1778 the deficiencies amounted to 645,920 pounds in the cargoes of seven fleets supposed to be carrying 10,644,700 pounds. The missing flour would have fed 20,000 men for over a month.[24]

After 1779 complaints from the army about the provisions declined significantly. During 1780 and 1781 reports

[21] AO 16/10, 98-100, Robinson to Gordon, 6 May 77; HSP, Wier Letter Book, Wier to Robinson, 1 Sept 77.

[22] HSP, Wier Letter Book, Wier to Robinson, 25 Oct 77.

[23] HSP, Wier Letter Book, Wier to Robinson, 29 Nov 77. The Treasury replied that the shortage was probably due to a "natural shrinking process" in the meat while it was in the brine, but Wier replied that the navy, which had long experience with salt meat, had also complained about the deficiencies in some meat loaned to them by the army (*ibid.*, Wier to Robinson, 14 Dec 77).

[24] T 64/114, 136, Wier to Robinson, 14 Feb 79.

of provisions of bad quality seldom involved more than the cargo of a single ship in a convoy and complaints of short-weighted barrels fell off. Not until 1782, when John Morrison, the commissary at Charleston, reported that the flour delivered to the army in the South was generally bad, did another serious complaint arise.[25]

In an operation as complex as that of supplying provisions for an army, it is unlikely that responsibility for any major failing can ever be assigned to any one factor. Such is the case with the problem of bad and short-weight provisions. Initially the responsibility lies with the war itself. The demand for provisions of the highest quality prepared and packed with more than ordinary care was sudden and heavy and it should not come as a surprise that the attempt to meet it involved some failures. But it is also true that the demand was well within Britain's capacity and, as Professor Baker's study of the British end of army logistics points out, contractors, sub-contractors, and agents who cut corners in order to increase profits or just to stay solvent in what became a highly competitive business were also to blame.[26] Responsibility must also lie heavily on Robert Gordon, to whom the task of inspecting the provisions as they were received from the contractors was assigned, and to a much lesser extent on his Navy Board successors. All rejected large quantities of provisions for a variety of reasons: flour because it was inadequately dried or of inferior quality and in one case because stones had been added to the barrels to make up weight and in another because pease had been added; meat because of the inclusion in the barrels of heads, necks, shins, marrow bones, and feet; and pease because they were green and lacked "substance" when boiled. But clearly Gordon also missed much—too much. Not until the Navy Board assumed the task of inspection did bad provisions cease to be a major army problem. Gor-

25 T 1/577, 294-295, Morrison to Chamier, 12 Mar 82.
26 Baker, 116-123, 241-248.

don had many problems to contend with. To him fell the task of setting up the provisions' reception and shipping depot at Cork, and he had regularly to deal with ship captains and contractors whose honesty could not be depended on. Nevertheless, Professor Baker, who includes Gordon's operations in his study, comes to the conclusion that he "failed to give his task the full attention that it demanded, was confused in method, generally inefficient and quite possibly dishonest."[27]

The greatest responsibility for the bad provisions must rest in the end, though, with the Treasury. As the problem grew, Gordon and the commissary at New York each came to place responsibility for it on the other, the commissary claiming that Gordon's inspections were inadequate and Gordon claiming that the fault lay in bad handling and storage at New York.[28] As charges and countercharges flew, the Treasury had some reason to be confused, but the persistence of the complaints from New York, backed up by the authority of the commander-in-chief there, should have led it to a comprehensive investigation of the problem. Yet beyond delivering an occasional rebuke and passing on Gordon's charges to the commissary and vice versa, it did nothing until 1779, when it turned the whole problem over to the Navy Board. Further, the Treasury was even reluctant to take punitive measures against contractors who were proved delinquent; as a result the delinquencies continued. Although contractors were required to replace provisions that were found to be bad at any time up to six months after delivery at Cork, that was no consolation to a soldier who had to eat mouldy bread because nothing else was available or to a commander-in-chief who found that the reserves of food he counted on in the planning of a campaign were inedible. Bad provisions could have serious results even when they were discovered during inspection at Cork, for deliveries were then delayed while replace-

27 *Ibid.*, 95-115.   28 *Ibid.*, 114-115.

ments were collected. Not until 1780, however, and then only when it was suggested by the Navy Board, were penalties instituted even for late deliveries.[29] Similarly, although the problem of inadequate containers first came up in 1776, it was still around in 1779, for John Marsh, the Navy Board agent, to deal with. The quality of the pease and the flour were acceptable, he wrote to his superiors, "yet that of the casks throughout is totally insufficient for the service they are intended, from their being in the main too weak, the timber green and unseasoned when made up, and the heads for the most part of deal, the turpentine whereof not only infects the exterior but to the very heart of the flour."[30]

There can be no question of the ill effects of bad provisions. Because they came to expect that a high proportion of the provisions delivered by the contractors would be bad, the Navy Board inspectors felt bound to open every barrel that went through their hands, a time-consuming process that could delay the loading and sailing of ships. When the rejection rate was high, as was the case when Marsh rejected 2,928 barrels of pork, sailings were delayed while the contractors provided replacements.[31] With the army the effect was even more serious. Although repeatedly informed that he was to refuse to accept all provisions that

[29] T 1/560, 199-203, Navy Board to Treasury, 4 Aug 80.

[30] T 64/200, 52-53, Marsh to Navy Board, 17 Dec 79. It is probable that poor barrels were a major cause of short weight in dry provisions. Gordon reported in May 1779 that "the agents for the contractors in England still continue to send very bad casks under their flour & pease; the flour casks so ill coopered that when they come to be pressed and worked in the ship, a great quantity of the flour works out . . . the pease casks are so very thin & made of such brittle stuff, . . . the pease all work through the joints . . ." (T 1/555, 300).

[31] T 64/200, 74, Marsh to Navy Board, 12 Feb 80; *ibid.*, 99-100, George Cherry (Navy Board Agent at Cowes) to Navy Board, 20 July 80. In addition, between 3,000 and 4,000 barrels of flour were rejected the previous autumn, and large quantities of butter and beef in February 1780. (*Ibid.*, 45-47, Harris to Navy Board, 23 Oct 79; *ibid.*, 74, Marsh to Navy Board, 12 Feb 80.)

were not of the best quality and in perfect condition on their arrival,[32] the commissary in America must have considered such instructions as almost facetious. He seldom had more than a few months' stock of provisions on hand, could not count on collecting any in America, and by experience knew that the regular shipments from Britain were often delayed. To direct the return of food that, although bad, was still edible under such circumstances was to invite disaster. While he had necessarily to reject that which was totally inedible, for the rest he usually had little choice but to issue it.[33] The effect of bad provisions on the British troops and their German allies is, unfortunately, not well documented. Accounts of experiences in the war on the British side are usually by officers, who could afford to supplement or even totally replace their rations by purchases on the local markets. It was the enlisted men who had to eat the government rations regularly and few of them were literate. Nevertheless, a few indications do exist. Like all soldiers, the British were able at times to make light of their difficulties, as was the case at Rhode Island in 1777, when the soldiers composed an irreverent version of the Lord's Prayer to express their opinion:

> Our Commander who art in Newport,
> Honoured be thy name.
> May thy work be done in Newport
> As it is in York.
> Give us each day our dayly bread,
> And forgive us our not eating it,
> If we don't like it;
> But deliver us from mustiness and bad bakers.
> For thine is the power to get wood and good flour,
> For some time to come. Amen.[34]

[32] For example, T 64/119, 12, 36-37, Robinson to Wier, 30 Apr 78, 7 Aug 79.

[33] T 64/108, 143, 145; T 64/114, 20-22, 34-37, Wier to Robinson, 4 Mar 78, 16 Apr 78.

[34] CP, Sir Charles Hastings to [?], spring 1777.

Still, one can speculate that the humorous approach diminished in proportion as the problem continued, to be replaced by a more bitter attitude leading to a decline in morale, an increase in the rate of desertion[35] and, as was the case with one Hessian soldier, to an increased temptation to pillage the civilian population.[36] It also promoted a measure of distrust among both officers and men: distrust of government, which they could believe cared little for their welfare, and of commissaries, from whom they refused to accept barrels of provisions without first opening, inspecting, and weighing the contents.[37]

Bad provisions and American captures of supply ships had their most serious effect on British operations in 1776. Although the Treasury believed the army to be well supplied, these problems, along with the storm damage to Mure, Son & Atkinson's grand fleet, left it in fact seriously short of provisions. It suffered heavily from disease and desertions over the winter of 1775-1776 and when spring came the evacuation of Boston was forced as much by the state of the provisions' reserves as by the American occupation of Dorchester Heights. With less than six weeks provisions in stock, Howe could not afford to wait much longer for a supply fleet from Britain.[38]

That the army had to leave Boston was no disappointment in itself: that move had been decided on the previous fall.[39] What was affected was its destination. Had provisions been sufficient to last the army into the summer, as was expected, Howe might have moved directly into New York, but as it was that was out of the question. He could not move against the enemy without being sure of his provi-

[35] Lt. Gen. Charles Stuart, *New Records of the American Revolution* (London, 1927), 48; Uhlendorf, 213.

[36] Pettengill, 164.

[37] T 64/120, 3-6, Paumier to Robinson, 7 Aug 79; T 64/114, 190-192, Wier to Robinson, 26 Aug 79.

[38] CP, Howe to Clinton, 21 Mar 76; T 64/108, 29-31, Howe to Robinson, 8 May 76.

[39] *Supra*, 62-63.

sions and the experience of the army in the previous year
in attempting to obtain supplies from the Thirteen Colonies had demonstrated that he would meet hostility wherever he went, hostility at least strong enough to make it
impossible to depend on local supplies. This analysis had
led him in December to request that he always be kept six
months ahead in provisions.[40] He had no doubt of his ability to overcome the Rebel opposition wherever he chose to
land, but the few weeks' provisions he had in March gave
him little opportunity to maneuver and no margin for
error. In fact, he was probably so confident of victory that
there seemed little point in risking a setback for want of
provisions. Thus, when forced out of Boston he had little
choice but to go to Halifax, although he knew that it had
been "stripped of provisions during the winter and afforded
few conveniences for so numerous a body."[41] It was at least
friendly.

Howe's sojourn at Halifax should not have been a long
one, but logistical problems on the other side of the Atlantic kept him there for over three months. Four victuallers
that should have sailed from Cork in January were un-
explicably delayed until April,[42] and the Treasury put off
hiring shipping needed for the transportation of troops and
stores because of a rise in shipping rates.[43] These failures
cost the army two months of good campaign weather, and
in 1776 those two months might just have made the difference between victory and defeat. Britain's most successful
year in the Revolution was 1776. Washington was battered
at Long Island and White Plains and ended up in pre-
cipitous flight across New Jersey. He escaped only by crossing the Delaware River and destroying the boats by which
the British might have followed him. But lack of boats

[40] T 1/518, Howe to Treasury, 1 Dec 75.

[41] CO 5/93, 173-182, Howe to Dartmouth, 21 Mar 76.

[42] T 64/106, 26-28, Robinson to Howe, 12 Apr 76.

[43] Dartmouth Papers, D1778/11/1819, "An Account of what has been
done by the Treasury Board...," 1 Jan 78.

would not have stopped the British for long. What really halted them was the arrival of winter and the end of the campaign season. Had there been two more months of good weather, the British would surely have followed closely on Washington's heels and perhaps brought both him and the Revolution to bay.

There were no further shortages of provisions in 1776. Stocks of salted rations fell sharply in September because a number of victuallers that arrived in Halifax after the army left did not have instructions to follow the army and refused to do so. But that caused no problems since the army was by then reaping the harvest of the New York area.[44]

The best year of the war for the army on the Atlantic coast in terms of provisions' reserves was 1777 but the following year was the worst. The shortages in 1778 began in the spring and continued right through until the end of the year. In part they were due to bad and deficient provisions, but more basically they resulted from administrative failings on the part of the Treasury and the army commissaries. The failings were fundamental. On the part of the commissaries they included the inability to determine the stocks of provisions on hand and the numbers being fed, and on the part of the Treasury the inability to interpret and act effectively on the information it did receive. There had been earlier problems of this sort, especially in 1775, when

[44] T 64/118, 31-32, Robinson to Chamier, 25 Nov 76. The problem in part was due to the Admiralty licenses referred to in the conclusion. A number of ships were dispatched in the early summer to Halifax although it was known that the army was probably not there, because that was the destination named in their licenses. Robinson had strongly warned Gordon against changing the destination because ". . . you will unhinge the whole arrangement. Ye Admiralty licenses sent you will in that case not answer, and you will by such measures throw all into confusion." AO 16/10, 49, Robinson to Gordon, 29 July 76.

it seemed at times that neither the Treasury, the Secretary of State nor, indeed, the army itself knew how many men were being fed or what stocks were in store or in transit. In the political and administrative confusion of 1775, in the welter of contractors, contractors' agents, and commissaries such a failure was not at all remarkable. War brings confusion and demands reorganization. By 1778, however, these problems should have been overcome. Not only was the Treasury aware that most provisions would have to be provided from Britain but the system, as reorganized in 1776, eliminated contractors' agents in America[45] and placed more responsibility for organizing provisions' shipments on the Treasury. Thereafter the commissary general was the chief provisions officer with the army, responsible for reporting regularly to the Treasury the stocks of provisions on hand and the length of time they were expected to last, and for anticipating, as far as he could, future needs. As the administration in Britain adjusted to the war, the Treasury was regularly informed when reinforcements were being sent out and made a practice of sending several months' provisions with each group.[46]

The new system was indeed an improvement in that it concentrated responsibility and thus shortened lines of communication. But it by no means eliminated the problem. If the Treasury was to keep the army adequately supplied, it had to know how many people were being fed at any time and even in 1776 it had difficulty discovering this essential fact. Early in that year the Treasury was informed that Howe's army was to be increased to 36,000 men and accordingly let provisions' contracts for that number. Thus John Robinson, the Treasury secretary, was surprised to

[45] There were still contractors' agents with the army, but they no longer had charge, as they did previously, of the reception and distribution of the provisions. From 1776 on they merely looked after the contractors' interests.

[46] T 64/106, 29-44, Robinson to Howe, 1 May 76.

receive from Chamier reports dated September 4 and 24 that gave the stocks of provisions on hand and calculated the length of time they would last only 27,000 men.[47] Just what the ration strength of the army was at that time is not entirely clear, but it might well have been 27,000 since all of the reinforcements had not arrived. On the 18th of October, however, the last major division—some 8,000 men[48]— put into New York, yet Chamier's next return, dated November 24, calculated the provisions on hand for the length of time they would last only 30,000 men,[49] and this was patently wrong. A return of the army of 20 March 1777 gave a rank-and-file total of 28,857, which is probably representative of the whole period from October 18 since losses during the winter were about balanced by the steady trickle of replacements from Britain and the arrival of the 6th Regiment from St. Vincent on November 20.[50] But the figure 28,857 in no way represented the total ration strength of the army. Officers, noncommissioned officers, and drummers, never counted with the rank and file, constituted on the average fourteen percent of regimental strength; this would add 4,697 to the strength given above, bringing it to 33,554. Still not included are headquarters and hospital personnel, civilian employees of the various army departments, and servants of general officers (all of whom were entitled to full rations), wives and children of the soldiers (the former entitled to half rations, the latter to half that), and prisoners of war and destitute refugees (usually provided with two-thirds rations). The numbers could obviously vary widely and unfortunately were seldom accurately determined. However, it seems quite clear that over the whole war there were never less than 3,000 and at times—such as the evacuation of Philadelphia, when the

---

[47] T 64/118, 31-32, Robinson to Chamier, 25 Nov 76.

[48] Searle, 125-126.   [49] T 64/118, 34.

[50] HMC, Stopford-Sackville Mss., Return of Howe's army in 1777; Searle, 144.

numbers of refugees dependent on the British increased tremendously—as many as 10,000. A conservative average of the number at any time would be 4,000, thus bringing the ration strength of the army over the fall and winter of 1776-1777 to the neighborhood of 37,500.[51]

When confronted with his inaccuracies, Chamier explained that they resulted from "the distant and dispersed situation of the army," lack of conformity in the periods for which different units drew rations, and the practice of some army departments of drawing large quantities of food in anticipation of future needs and submitting only quarterly accounts of actual issues.[52] These excuses had some validity for the latter part of 1776. The army, constantly in the field, grew steadily in size that fall, and service departments were being organized and expanded. But they certainly do not hold for the early months of 1777, when the situation was relatively static. Yet in a return of March 9th Chamier still computed his provisions' returns on the basis of 30,000 men. Not until two weeks later did he begin to work on the basis of even 36,000.[53] Just why Chamier's returns at this time were so inaccurate is not clear. It might well have been that he had to deal with unit commanders

[51] Detailed breakdowns of the ration strength of the army are few and far between. The commissary generals' returns usually only distinguished between men, women, and children, and headquarters returns often omitted civilian departments and other lesser groups. The average of 4,000—a conservative figure—has been put together from various returns throughout the war and is confirmed by the few detailed breakdowns that do exist. One of these, for the fall of 1778, gives the total number of officers and men as 36,020. To this are added 2,975 other personnel and 3,946 women, thus adding 4,948 to the ration strength of the army. (CP, Return prepared by Sir William Erskine. Filed at the end of 1776 in the papers but most certainly dating from August or September, or early October 1778.) Since the return does not include either children or headquarters personnel, the figure for ration strength was probably even higher.

[52] T 64/118, 36-40, Chamier to Robinson, 31 Mar 77.

[53] T 1/534, 99; T 64/118, 23.

and department heads who were reluctant to take the time and trouble to make out regular and accurate returns of the rations used. But that reflects as badly on Chamier as a simple lack of organization on his part, for it indicates a failure to convince the people involved, especially the commander-in-chief, of the absolute necessity of such returns. The Treasury apparently realized this also, for in 1777 Chamier was eased out of office, to be replaced by Daniel Wier. Unfortunately for the British army, Chamier's inefficiency was not confined to inaccuracies in reports of numbers drawing rations; nor did the effects of his mistakes end with his removal from office.

Wier arrived in America just in time to plunge into preparations for the 1777 campaign and the hurry of the moment led him to accept a number of inaccurate accounts compiled under Chamier. First, as he reported later, although he demanded a complete inventory of all commissary stores, the confusion of accounts and the bad state of the provisions in one of the major warehouses in New York City led him to accept an earlier inventory of that warehouse which proved to be highly over-optimistic. Further, large quantities of provisions were kept on board a number of troop transport ships that were always available for the army's use. Since it proved impossible to obtain up-to-date accountings from their captains, Wier also accepted the latest inventory of their contents, despite the fact that considerable quantities had been used. The result of these and a few other minor errors was that Wier began his administration believing that he had on hand about a million more rations than was actually the case.[54] Wier made a second error in trusting, again in the stress of the moment, the procedures developed by Chamier for determining the numbers of rations drawn daily. The figure his accountants first presented to him—36,858—Wier estimated later was short

<hr/>

[54] HSP, Wier Letter Book, Wier to Robinson, 12 July 77; T 64/114, 128-134, Wier to Robinson, 14 Feb 79.

by at least 7,000.[55] It was on the basis of these errors inherited from Chamier that the provisions crises of 1778 were founded.

The first person to become aware that a problem was building up was Wier himself. The awareness came in the early fall of 1777, when for the first time he was able to turn his attention to the reorganization of the accounting processes in the department and found that he was feeding not 36,858 as he had originally assumed but at least 41,794. In a report dated October 10th he informed the Treasury of the new figure, and of the fact that new provincial corps were being recruited and warned that unless the existing provisions' contracts for 36,000 were extended the army would inevitably suffer shortages.[56] He took up the warning again in letters of December 4, 1777, January 20, March 4 and 25, April 16 and 26, and May 22, 1778, and in them gave further reasons why his stocks were lower than the Treasury might estimate: large quantities of provisions had been damaged by exposure to weather during the fall, when the army in Pennsylvania had to be supplied via Head of Elk, where there was no warehousing, and more had been pilfered at the same time; the month-long voyage from New York left the army transport ships short on provisions and they had to be restocked from army stores; because the army spent so much time in the field, where extra meat was issued in lieu of small species, that item was low, as were dry provisions, as a result of bad and short-weight deliveries. He also noted that not only was the army for which he was directly responsible steadily increasing in size but that he was also called upon to provide provisions for Burgoyne's army (which, because it submitted to a convention rather than surrendered, was still a British responsibility to feed), and that he had to send a large quantity of provisions to Florida to relieve a provisions' shortage there even

[55] HSP, Wier Letter Book, Wier to Robinson, 20 May 77; T 64/114, 128-134, Wier to Robinson, 14 Feb 79.

[56] HSP, Wier Letter Book, Wier to Robinson, 25 Oct 77.

though the troops were supposed to be victualled under a separate contract.[57] In a February 1779 recapitulation of his provisions' situation since he took office, Wier summed up these drains on his supplies, adding to them such other items as rations issued to American prisoners, lost in various actions and accidents and loaned to the navy, and the loss in weight that occurred when flour was baked into hard bread. Since July 12, 1777, when he made his first comprehensive return, they accounted for 4,880,068 pounds of flour, 497,911 of beef, and 674,425 of pork.[58] If to this is added the over-estimation of stocks that resulted from Chamier's errors, the total amounts to almost twenty percent of the bread and flour, twelve percent of the beef, and eight percent of the pork that it might otherwise be assumed the army had available to it between July 12, 1777, and the end of 1778. This was an immense amount of food and its loss to the army amply accounts for the shortages of 1778.

The problem was that Wier, while he saw the provisions' shortages building up, did not discover Chamier's errors, or the main reasons for them, until 1779; nor was he able to give accurate figures for the various drains on his stocks that he reported until the same time. Further, because the army was divided and the headquarters of the commissary department was in New York while Wier was in Philadelphia with the commander-in-chief, accurate provisions' reports were almost impossible to compile. As a result the Treasury, on whom the relief of the situation depended, based its estimates of the army's provisions' situation on Wier's initial report of provisions on hand compiled when he took office. To that it added the provisions Wier reported purchasing in America and those Gordon shipped from Cork, and came up with a very satisfactory picture of the army's supply situation. Thus Wier's report of October

[57] HSP, Wier Letter Book, Wier to Robinson, 14 Dec 77; T 64/114, 1-5, 20-22, 33, 34-37, 46, 52-53, Wier to Robinson.
[58] T 64/114, 128-134, Wier to Robinson, 14 Feb 78.

10, 1777, which showed the numbers being fed as 41,794 rather than 36,858, caused some recalculation but little worry when it was received in London. Because it was working from the earlier erroneous returns and its own knowledge of provisions then at sea, the Treasury estimated that the army had, or would shortly have on hand, provisions sufficient to feed 45,000 until the end of December 1778, exclusive even of any fresh provisions Wier might have purchased. While it was recognized that some of this would have to go to Burgoyne's army it nevertheless appeared to everyone in London that, despite Wier's apprehensions, the army was adequately provided for.[59] Not until June 1778 was Wier able to provide the Treasury with accurate accounts of his stocks in an effort to convince that department that the army's provisions' situation bordered on the desperate. Even so, on June 5 Robinson wrote that although he could not be sure, since the partial returns he had received to that point did not indicate which provisions' ships had arrived, it appeared that while Wier's stock was "drawn lower than it was the intention of the Board . . ." nevertheless, "there appears to be no reason to fear your wanting provisions."[60] The Board apparently saw no reason, either, for reconsidering the 1778-1779 contracts that had just been let again for only 36,000 men.[61] It was not until June 12, when it received a complete return from Wier dated April 26, that the Treasury realized that a serious situation had developed. That report showed 45,455 people being fed for whom there were only sixty-four days' bread and ninety days' meat left in stock.[62] At that point the Treasury began to worry, and directed the contractors to supply all of the current year's provisions as soon as possible.[63]

[59] T 64/119, 6-8, Robinson to Wier, 6 Dec 77.

[60] T 64/119, 15-16, Robinson to Wier, 5 June 78.

[61] T 64/119, 12, Robinson to Wier, 30 Apr 78.

[62] T 64/114, 46, Wier to Robinson, 26 Apr 78; CP, Robinson to Clinton, 31 Oct 78.

[63] T 29/47, 12 June 78.

However, even though it began to worry, the Treasury did not see the situation as desperate. It calculated that since twenty-four victuallers, in three fleets, had been dispatched since April 26[64] and eight more were being prepared, stocks in America would soon be well up again. Indeed, Robinson calculated that with the supplies already on the way, it would require only provisions for 31,000 men for twelve months out of the current year's contracts for 36,000 to give Wier sufficient stocks to feed 40,000 until the end of May 1779. He figured the army's ration strength at 40,000 rather than the 45,455 Wier gave in his return of April 26 because Clinton had been ordered to send a detachment to Georgia and the West Indies that summer. So confident was the Treasury in its analysis of the situation at New York that it decided that the "extra" 5,000 rations in the 1778-1779 contract could be safely cancelled, and, rather than hire more ships to carry to the army immediately the provisions then being collected at Cork, it determined to await the return of vessels dispatched earlier in the year.[65]

The Treasury's analysis was, for the most part, sound within the context of the information it had on hand. Yet it erred in its assumption. It assumed that the number fed would remain static until August, when it would decline to well below 40,000. But such, as it proved, was not the case. First, several thousand refugees went with the army when Philadelphia was evacuated and these had to be fed for a time from army stores.[66] Second, the detachments for

---

[64] The first six of these vessels, the *Sibella's* fleet, dispatched May 31 and arrived Aug 26, carried the last quarter of the 1778 provisions. The next two fleets, with the *Francis* and the *Roehampton* as commodores, were dispatched June 28 and July 31. The *Sibella's* fleet was directed to Philadelphia and sailed into Delaware Bay after the British evacuation. Only good luck saved it from capture. The *Francis'* fleet arrived at New York sometime in September and the *Roehampton's* on Oct 19.

[65] T 64/119, 13-15, Robinson to Wier, 27 July 78.

[66] Unfortunately Wier never gave the exact number of refugees fed at this time. He probably did not know himself. (T 64/114, 63-64, 65-66, Wier to [Robinson], 15 June, 7 July 78.)

Georgia and the West Indies, 11,000 men in all, were delayed at New York by the presence of d'Estaing's fleet on the Atlantic coast and did not leave until almost the end of October. While they waited they consumed two more months' provisions and when they did leave took a further three months' supply with them; none of this figured in the Treasury's analysis.[67] Further, the Treasury's information was not entirely sound. Robinson believed that eight victuallers beyond the twenty-four that had already sailed were preparing; he was mistaken.

The result of these various failings was that the army lived a truly hand-to-mouth existence throughout most of 1778. On the 6th of May, just before the arrival of a fleet dispatched in February, it was reduced to 25 days' flour and 86 days' meat and was at almost exactly the same position again on the evacuation of Philadelphia a month and a half later. On the 26th of August, on the arrival of the next fleet, there were 22 days' flour and 33 of meat in the stores, a situation that would have been graver had not ten days' provisions been foraged from the countryside on the march from Philadelphia. On the 19th of October, when the last fleet of the year arrived, there were only 26 days' flour and 55 days' meat on hand. When the next fleet arrived on the fourth of January 1779 the army had only four days' provisions in store.[68] And the timely arrival of that fleet was largely a stroke of luck. In late August of 1778 the Treasury, confused by some of Wier's returns, came to the conclusion that he might be feeding as many as 56,000 men. Thus instead of waiting the return of victuallers from America before dispatching the next fleet as intended, it ordered additional shipping taken up and dispatched as soon as possible.[69] This fleet arrived on January 4th and literally saved the British army. Unable to evacuate because

67 T 64/114, 128-131, Wier to Robinson, 14 Feb 79.
68 *Ibid.*, 65-66, 101-102, Wier to Robinson, 7 July, 23 Nov. 78.
69 T 64/119, 17-18, Robinson to Wier, 3 Sept 78.

most of his troop transports had gone with the detachments to the South, Clinton really had no choice had the ships not arrived but to strike inland in search of provisions. Clinton recalled his position in his memoirs: he looked to get ten days' provisions by scouring the environs of New York and perhaps a week's further supply from pillaging Philadelphia. "After that *bas les armes* if the Delaware Neck could not have supplied us."[70]

The responsibility for the crises of 1778 did not lie in any one place or with any one man. The original failing was Chamier's inability to keep track of either the quantity of provisions he had on hand or the number of men eating them. But Wier must bear considerable responsibility also, for accounting procedures under his administration were only marginally better than Chamier's. He was plunged into campaigns immediately on his arrival and thus the reform of the system was necessarily delayed. It was not until the end of April 1778 that he was able to produce an accurate and comprehensive account of the provisions the army had on hand and not until the following February was he able to track down the errors he inherited from Chamier. Similarly, although he reported to the Treasury that large quantities of provisions were bad or short of weight on receipt and that other quantities were lost as a result of bad weather, enemy action, and, in the case of flour, shrinkage during baking, he was not able to give the Treasury an exact account of these losses until February 1779. And even his accounts of the numbers being fed were not always consistent. He rectified one of Chamier's errors when he reported in October 1777 that he was feeding 41,794 and he did not change that figure until April 26, 1778, when he reported a ration strength of 45,455. Yet in February 1779, in reply to Treasury criticisms of his accounting methods, he insisted that he had never issued less

[70] Clinton, *American Rebellion*, 112.

than 45,000 rations a day during his whole term as commissary general.[71] There were reasons, then, for the Treasury's inability to foresee the impending crises.

Nevertheless, the Treasury was not entirely innocent in this affair. Unless given precise figures of deficiencies, that department insisted on believing that every pound of rations ordered out was available for issue to the troops. Yet there was ample reason for it to believe otherwise. Reports of bad bread and flour were as continuous from Wier as they had been from Chamier, and Wier first brought up the problem of short weight in a letter of 29 November 1777.[72] It also knew he was sending provisions to Florida—at one point 2,500 barrels—and to Burgoyne's army at Boston, and Germain had long since authorized the army to issue provisions to destitute refugees.[73] Treasury officials were also aware of the hazards of war on land and on sea. Wier had informed them of "substantial losses" at Head of Elk due to exposure to weather and pilfering, and they knew also that the arming of victuallers had not entirely ended losses to American privateers. Yet, despite this knowledge, the department sent to America on three separate occasions computations of provisions that proved, by adding together every pound of provisions sent out, that the army could not possibly be short of food.[74] Perhaps the Treasury was justified in this since Wier so seldom provided details of his problems, but justice and wisdom do not necessarily

[71] HSP, Wier Letter Book, Wier to Robinson, 25 Oct 77; T 64/114, 46, 128-131, Wier to Robinson, 26 Apr 78, 14 Feb 79. He reported the losses from short deliveries and bad provisions as 1,658,515 pounds of flour and 346,802 rations of meat.

[72] All of this information is contained in letters from Wier to the Treasury from 20 May 1777 through to the end of 1778. Those from 20 May 1777 through 11 Dec 1777 are in a letter book of Wier's at the Historical Society of Pennsylvania. The remainder are in the Treasury letter book T 64/114.

[73] BAHQP, 209, Germain to Howe, 11 June 76.

[74] T 64/119, 17-18, 21-25, 29-31, Robinson to Howe, 3 Sept, 31 Oct 78, 19 Jan 79.

coincide. Wier, the man on the spot, emphasized in every letter from 25th of October 1777 on, that he feared a provisions' crisis was building up, but the Treasury could always find reasons to ignore the warnings. While the Treasury basked in a pedantic sense of righteousness fostered by 3,000 insulating miles of ocean, the army slid to the brink of disaster.

The results of the logistics debacle of 1778 were various. In Britain it probably determined the Treasury to renew its appeal to the Navy Board to take over the organization of provisions' transportation to the army, an appeal that on this occasion was successful. In America it brought some unrest among the troops. The shortage of flour made it necessary to issue rice in place of flour two days a week as early as the summer of 1778, and as the crisis deepened in December a "bread" made of oatmeal, pease, and Indian corn was all that could be provided.[75] Wier fully expected "murmurings and discontent" and was agreeably surprised to find that the British troops at least bore this hardship without a word of complaint.[76] Perhaps because they were less interested in the war, or less adept because of the language barrier at finding alternate sources of food, the German troops found the shortage more galling. Several German officers' diaries report increased desertion along with the "murmurings" at this time.[77] Shortages seem also to have driven some civilians to move out of the British enclaves to areas where food was available.[78]

The effect on operations appears to have been negligible. The entry of France into the war had changed the whole

[75] *Ibid.*, 107-108, Wier to Robinson, 21 Dec 78.

[76] *Ibid.*, 117-120, Wier to Robinson, 19 Jan 79. The troops did not always accept the substitution of rice for flour so well. General Prevost, campaigning in Georgia in March 1779, noted that he had been forced to this resort several times and that it was not always agreeable to the troops "who have frequently murmured at it." (BAHQP, 1,829, Prevost to Clinton, 15 Mar 79.)

[77] N-YHS, "von Kraft Journal," 75-77; Uhlendorf, 248.

[78] Mackenzie, 397.

direction of strategic thinking in London and the army in America, turned over from Howe to Clinton in the spring of 1778, had been ordered on to the defensive.[79] Admiral d'Estaing's fleet, which blockaded New York in the summer and shortly afterwards combined with the Americans in an attack on Rhode Island, was far more important as a determinant of events. Clinton did have to make several extensive foraging expeditions, but these were completely consistent with his orders to carry out harassing operations. General Grey, after relieving Rhode Island, proceeded on to raids that resulted in the partial burning of the towns of New Bedford and Fairhaven and the collection of 10,000 sheep from Martha's Vineyard. Towards the end of September Cornwallis took a considerable force into New Jersey for the same dual purpose.[80]

The most serious effect of the crisis was probably on General Clinton. He took over as commander-in-chief at Philadelphia on May 8 and his first orders from London directed him to evacuate that city and fall back on New York. From New York he was to dispatch large detachments to Georgia and the West Indies to defend those areas against possible French attack and then if New York itself proved to be indefensible he was instructed to retire with the rest of the army to Halifax.[81] This was clearly not what he expected when he agreed to take over command. Although the excitement of the summer—the evacuation of Philadelphia, Monmouth, d'Estaing's blockade, the relief of Rhode Island—kept his thoughts on other matters, by autumn he was so disillusioned that he asked for his recall.[82] The detachments he had been ordered to make, he wrote to Germain, had destroyed "the very nerve of this army"; he was prevented by his orders, and the size and quality of

[79] Willcox, *Portrait of a General*, 224.
[80] Ward, 592-593; Uhlendorf, 216-218.
[81] Willcox, *Portrait of a General*, 224.
[82] *Ibid.*, 261.

the force left him from doing anything constructive.[83] Clearly, Clinton could see, the West Indies had assumed priority over America in the minds of the men at Whitehall. His provisions' situation seemed to confirm this and hence increased his despondency. When he took over, the first provisions' crisis of the year was building up. Thus one of his first worries was the feeding of his army and it remained so throughout the year. On three separate occasions even before the grand crisis of December-January his provisions' reserves fell to less than forty days' and on only one brief occasion stood at over 100 days'. Fleets arriving from Cork never brought more than several months' supplies, enough to relieve the crisis but never sufficient to give him peace of mind. At least one of these crises brought with it the spectre of defeat. On his return from Philadelphia Clinton found himself short on supplies and bottled up by d'Estaing's fleet. The only apparent hope of relief was the arrival of promised naval reinforcements under Admiral Byron. William Eden, one of the erstwhile peace commissioners sent out from London, put the prospects of the army at the time very succinctly: "If Byron arrives before the messieurs depart, I hope that Messrs. d'Estaing and Bougainville will shortly afterwards dine with me as prisoners of war. If he should not arrive, and if we cannot beat them without waiting for him, I must dine with them; for I shall not have any means of dining elsewhere."[84]

The French fleet gave up the blockade after less than two weeks but nevertheless its continued presence in North American waters was a cause for acute anxiety. As long as victuallers had nothing to face but American privateers and the occasional American frigate, Clinton's provisions' situation was, if not desirable, at least tolerable. With the

[83] B. F. Stevens (ed.), *Facsimiles of Manuscripts in European Archives Relating to America, 1773-1783* (London, 1889-1898), XI, no. 1175, Clinton to Germain, 8 Oct 78.

[84] *Ibid.*, V, no. 504, Eden to [?], 19 July 78.

French navy at large, the loss of a whole victualling fleet became a possibility, and only one such disaster was needed to bring the army to destruction. Never a man to suffer in silence, Clinton protested his situation by letter and by personal emissary. The main burden of his messages, of course, was the position assigned to him and his army in the new strategy, but the logistical complaints were always included.[85] He recommended that he never be left with less than six months' provisions on hand and preferably twelve, and Eden carried the same message personally to Germain.[86]

Strangely enough, the most serious crisis of the year, that of December-January, did not elicit any further recriminations from Clinton. In a letter written just after the relief fleet arrived he described briefly the position he had been in and its possible consequences, but then went on to express the confident hope that the government would "for the future order us more ample and regular supplies."[87]

The following years proved that Clinton's confidence was not justified: the first nine months of 1779 were almost a repetition of 1778. Although six convoys of victuallers arrived between January 19 and September 10 the army's reserves were never sufficient for more than five months and on several occasions dropped below the sixty-day level. Not until the arrival in September of the first fleets organized by the Navy Board did the situation improve. The provisions brought by that fleet, along with those already in stock, gave the army seven months' reserves.[88] The next

[85] T 64/114, 74-76, Wier to Robinson, 5 Sept 78; BAHQP, 1,350, Clinton to Germain, 15 Sept 78; T 64/109, 122-123, Clinton to Robinson, 16 Nov 78; Willcox, *Portrait of a General*, 261-265.

[86] CP, Eden to Clinton, 23 Jan 79.

[87] CP, Clinton to [Eden], 10 Jan 79.

[88] See chart, appendix 1. There were 29 ships in one fleet, escorted by Sir Andrew Hammond in the *Roebuck*; T 64/114, 211, Wier to Robinson, 10 Oct 79.

convoy arrived in March 1780, but there was not another one until November 13 and by that time the reserves had been perilously low for almost four months. And those four months encompassed most of the campaigning season of 1780.

As was the case with earlier shortages, those of 1779 and 1780 can be traced to a number of failings. One was, again, the reports of the commissary general. Wier finally began, in late 1778, to submit detailed monthly reports of his provisions' state. By early 1779 they had become reasonably comprehensive and uniform but were still often inaccurate in terms of the numbers drawing rations. After the departure of the expeditions to the West Indies and Georgia, Wier gave the ration strength of the army as 33,000 and with only minor variations he stuck to that number throughout the following winter and spring.[89] On May 2, however, in response to a letter from the Treasury criticizing his returns, he stated that his consumption was and had been "in one way or another" close to 36,000.[90] The figure of 36,000 was probably the correct one. Provincial units were being built up to compensate for the troops sent south[91] and refugees and casual laborers, the latter employed on the construction of new defensive works, were a steady drain on supplies at this time. It was probably very difficult to keep track of the number of these people, but Wier's failure even to mention them in his returns or estimate their numbers was indefensible.[92]

[89] T 64/113, 101-102, 128-136, 150-151. Wier did mention in one return that the figures given did not include the "families," that is personal staffs, of the general and headquarters officers (T 64/114, 96-99, 14 Nov 78).

[90] T 64/114, 162-166, Wier to Robinson, 2 May 79.

[91] Willcox, *Portrait of a General*, 286-287.

[92] There are no accurate returns of refugees fed until late 1779, when an inspector of refugee claims was appointed. Before that time, apparently all that a refugee needed to obtain rations was a certificate from a senior officer stating that he was "destitute." The first inspector was

A second failing lay with the contractors. When in June 1778 the Treasury first became aware of the provisions' crisis in America it directed the contractors to supply all of the provisions then on order as soon as possible. The provisions' year ran from 1 June to 30 May and three quarters of the 1778-1779 supply was still outstanding on the contracts. On December 6 Gordon wrote to the Treasury that he was still awaiting the delivery of considerable quantities of provisions at Cork and not until well into January 1779 could he report that the last quarter of the 1778-1779 provisions were ready for shipment.[93] Since these provisions could not possibly reach the army before the middle of March and were meant for consumption in March, April, and May, the contractors not only failed to meet the advanced delivery dates requested by the Treasury but were even months late on their regular delivery date. The Treasury had stated that it intended to follow the commander-in-chief's wishes and keep the army always six months ahead in provisions[94] and if it intended to live up to that the deliveries at Cork should have been completed by September at the very latest.

But the most important reason for the shortages was shipping and its cost. When the Treasury came to the conclusion that the army in America would have to be supplied from Britain for an indefinite time and hired and armed victuallers to carry the supplies, it confidently assumed that each ship could make two round trips to America a year. The ships were to be divided into two fleets and the provisions for a year into four quarters; the first fleet would take the first and third quarters and the second fleet the second and fourth.[95] Like so many plans conceived in the rarefied

---

Roger Morris and his returns for January and February of the numbers drawing rations vary from 758 to 868 (CP, 28 Feb 80).

[93] T 29/48, 17 Dec 78; T 64/107, 24, Robinson to Clinton, 19 Jan 79.
[94] T 64/119, 2-3, Robinson to Wier, 26 Sept 77.
[95] T 64/106, 29-44, Robinson to Howe, 1 May 76; Dartmouth Papers, D1778/11/1819, "An account of what has been done by the Treasury Board. . . ," 1 Jan 78.

air of higher administrative circles, this one broke down immediately when it came into contact with reality. In Britain schedules were upset by contractors who failed to meet delivery dates and by adverse winds that on occasion held up sailings for weeks and even months.[96] In America the possibilities for upsetting the schedules were even greater. One of the first fleets went to Halifax, but arrived there after the army had left. Not having orders to cover this contingency it dropped anchor and waited there for over a month instead of following the army to New York.[97] On other occasions victuallers on their arrival were directed to accompany detachments or take their provisions to detachments already established. This again could cause long delays. New York harbor was a tremendous bottleneck. Unloading and warehousing facilities were hopelessly inadequate and ships not uncommonly rode in the harbor for up to eight weeks waiting to discharge cargo. Unloading itself could be a painfully slow process due to broken and damaged barrels and the necessity of inspection. Coal, while it was shipped, also caused delays: it was loaded into the hold loose and had to be bagged for removal.

The Treasury thus found it necessary to hire far more ships than originally intended and even then had to dispatch provisions not in neat quarterly convoys but in odd lots as ships could be collected and loaded. By 1778 shipping schedules were in such disarray that the last quarter of the 1777-1778 provisions was not dispatched until May 29, 1778 and the first fleet with 1778 provisions did not sail until June 28.[98] The next fleet did not get away until July 31 and, because of a shortage of ships, the next one not until October 12. Four more sailings were required to complete the 1778-1779 provisions, the last not getting away until late in January 1779. The first four months' provisions of the 1779-1780 contract were equally dispersed, sail-

[96] For example, T 64/106, 26-28, Robinson to Howe, 26 Apr 76.
[97] T 64/118, 31-32, Robinson to Chamier, 25 Nov 76.
[98] T 64/119, 13-15, Robinson to Wier, 27 July 78.

ing in four convoys between March 5 and May 28. The result of this was, as Wier complained, "that the provisions of one convoy are consumed before the arrival of another. . . ."[99]

Although the Treasury came to recognize that some delays were inevitable, it put most of the blame for the disruption of its shipping schedules, and the consequent provisions' shortages, on unnecessary delays of the ships while in America. The army, it claimed, was not doing all that it could to speed the return of victuallers to Britain. In some cases the Treasury's charges were completely unjustified. For instance, it laid part of the blame for the provisions' problems of 1778 on the failure of the army to return a fleet of nine ships that sailed from Cork on February 25 and arrived at Philadelphia on May 21. Instead of being unloaded immediately, and returned to Cork for a planned second voyage in July, they were, Robinson complained, kept with the army, returned with it to New York, and were there penned up by d'Estaing for the best part of the summer. Had they been dispatched when they should have been, he wrote, the army would have been spared at least one of its crises that autumn.[100] The Treasury's anger would better have been directed at Germain for failing to notify it that Clinton had been ordered to evacuate Philadelphia by sea. To have unloaded the fleet, which arrived only three weeks before the evacuation, would have been madness even if other ships had been available to accommodate the provisions. In any case, there was barely enough shipping available for the army's stockpile of supplies and the Loyalist refugees of Philadelphia; the army itself had to march back to New York.

In other cases the Treasury's complaints were more justified. For instance, the great fire that occurred at New York immediately after the British occupied the city destroyed,

99 T 64/114, 107-108, Wier to Robinson, 21 Dec 78.

100 CP, Treasury Correspondence Letter Book, 31 Oct 78; T 64/119, 21-25, Robinson to Wier, 31 Oct 78.

among other things, a large number of warehouses. The warehouses were not only difficult to replace but since it was believed that the fire had been started by Patriot incendiaries the army was not inclined to put all its provisions' reserves in such vulnerable places. Hence it turned to using ships as floating warehouses and in early 1777 thirty-nine victuallers were so employed.[101] Clinton apparently cut down on this practice, but had his own reason for retaining ships. The various provisions' crises of the fall of 1778 made him acutely aware of the danger of being without transport. All the ships usually with the army were engaged in carrying troops to the South during the last part of that year. None were available for the evacuation of New York had provisions finally run out. Without the option of evacuation there were only two courses of action open: to surrender or to strike out inland in search of food and probably meet the same fate as overtook Burgoyne. "I have not transports sufficient for 4,000" he wrote in frustration and anger to Newcastle at the end of the year.[102] To Eden he wrote on January 10, 1779 ". . . [that] transports in case embarkation should be necessary we have none of L[ord] Howe will have represented & we shall no doubt be supplied. . . ."[103] As transports of any sort arrived he apparently detained them. His action was not well received in London. In May he received a letter from Robinson protesting his retention of victuallers for use as magazines "or to attend the army as common transports." From Germain he received a letter that concluded a confident resumé of the total disarray of the American cause with the assertion that he (Clinton) should no longer find it necessary to keep with him transports "sufficient to carry off the whole army and stores at one embarkation. . . ."[104] But despite these and even more categorical orders not to detain ships, and

101 T 64/108, 103-105, Howe to Robinson, 5 Apr 77.
102 CP, end of 1778.
103 CP, 10 Jan 79.
104 T 64/107, 15-19, 19 Jan 79; CP, 3 Mar 79.

his own protests that he always directed that the ships be sent off as soon as they were unloaded, there is some evidence that Clinton did indeed continue to keep a substantial fleet on hand. Sometime in late 1780 the Navy Board, concerned about the shortage of shipping, apparently requested its agents there to make a quiet survey of the shipping in the British-held ports in America. The returns were transmitted to the Treasury in April 1781: eleven vessels amounting to nearly 4,000 tons were in use as prison ships, hospitals, and magazines.[105]

The effect of the provisions' problems of 1779 was again largely in terms of morale and must be understood in the context of the size of the army available to Clinton. Clinton had reacted most strongly to the withdrawal of parts of his army for operations to the South in 1778 and his complaints and threats to resign finally drew from Germain a promise of reinforcements. They would be convoyed by the fleet carrying the new naval commander for America, Admiral Marriot Arbuthnot. On the basis of this promise Clinton designed his 1779 campaign. In early May he sent a large detachment to attack Portsmouth, Virginia, and on its return, in the later part of the same month, launched an attack on Verplanck's and Stony Point. These attacks were designed to throw Washington off balance, interrupt his supplies, and force him to a decisive battle. At this point, June, the reinforcements from Britain were supposed to arrive, but the fleet that was to convoy them to America was drawn off by a report that the French were attacking the island of Jersey. As a result June, July, and most of August passed before Clinton received his new troops.[106] By then the opportunity had passed; the early effort had been wasted. To this disappointment was added the failure of provisions. Despite his urgent pleas for a large reserve there were less than four months' supplies for the army in the warehouses at New York at the beginning of June and

[105] T 64/107, 65, Commissioners of the Navy to Treasury, 2 Apr 81.
[106] Willcox, *Portrait of a General*, 274-277.

they dwindled to a sixty-day supply before the next fleet arrived. With the activities of the Rebel navy and privateers increasing—a fleet of victuallers from New York to Georgia was captured in April—Clinton had cause to worry.[107] When the next fleet did arrive it brought less than two months' supplies and by September the army was again with less than two months' reserves. When Arbuthnot's fleet finally arrived it carried but half the 6,600 men promised by the government and most of them were sick.[108]

So collapsed the campaign of 1779, and with it Clinton's morale. To him, the failure of reinforcements and of provisions were of the same order; both indicated that his needs were of the lowest priority for the government. " 'Tis needless to complain of your total neglect of us," he wrote to Eden in complete dejection in July. "With what you send us, when it arrives, we will do the best."[109] In August he wrote to Germain requesting that he be relieved of his command: "To tell the truth, My Lord, my spirits are worn out by struggling against the consequences of many adverse incidents which without appearing publickly to account for my situation, have effectually oppressed me."[110]

With the arrival of large quantities of provisions in September Clinton's humor returned and in December he mounted the attack against Charleston, his most successful operation as commander-in-chief. He returned to New York in June 1780 anxious to build on that success. Instead he moved into his most frustrating provisions' crisis.

When the Treasury turned the task of accepting, inspecting and delivering provisions over to the Navy Board, it was its hope that the problems of feeding the army had come to an end. The Navy Board took up its new task in the middle of 1779 but in 1780 the army suffered a provi-

[107] Clinton, *American Rebellion*, 127; CP, Clinton to Eden, 2 July 79.
[108] Willcox, *Portrait of a General*, 283.
[109] CP, Clinton to Eden, General Conway, and Duke of Newcastle, 2 July 79.
[110] CP, Clinton to Germain, 20 Aug 79.

sions' crisis that lasted through most of that year's campaign season.

The cause of the crisis was again shipping. The Navy Board's plan was to send the victuallers, now disarmed and protected instead by ships of the Royal Navy, in two large convoys each year, the first leaving in the late spring or early summer and the second in the late summer.[111] In 1779, however, even though there were only eight months' provisions of the 1779-1780 contracts remaining to be delivered when the Board took over, both the convoys were late getting away. The first, perhaps because the system was new and because there was a delay while the victuallers were disarmed, did not depart until July 19 or arrive in New York until September 22. The second convoy, although it was ready at Cork by the middle of September, did not depart until December 24 and then, to avoid the winter storms of the North Atlantic, was directed to take a southern route to America. It arrived in Charleston in early March 1780. Thirteen of the twenty-eight ships in the convoy remained with the army there and the rest proceeded immediately on to New York. The delay of the second convoy was a graphic demonstration of the more subtle ways in which the war in Europe could affect the war in America. The convoy did not sail because its naval escort was not available, and that the Admiralty blamed on "the circumstance of the United Fleet being masters of the Channel and contrary winds. . . ."[112]

But the significance of the delayed sailings of these two convoys was not so much that the provisions they carried arrived late in America but that the ships that carried them were not available on time for the 1780-1781 deliveries. Although the first half of the new year's provisions were ready at Cork by June 1780 not a single ship of the Navy Board's 1779 convoys had returned.[113] For the convoy, which did not leave Cork until December 24, this is not

111 Syrett, 154.   112 *Ibid.*, 156.
113 T 64/200, 113, Navy Board to Treasury, [Sept] 1780.

surprising but what of the ships in the first convoy, which arrived at New York on September 22? Wier wrote to the Treasury on October 10 to report the arrival of that convoy and, aware that shipping was in short supply, noted that the empty victuallers would be dispatched "with all expedition."[114] A month later he reported that the unloading had been completed and the vessels would sail "as soon as a convoy is appointed." Along with them were to go seven other ships—the *Maria's* convoy—which had arrived on September 10 and had been kept for use as transports for a time.[115] In all, then, there were twenty-seven ships at New York on November 11 ready for return to Cork. Just what happened to these ships is not entirely clear, but it is very probable that they were used to carry Clinton's expedition to Charleston. Certainly it is clear that there was a shortage of transports in America that fall since it was the Navy Board's agent at New York, responsible for supplying transports for the army, who had detained the *Maria's* convoy. With a major expedition in the offing even more ships were necessary and the September 22 convoy and the *Maria's* convoy were probably impressed for that service.[116] But it was not just the army's expedition that delayed the ships. Clinton and the transports were back in New York by June 1780 and two months later, responding to a charge that he was detaining the ships unnecessarily, Clinton noted that the fault lay with Admiral Arbuthnot, who would not provide a convoy for them. "They have . . . been discharged from us these three months," he wrote, "& the Admiral does not send them home, tho' we repeatedly apply."[117]

114 T 64/114, 211, Wier to Robinson, 10 Oct 79.

115 *Ibid.*, 215-219, 11 Nov 79.

116 Although specific convoys are not mentioned, this is strongly suggested in a letter from Clinton to Eden dated 14 Aug 80. In the context of a complaint about his provisions' situation Clinton wrote, "perhaps you blame us for not returning the victuallers to Corke; it cannot be, while expedition goes on, they must attend it" (Newcastle Papers, NeC, 623).

117 *Ibid.*

The delay of the victuallers in America would not have been significant had it not coincided with a severe shortage of shipping in Britain. When the Navy Board tried to hire more ships to carry out the 1780-1781 provisions it found that none were available "although every encouragement by premium & other ways hath been offered for months past to all parts of the Kingdom. . . ."[118] The summer was almost over before a convoy was finally collected and it did not arrive at New York until November 13. By that time, even by the Treasury's habitually generous calculations, the army had been out of preserved food for three months.[119]

The effects of the shipping delays of 1780 were serious. Not since 1776 and 1777 had the British had a better chance to deliver a mortal blow to the Rebel cause. The capture of Charleston and with it General Lincoln's army—a disaster for the Americans equivalent to Saratoga for the British—sapped Rebel morale and gave a corresponding lift to the hopes of the British and their Loyalist supporters. In June, with Cornwallis well started on the reduction of the interior of Georgia and the Carolinas, Clinton returned to New York full of enthusiasm and eager to build on the winter's successes.[120] But the whole summer and fall passed without a major stroke against the enemy undertaken: General Alexander Leslie was sent with 2,500 men in October to create a "diversion" in the Chesapeake to take pressure off Cornwallis and the ill-fated attempt to exploit Arnold's treason was undertaken, but beyond that nothing.

The inactivity of the first two months after Clinton's return to New York was probably not due to provisions' problems but rather to the worsening of the long-smoldering feud between Clinton and Arbuthnot, the admiral commanding on the American station. The most pressing busi-

118 T 64/200, 113, Navy Board to Treasury, [September], 1780.
119 T 63/201, 3-11, Treasury Board to Commissioners of the Navy, 27 Feb 79.
120 Willcox, *Portrait of a General*, 321-322.

ness of the army at this time was a move against Rhode Island. Word had been received that a French squadron under the Chevalier de Ternay, convoying 6,000 troops under the Comte de Rochambeau, was on its way to America. Its destination was known to be Rhode Island and Clinton wanted to disrupt the enemy's plans by retaking Newport (abandoned by the British the previous fall) before the French arrived or, if that proved impossible, to attack them there once they had landed but before they were established. Either operation, however, required a high degree of cooperation between the army and the navy and Clinton's stiff-necked contempt on one side and Arbuthnot's senile incompetence on the other made that impossible.[121]

But then on September 14 Admiral Sir George Rodney arrived unexpectedly at New York with ten ships of the line. The way should have been open for a major stroke against Rhode Island or elsewhere, for not only did the ships give the British immense naval superiority in American waters but Rodney automatically superceded Arbuthnot in command of the American station, and he was one of the few men Clinton found it possible to work with.[122] But the stroke that was now possible in terms of men and ships had become impossible in terms of logistics.

When Clinton returned to New York in mid-June the army had about two and a half months' provisions in stock, well below the desired reserves but not a critical situation. But July, August, September, and most of October passed without even word that a fleet was on its way;[123] not until November 13 was the situation relieved. The army was saved from starvation only by the energetic actions of the

---

[121] *Ibid.*, 323-330.   [122] *Ibid.*, 337-338.

[123] The provisions' convoy sailed from Cork on August 14 but the army did not get news of it until the middle of October and then only from a civilian ship that left Britain about the same time. (T 1/559, 214-219, Wier to Robinson, 27 Oct 80; CP, draft of a letter from Clinton to Dalrymple, [November] 1780).

commissariat in collecting provisions, the coincidence of the shortage with harvest time, and the timely arrival of a civilian fleet at New York in October.[124] From July to November, Wier was able to purchase over a million and a half pounds of flour and 400,000 pounds of meat. But the impossibility of depending indefinitely on local resources was indicated both by a steep rise in food prices at New York over the period and by the depletion of such reserves as there were in the army storehouses.[125] In mid-July there were fifty days' provisions in stock and a month later, thanks to Wier's purchases, that amount had not decreased. By September 20, however, the stock was down to twenty-two days and a month after that to thirteen days. When the provisions' fleet from Britain finally arrived there were only six days' food in the warehouses and even though he expected to be able to obtain a month's provisions from the navy, Wier despaired of being able to feed the army beyond Christmas.[126]

The adverse effects of the provisions' shortage became apparent at least as early as August. At that time, although Clinton was still trying to plan a move against Rhode Island with Arbuthnot, his initiative, as W. B. Willcox notes, was ebbing. Willcox attributes this to a resurgence of Clinton's normally conservative approach to operations,[127] but a letter Clinton wrote to Eden at this time reveals in fact an intense concern about his provisions' situation: "What is this new contract of supply? Had not Mr. Wier exerted himself all was finished on the 7th of this month; no hint even of a Cork fleet. Why all this neglect? Perhaps

[124] *Ibid.* Wier purchased about 3,000 barrels of beef and flour from the provisions brought by this fleet but that drove prices up drastically.

[125] CP, Returns of provisions in store, 19 July to 21 Aug, 26 Sept to 2 Oct, 6-19 Nov 1780; Mackenzie Papers, Return of provisions, 22 Aug to 25 Sept 80.

[126] T 1/563, 141-144, Wier to Robinson, 9 Nov 80.

[127] Willcox, *Portrait of a General*, 330.

you blame us for not returning the victuallers immediately to Cork; it cannot be, while expedition goes on, they must attend it; they have however been discharged from us these three months, & the Admiral does not send them home tho' we repeatedly apply. Well I will endeavor to forget we have missed an opportunity of attempting an important stroke, and in perfect good humour attend the Admiral. . . . For God's sake send us money, men, and provisions, or expect nothing but complaints."[128]

Two weeks later he wrote again, expressing even greater pessimism: "I have no money, no provisions, nor indeed any account of the sailing of the Cork fleet, nor admiral that I can have the least dependence on, no army. In short, I have nothing left but the hope for better times and a little more attention."[129]

By the time Rodney arrived, the situation, at least as far as offensive operations was concerned, was hopeless. Although he was prepared to attempt to exploit Arnold's treason if that had proved possible, and went through the motions of planning operations with Rodney, Clinton obviously could attempt nothing substantial when, as Wier put it, the army was "living hand to mouth."[130] He did not even dispatch Leslie to the Chesapeake until he knew that provisions were definitely on the way and then could not provide him with more than a meagre reserve of the "salt beef, and oat-grits meal and bad zweiback" on which the army was then existing.[131] When the provisions' convoy arrived on November 13 not only was the campaign season over but Rodney had to return to the West Indies.

So ended one of the best opportunities of the war for decisive British action. And not only had nothing been accomplished in the summer, but with a French fleet now

---

[128] Newcastle Papers, NeC, 623, Clinton to [Eden], 14 Aug 80.
[129] Clinton, *American Rebellion*, 456, Clinton to [Eden], 1 Sept 80.
[130] T 1/559, 214-219, Wier to Robinson, 27 Oct 80.
[131] N-YHS, "von Kraft Journal," 121, entry of 15 Oct 80.

firmly established at Rhode Island the British army was in a more dangerous position than it had ever been before.

With the arrival of the provisions' fleet in November the army's problems with provisions shipped from Britain virtually came to an end. There were still occasional batches of bad flour and meat, but generally the provisions received in America in the last years of the war were, as Nathaniel Day, the commissary general in Canada, commented in 1783, "sweet, sound & wholesome . . . in every way fit for issuing to His Majesty's Troops, the packages in good condition being the strongest & best that have yet come. . . ."[132] And although the provisions' reserves of the army at New York dropped to sixty-six days in April 1781, thereafter it never had less than nine months' food on hand and often more. Thus by 1781 an adequate organization for supplying the army in America had been developed. The problem was that by that time opposition to the war was building rapidly in Britain and it needed only Cornwallis' surrender at Yorktown to bring Parliament to demand that it be brought to an end. The loss of Cornwallis' army was not a terrible military disaster, however. What made it so significant was the five years of indecision that had preceded it. The failures of supply that occurred while the provisioning organization was being developed helped significantly to make those years indecisive.

In this consideration of the problems of supplying the army with food from Britain, one more point requires consideration. In a memorandum Sir Henry Clinton once noted that "economy is a word which ought not to be found in [the] military dictionary in time of war."[133] The idea is not entirely defensible. When war is used as an instrument of national policy, its prosecution must be limited by the resources the nation is willing to divert, just as its aims

[132] T 1/580, Day to Robinson, 4 Aug 83.
[133] CP, undated memorandum filed at the end of 1777.

must be limited to those the nation sets. Generals, however galling it may be to their pride and ambition, must be satisfied to work within those limitations. Nevertheless, when a nation does make a military commitment it has a responsibility to support the forces involved to the best of its ability. The British government, and particularly the Treasury, most certainly recognized this. Time and again the Treasury in its role as chief organizer of the army's logistical support expressed to the commander-in-chief its desire to provide the army with everything it needed. Yet the Treasury was also, and more traditionally, the comptroller of the national treasury and thus deeply interested in economy, and it is clear that in its dichotomous role that department not infrequently allowed relatively minor considerations of economy rather than the good of the army to guide its decisions.

Of course the Treasury was under considerable pressure to reduce expenses. In 1775 and 1776, when it seemed to government, to Parliament, and to most Englishmen that the impertinent rebellion of the American colonies could be put down with a minimum of effort, there was apparently little regard for cost: the elaborate arrangements involved in Mure, Son & Atkinson's ill-fated provisions' fleet of 1775 indicate a "nothing is too good for the army" attitude, and Parliament quickly voted a four-shilling land tax to cover expenses. But even by 1776 the attitude had begun to change. A year and a half of war had apparently produced little more than the exchange of Boston for New York; the campaigns had been enormously expensive and at least one and probably more was necessary. The national debt, already large as a result of the Seven Years' War, and regarded then as an indication of the financial irresponsibility of the government and the country, was building up again at an alarming rate. Responding to this pressure the Treasury became much more conscious of cost and passed its concern on to the commander-in-chief. As the war dragged on and opposition to it built up, costs became even more important.[134] Germain, writing to Clinton in 1779 to urge the reduction of the number of transport ships with the army and giving the cost of maintaining them as the reason, noted that any reduction of expenses was desirable since "the indispensably necessary charges of the war require the utmost exertion of the finance ability of this country to provide for them."[135]

But unless the Treasury was prepared to accept the political and military consequences of such actions, it could not translate the desire for economy into a reduction in the quality or quantity of the supplies and services it provided for the army. That it was not prepared for this is indicated in repeated letters to the commander-in-chief and the commissary general in America that, although expressing deep concern over costs, also asserted the determination of the Treasury Board to provide everything the army required.[136] But, nevertheless, it is clear that when decisions had to be made in which an element of doubt existed, North's notorious "parsimony of the public treasury" came into play and the Treasury regularly came down in favor of economy.[137] Such was the case on several occasions in respect to shipping. In the spring of 1776, for instance, when seamen's strikes and the increased demands of various government departments for shipping drove the cost of hiring transports up from eleven shillings to twelve shillings and sixpence a ton a month, the Treasury decided to put off hiring the shipping it required for the 1776 provisions. The decision was in part motivated by a consideration peculiar to this age of limited war: by offering twelve shillings and sixpence a ton the Treasury could get all the shipping it required but it would be drawn away from civilian uses and the government wished as much as possible to avoid "distressing

[134] Mackesy, 22, 170, 313-314, 369-370, 435-436, 460-461.

[135] CP, Germain to Clinton, 3 Mar 79.

[136] T 64/106, 67-71, Robinson to Howe, 14 Jan 77; BAHQP, 426, Robinson to Howe, 4 Mar 76; T 64/119, 4-5, Robinson to Wier, 29 Oct 77; T 64/107, 49, 60-61, Robinson to Clinton, 17 Nov 79, 31 Mar 81.

[137] Mackesy, 22.

the commerce of these kingdoms. . . ." But equally it was motivated by the hope that the price would come down by early summer.[138] The Treasury probably assumed that the army was well stocked with the provisions sent out the previous year—it did not know then of the various disasters of the winter—but it also knew that those provisions were not intended to last beyond June and that Howe wanted six months' reserves on hand for the beginning of the 1776 campaign.

A similar situation occurred in 1778. Although it was reasonably sure in the summer of that year that the army's provisions' situation was satisfactory, the Treasury also knew that the estimates of the army's provisions' stocks had been highly inaccurate. Yet when it came to choose between hiring more ships to carry out provisions then in stock at Cork or waiting for the return of ships from America it chose to follow the latter course.[139] Robinson explained the decision in a letter to Wier: "The great expence and increasing difficulty of arming & manning new ships render the taking up others by the [Treasury] Board very unwarrantable whilst there is any just ground to expect the return of those already in the service. . . ."[140]

The same penny-wise, pound-foolish attitude is seen in another Treasury decision during the provisions' crisis of the fall of 1778. Attempting to determine how many people were being fed by the army so as to govern its dispatch of extra provisions, the Treasury found ambiguities in Wier's returns that precluded an accurate determination. "After the most thorough revisal of your correspondence," Robinson wrote to Wier, "it cannot be determined with certainty whether you are consuming about 46,000 rations per day or about 56,000 & the circumstances favoring either opinion are so nearly equal that it is with great diffidence a judge-

---

138 T 64/106, 29-44, Robinson to Howe, 1 May 76; Dartmouth Papers, D1778/11/1819, "An account of what has been done by the Treasury Board. . . ," 1 Jan 78.

139 *Supra*, 117.   140 T 64/107, 12-14, 31 Oct 78.

ment is formed in favor of the smaller number."[141] As it turned out, the choice of numbers was the correct one, but clearly, also, the Treasury was prepared to risk further shortages rather than the possibility that provisions would go to waste.[142]

But the most serious effect of the Treasury's parsimony was in its attitude towards provisions' reserves for the army. When in 1780 that department attempted to blame the Navy Board's shipping arrangements for one of the perennial shortages of provisions in America, the Board replied with some asperity that: "admitting the troops in either America or the West Indies to be in distress because a convoy has been detained in this country by an enemy fleet, winds, or any other circumstance for 2, 4, or even 6 months is a reflection on those who have the management of provisions for keeping so little as two months in store. . . ."[143] The analysis was astute: too often provisions' crises had occurred because there was no commitment to maintain adequate reserves with the army. In response to the request by Howe that the army be kept always six months ahead in provisions, the Treasury had asserted in 1777 that a six months' reserve was in the "general plan"[144] but it never

[141] T 64/119, 21-25, 31 Oct 78.

[142] The Treasury displayed a somewhat similar attitude with respect to the purchase of provisions in America by the commissary general. Although the Treasury's fondest hope was that the army would be able to supply itself with food from America and thus cut down the expense of shipping it from Britain, its first response on several occasions to reports of considerable purchases by the commissary general was concern that the purchases might duplicate provisions already ordered out from Britain and hence result in waste. When the army was forced by failure of provisions from Britain to exist on what it could purchase in America, among the first concerns of the Treasury was that the purchases were made ". . . in the best manner and with the utmost economy, and saving to the public." (T 64/106, 67-71, 135-138, Robinson to Howe, 14 Jan 77, 14 Mar 77; T 64/119, 40-42, Robinson to Wier, 13 Mar 81.)

[143] T 64/200, 102-105, Navy Board to Treasury, 4 Aug 80.

[144] T 64/119, 2-3, "General state of provisions . . . ," Robinson to Wier, 26 Sept 77.

seemed committed to the plan and in fact admitted to the commissioners of the navy in September 1780 that, "This board do not contract for greater quantities of provisions than may be ample supply for the troops on the respective service, and if possible to keep such supply a few months ahead."[145]

What happened to the general plan of 1777 is not clear. If the Treasury Board took it up and rejected it there is no record of the decision in the Board's minutes. It would seem, rather, that it was a silent victim of an approach to problems that tended to favor accounting logic over war realities. This approach is seen very clearly in the size of the 1779 provisions' contracts. In the summer of 1778 Wier informed the Treasury that he was issuing 46,000 rations a day. The Treasury thought the number should be no more than 42,000 (and, indeed, that was approximately the number of troops in Clinton's army but, as pointed out earlier, the army always had large numbers of auxiliaries to feed), but, nevertheless, it acquiesced in Wier's figure and computed the number of extra rations it would have to get to the army to relieve the crisis of that year on that basis.[146] In the fall of 1778 some 11,000 men were detached from Clinton's command for the campaign in Georgia and the West Indies, thus considerably reducing the number for whom Wier was directly responsible. For accounting purposes, however, both detachments were considered as part of the main army at New York and hence the overall number to be contracted for remained the same. Despite this, however, the Treasury let contracts for 1779 for only 42,000 men.[147] Wier must bear some responsibility here, of course, since he failed to account for the discrepancy between the number of troops on the establishment and the number of

[145] T 27/33, 236-237, Robinson to Commissioners of the Navy, 22 Sept 80.

[146] T 29/47, 12 June 78; T 64/114, 65-66, Wier to Robinson, 7 July 78; T 64/119, 13-15, 17-18, Robinson to Wier, 27 July, 3 Sept 78.

[147] T 64/107, 15-19, Robinson to Clinton, 19 June 79.

rations issued but, nevertheless, the Treasury knew that there was a discrepancy and chose to ignore it. In short, the Treasury was not prepared to allow the army even a small margin of provisions to cover emergency or extraordinary situations.

The same mode of thinking characterized the department's attitude towards bad and short-weight provisions received by the army. The Treasury required that the contractors replace bad provisions and make up short weights, but from the beginning of the war insisted that it could only direct them to do so when it received from the army formal surveys of the provisions involved. This was reasonable but inadequate, since the process of survey, communication with the Treasury, communication with the contractor, and, finally shipment of the replacement provisions could take months, and in the meantime the army did without.[148] Hence after the crises of 1778, which were in part caused by bad and short-weight provisions, Wier requested that "at least one eighth of dry provisions and one sixteenth of wet should be sent in addition to the quantities specified in the contract."[149] This would ensure that the army was not left short when provisions proved to be bad on arrival in America. The Treasury's response to this initiative was myopic in the extreme. Writing to Clinton in January 1779, Robinson noted that "it is admitted that large allowances must be made for waste, & damaged provisions . . . ," but went on to insist that the department could act on the problem only after the event: when the army sent surveys it would direct the contractors to supply replacements.[150] Wier's request for specific extra allowances of provisions brought no direct response at all.

The Treasury's reluctance to supply the army with ade-

[148] For instance, the contractors were ordered to replace the bad flour received by the army in the fall of 1775. It did not arrive until May 22, 1777.

[149] T 64/114, 162-166, Wier to [Robinson], 2 May 79.

[150] T 64/107, 15-19, 19 Jan 79.

144

quate reserves and its implicit refusal of even a buffer supply could have made the provisions' crises of 1779 and 1780
more serious than they were but for two happy accidents.
In the spring of 1779 Clinton was informed that he was to
receive reinforcements in the order of 6,600 men and was
ordered also to step up the recruitment of provincials. To
feed this extra force the Treasury increased its 1779 contracts by 10,000, from 42,000 to 52,000.[151] As it turned out,
however, the promised 6,600 men became little more than
half that number and instead of arriving at the beginning
of June as intended, they did not start to draw rations until
the end of August. Clinton, whose plans were frustrated by
the late arrival of the troops, probably never appreciated
it, but the provisions thus saved—sufficient for 30,000 men
for over a month—probably prevented the shortages of that
year from turning into a disaster. The second fortunate
occurrence was the discovery by the army operating in the
interior of South Carolina that by the devices of the commissary of captures and the commissary of sequestered
estates it could very largely feed itself from the countryside.[152] Four to five thousand salt rations a day were thus
saved and they also helped to save the situation in 1780.

In the background of many of the provisions' problems,
then, lay the Treasury's long-standing desire for economy
in government expenditures. There was nothing necessarily
wrong in that desire for economy; governments need departments whose main concern is just that. But the econo-
mizing must be rational, and is best decided on by dialogue
between the advocates of economy and those whose expenditures are at issue. The problem was that the army had no
advocate in the government whose task it was to oversee
its logistical interests. Insofar as that did belong to anyone,
it belonged to the Secretary of State, but he was far too
busy with other concerns to pursue it with the diligence it
required. It fell by default, then, to the Treasury, the prime
advocate of economy.

[151] T 29/48, 26 Jan 79.   [152] See Ch. II, 86-91.

145

IV

BRITAIN AS A SOURCE OF SUPPLY:

Camp Equipment, Clothing, Arms,
Ammunition, Money

WITHOUT QUESTION, THE MOST SERIOUS AND PERSISTENT supply problem of the army in America was provisions. In most other areas of supply the system, perhaps because demand was less insistent, seemed to work better. Nevertheless, over the long years of the war, virtually every item used by the army came into short supply at one time or another. For the most part such shortages were more annoying than anything else. Occasionally, however, they had serious effects on the capacity of the army to carry out its task.

One of the earliest problems to bring serious repercussions involved camp equipment. Because governments are usually reluctant to allocate more than is absolutely necessary to the military budget in peacetime, armies seldom begin wars with equipment that is adequate in either quality or quantity. Such was the case in 1775. Although regiments were supposed to possess full sets of camp equipment, those which assembled at Boston in early 1775 were badly deficient in tents, and the regiments that came late in the year brought tents with them that proved to be old, worn, and of very poor quality, "made of such very bad stuff," William Shirreff, the deputy quartermaster general reported, "that they would not turn the rein [sic] and the men in bad weather were constantly wet."[1] This was a serious deficiency because there was insufficient housing for

---

[1] WO 1/2, 158.

the army at Boston, and many soldiers had to remain in tents through the winter. The miserable quality of those accommodations probably contributed to the high disease and desertion rates of that period.[2]

But the most serious consequence of the camp equipment situation in 1775 was that it contributed to the delay of the 1776 campaign. Howe's earliest plans called for that campaign to begin in April with a move against New York,[3] but his food situation made that impossible: he left Boston only to be stuck in Halifax. At Halifax he received orders to hold off the campaign until his force was augmented by the return of Clinton and Cornwallis from Charleston and the arrival of the recently hired German troops.[4] When his food situation improved, he moved to Staten Island but no farther. After almost a month, however, even the phlegmatic Howe began to grow impatient, and when Clinton arrived on July 31, he would have begun the campaign almost immediately but for one problem: he was without adequate camp equipment and, like most other eighteenth-century commanders, was reluctant to undertake a campaign without it.[5] Losses by disease on campaign were always heavy, but the British had learned that they could be kept within manageable proportions by the provision of good camp.[6] The poor equipment brought out with the army in 1775 made it necessary to order a complete re-equipping for 1776, but the same shortage of shipping that delayed the buildup of food supplies and the arrival of the Hessians also delayed the camp equipment. Plans called for the dispatch of the equipment in March, but in fact it only arrived with Commodore Hotham's fleet and the Hessians in the middle of August.[7]

---

[2] Bad food was another cause. See *Supra*, 54.

[3] CO 5/92, 621-630, Howe to Dartmouth, 9 Oct 75.

[4] *Ibid.*, 231-239, Germain to Howe, 3 May 76.

[5] HMC, Stopford-Sackville Mss., Howe to Germain, 10 Aug 76; Clinton, *American Rebellion*, 40.

[6] Pargellis, 324-328.

[7] WO 1/890, 7-8, 27 Feb 76.

Although Ambrose Searle asserted that the want of camp equipment again held up the army in 1777,[8] in fact there were no further critical shortages of it after 1776. Some Hessian regiments had to put up with leaky tents on two occasions, and for a time the army at Savannah could not boil its rice rations for want of kettles, but neither was a serious problem.[9] Nevertheless the absence of problems involved more good luck than good management. The procurement of camp equipment demonstrated all the inadequacies of army administration. The equipment, particularly tents, seldom lasted through more than one campaign,[10] and hence a survey had to be made every fall and a requisition for replacements submitted to Germain's office. In several years early in the war, however, although the army required equipment, the quartermaster department failed to submit requisitions and only the willingness of the Secretary to order supplies sent out on the assumption that they would be needed saved the army from a repetition of the 1776 situation. In 1779 Germain finally protested to Clinton about the lack of returns, but by the following March still had no information and was driven to asking returning officers for their estimates of the situation in America.[11] But even when surveys and requisitions were provided by the army, procurement action in Britain could be incredibly slow. Clinton submitted a list of his requirements for 1781 in August 1780. It was received in Germain's office by October 4, but a month elapsed before it was sent on to the Treasury for procurement action and another month before that department finally completed negotiations with suppliers.[12]

[8] Dartmouth Papers, D1778/11/1758, Searle to Dartmouth, 20 May 77.

[9] Mackenzie, 212; Uhlendorf, 213.

[10] Alnwick Castle Mss., Percy Letter Book, II, Percy to [Howe], 9 Feb 77.

[11] BAHQP, 2330, Germain to Clinton, 28 Aug 79; WO 1/683, 395, Germain to Secretary at War, 3 Mar 80.

[12] CP, Clinton to Germain, 15 Aug 80; CP, Germain to Clinton, 4 Oct 80; T 29/49, 4 Nov, 2 Dec 80.

There were problems with clothing and barrack equipment also. At times these were unavoidable, as in early 1777, when a transport carrying clothing for eight regiments fell victim to the *Alfred*, an American naval vessel; the uniforms went to keep American soldiers warm while the clothing of several thousand British soldiers were reduced to tatters before replacements could be obtained.[13] More often, however, the problem was administration. The German regiments that arrived in 1776 fought through two campaigns without clothing replacements and then froze through the early months of the winter of 1777-1778 at Philadelphia because the quartermaster department failed to send the newly arrived stocks on from New York.[14] In 1779 the problem of quality arose when a whole shipment of clothing and bedding was found to be old and substandard. A board of field officers appointed to examine the shipment found 2,800 blankets damaged and many more so rotten that they could be shaken to pieces. Shirt linen in the shipment was "exceedingly coarse," stockings "of so flimsey a texture as to be of little service," and "shoes of the worst kind."[15] Perhaps it was some of these shoes that Cornwallis' force received in the following year and of which he complained that those which were not rotten were impossible to put on.[16] There were other problems with clothing throughout the war years also, but few of them and, indeed, few of those already discussed had any serious repercussions except in terms of uniformity and sartorial elegance. In desperate situations the army could often fall back on large stocks of cloth provided by the Treasury.[17] This was meant for making uniforms for provincial forces, but there were seldom the number of provincial troops

[13] WO 4/273, 253-254.

[14] Mackenzie, 212, 224; Uhlendorf, 131.

[15] CP, Report of a Board of Field Officers, 17 Dec 79.

[16] PRO 30/11/82, 81-82, Cornwallis to Balfour, 22 Nov 80.

[17] T 1/522, 182-185; T 27/31, 508; T 1/538, 164-165; WO 4/274, 9; CP, Germain to Clinton, 12 Dec 78; T 64/110, 89-99.

hoped for. If every other source failed, the troops could also turn to work clothes made from old tents.[18]

Problems with arms and ammunition occurred sporadically throughout the war. The first came up in July 1775, when Gage had to refuse the request of Governor Josiah Martin of North Carolina for arms and ammunition for a Loyalist force assembling there because he did not have sufficient supplies for his own troops at Boston. Any hope for an improvement in Gage's situation was lost when the Ordnance supply transport *Nancy*, carrying among other things 2,000 stand of small arms, was captured in November. Governor Martin eventually got 1,000 muskets originally intended for Lord Dunmore, but the force he assembled to use them quickly met defeat at Moore's Creek Bridge, and most of its arms ended up in the American armory also.[19] It would be difficult to attribute any great significance to either of these shortages, since Gage was immobilized in any case, and Governor Martin's Loyalists were so ill-organized that their defeat was almost inevitable.

A somewhat more significant problem, although impossible to pinpoint in its effect, concerned the quality of musket flints. A good flint could be used to fire sixty rounds without sharpening, but those provided to the army could barely be counted on for six. Colonel Lindsay of the 46th Regiment lamented that the valor of his men was often "rendered vain by the badness of the pebble stone." What was worse, the Americans seemed to be able to obtain good flints and among the rank and file of the British army the saying ran that a "Yankee flint was as good as a glass of grog."[20] Since the British tended to rely in battle on the volley, in which a few misfires would not be significant, and then on the bayonet charge, these complaints are difficult to relate to the major battles of the war. They must rather have referred to misfires during the *petite guerre* of

18 CP, Bruen to John Smith, 1 May 79.
19 CP, Gage to Martin, 29 July 75; Allen, I, 68-69; Ward, II, 662-664.
20 Curtis, 21.

patrols and forage, where individual fire was important. This type of conflict was a considerable part of the war, and bad flints would not only have a tactical effect but would also be, as the quotations above suggest, highly destructive of morale.

Shortages of gunpowder also occurred. Army stocks were somewhat low in 1778 and 1779, in part as a result of a shipment in the former year that had been in the damp hold of a ship so long that wooden packing cases had begun to fall to pieces and tin boxes of cartridges had rusted through, with the result that the powder was caked and useless.[21] A shortage in 1780 was more consequential. Clinton's inactivity in the summer and fall of that year had a number of causes, but primary among them was a steadily worsening supply situation. Although food, as discussed in the last chapter, was the main concern, an acute powder shortage also developed. General Pattison had ordered a supply in March, but in October it had still not arrived, and Clinton, writing to General Dalrymple, whom he had sent to London to impress on the government the need for regular and adequate supplies, complained that he had given up firing salutes and had not even enough powder to permit the troops to practice with their arms.[22]

Unquestionably, the most serious shortage of arms took place in the South in 1780 and 1781. After the surrender of Charleston and the defeat of Gates at Camden, Cornwallis hoped that all of South Carolina could be peacefully occupied. It was a vain hope. The guerrilla activities of Francis Marion, Thomas Sumpter, and Andrew Pickins made necessary the establishment of military posts throughout the interior of the province and the employment of Loyalist militia to garrison them. But not only garrisons were needed. The Rebels employed the now familiar tactics of surprise attack and terror that could be combatted only by strong cavalry detachments constantly on patrol and capa-

21 RAI, Ms. 7, 52, Pattison to Board of Ordnance.
22 CP, 30 Oct 80.

ble of moving quickly to trouble spots.[23] The problem was that there were few small arms available to equip either the garrisons or the mobile force and although horses were usually in good supply there were almost no saddles or other appointments for a cavalry force.

The reason for the shortage of small arms is somewhat obscure. In part it was due to the policy of demanding a loyalty oath from all South Carolinians after the fall of Charleston and then of distributing the large stock of weapons captured from the Rebels among those who took it. This not only did not produce an organized Loyalist force, but many took the oath only under duress and, once armed, went over to the Rebel side.[24] Also, there was an inexplicable failure on the part of both the government and Clinton to prepare adequately for the support of a large Loyalist force. Although it had been decided in 1779 that greater reliance would have to be placed on Loyalist help if America was to be returned to the King's peace, both Clinton and Germain each apparently assumed that the other would make the necessary logistical arrangements. As a result it was not until October 1780 that General Pattison submitted a demand for an adequate reserve of small arms—20,000 stand. These did not begin to arrive in America until April 1781.[25] In the meantime the consequences of the shortage began to appear. On October 1, 1780, Colonel Ambrose Mills arrived in Camden to collect arms for his newly raised militia. There were less than 200 old French muskets in store, and two other militia groups as well as Rawdon's Volunteers of Ireland were vying for them. Although he took away ammunition for 180, Mills had to be satisfied with sixty-one muskets.[26] By January, because of the short-

[23] PRO 30/11/82, 46-47, Cornwallis to Balfour, 16 Nov 80; CP, Balfour to Clinton, 31 Jan 81, 13 Feb 81; Ward, II, 704-711.

[24] Willcox, *Portrait of a General*, 321.

[25] CP, Leonard Morse to Benjamin Thompson, 1 Jan 81; PRO 30/11/5, 61, Balfour to Clinton, 7 Apr 81.

[26] PRO 30/11/3, 164, 172, Lt. Col. Turnbull to Cornwallis, 1 Oct, 2 Oct 80.

age of arms, Cornwallis was unable to raise further militia or provincial forces.[27] The shortage in the South was not attributable to hoarding in the North. When he began to dispatch expeditions to the Chesapeake in 1781, Clinton found it necessary to disarm the New York militia in order to provide the expeditions with a few extra weapons to arm the Loyalists expected to join them.[28]

The necessity of cavalry appointments to the prosecution of the war in the South was apparently not recognized until the summer of 1780. Then, in an attempt to speed up procurement, the army dispatched Major Charles Cochrane to Britain to follow through to completion the order for 1,000 sets of equipment. Cochrane did not arrive in London until mid-October, and although he set to work immediately, not until December 2 were designs and prices agreed on and contracts let by the Treasury.[29] After the contracts were let though, there still remained the actual procurement, collection, and shipping of the equipment, and by the end of May 1781 it had still not arrived in America.[30] By that time it was too late. Not only had Rebel guerrilla activities gone virtually unopposed for too long, but by April, Greene, his army recovered from Guilford Court House, was back in South Carolina. Although Rawdon was able to drive the American regulars from the field at the battle of Hobkirk's Hill in early May, his position in the interior of South Carolina had become hopeless. The guerrilla action virtually isolated the interior posts from each other and from Charleston; cut off from food, forage, and supplies, the army faced a future of starvation and surrender. Two weeks after his victory, Rawdon ordered the evacuation of Ninety-six and Fort Granby and himself evacuated Camden. The

[27] PRO 30/11/109, 9-10, Balfour to Clinton, 31 Jan 81; PRO 30/11/5, 61, Balfour to Clinton, 7 Apr 81.

[28] CP, Clinton to Germain, 13 May 81.

[29] PRO 30/11/6, 119, Col. Innis to Major Prevost, 26 May 81; T 27/49, 2 Dec 80.

[30] *Ibid.*

153

battle for the Carolinas was lost.[31] Only a major effort could reestablish British control there, and that was not forthcoming.

It would not be accurate, of course, to say that the war in the South was lost because of a shortage of muskets and cavalry equipment. The problems in that area began when Clinton demanded the oath of loyalty from everyone. In thus forcing everyone to choose, he led many who would otherwise have remained neutral to choose the Rebel side.[32] The actions of quartermasters and commissaries in expropriating supplies and equipment necessary for the army also tended to alienate many otherwise loyal Southerners.[33] Nevertheless, nowhere in the colonies were there more Loyalists; nowhere was there a better chance of reestablishing a loyal province. As long as outside forces could be held at bay, the decision was up to the South Carolinians themselves. Cornwallis seriously increased the possibility of outside interference by haring off to North Carolina and Virginia, but, as Rawdon demonstrated at Hobkirk's Hill, the regular force he left behind was at least adequate to keep the American regular army at bay. The decisive struggle, then, was between Rebel and Loyalist irregulars and militia, and here the Rebels won. They came to control the countryside and made the supply of a British army in the interior impossible—hence Rawdon's retreat after the victory at Hobkirk's Hill. The victory of the Rebel irregulars was due in large measure to better organization and audacious leadership, but in part it was due to the inability of the British to equip a Loyalist force capable of containing the Rebel guerrillas. Although repeated urgent requests were made for any sort of cavalry equipment to fill in the

31 PRO 30/11/5, 262, Rawdon to Cornwallis, 26 Apr 81; Mellish Papers, Major Hayes to Mellish, 30 Apr 81; PRO 30/11/109, 33-34, Balfour to Cornwallis, 6 May 81; Ward, II, 810.

32 Willcox, *Portrait of a General*, 321.

33 Wickwire, *Cornwallis*, 138-143, 230-240.

void until Major Cochrane's supply arrived, almost nothing could be done. Three hundred sets of appointments did arrive in November 1780, but the shipment was in bad order and had been plundered. Most of what was good had to go to replace the worn-out equipment of Tarleton's Legion, but the shortage was so acute that even the Legion's old equipment was salvaged and carefully parcelled out to militia groups in areas where Rebel pressure was heaviest. Forty sets of this equipment gave the garrison at Ninety-six its first mounted force.[34]

It may be asked, of course, why craftsmen in America were not turned to the production of the needed equipment. The answer is not difficult to find. Equipment was commissioned locally, but cavalry appointments, particularly saddles, were not within the competence of ordinary harness makers, and Colonel Alexander Innis found the equipment produced in America to be "at best a wretched expedient. . . ."[35] But equally important as a reason for not procuring this equipment in North America was the cost and a lack of cash,[36] and this leads to the consideration of a very different kind of supply problem.

As pointed out earlier, it was necessary throughout the war to supply the army with large quantities of specie.[37] This was the era before paper money achieved the respectability it now has, and, as the Americans found out with their continental currency, if the public came to suspect that paper money could not be readily exchanged for hard cash, confidence in the paper, and hence its value, dropped. The British never attempted to use paper money in the way that the Americans did—that is, for the day-to-day use of the public—but nevertheless it did seek to obtain the specie it needed by the sale in America of bills drawn on

[34] PRO 30/11/82, 6, 26, Cornwallis to Balfour, 4 Nov 80, Cornwallis to Major Dunlop, 11 Nov 80.

[35] PRO 30/11/6, 87, Col. Innis to Benjamin Thompson, 14 May 81.
[36] *Ibid.*   [37] *Supra,* 17-18.

London. In the prewar period, because there was usually ample specie available in the colonies, most of the needs of the army could be met by the sale of bills. Indeed, the bills could usually be sold at a premium.[38] During the war, though, specie tended to go quickly out of circulation all over America. It went into hoards and tended to move from British- to Rebel-held areas to pay for food, fuel, and forage obtained clandestinely or on foraging expeditions. But most of all, from both Rebel and British areas, it went to pay for goods obtained abroad that could no longer be paid for with American goods and services.[39] When cash became short, paper money sold at a discount. The American government, without a reliable source of hard cash, had to accept a progressive depreciation of its money that it both combatted and made worse by issuing more paper.[40] The British could maintain the value of their bills by regular infusions of cash from Britain into the enclaves they held. The Treasury was aware of the need to send specie and in the course of the war supplied the army, through Harley and Drummond, with vast sums. Still, on a number of occasions supplies in America fell very low, bringing huge discounts on army bills, and on two occasions the shortage continued for so long that bills could not be sold at all.

The list of items for which the army needed cash was a long one, and as the war progressed it grew longer. It required cash to pay the enlisted men and, from the middle of 1775 on, to pay officers also. In the pre-war situation the pay of officers serving in America was normally lodged with the regimental agents in London, an arrangement that suited the officers well as the bills that they drew on the agents could be exchanged at a premium. Very shortly after the outbreak of the war, the premium became a discount

---

[38] *Ibid.*
[39] T 64/108, 66-68, Howe to Robinson, 6 Aug 76.
[40] Ward, II, 595, 614, 626.

of fifteen percent or more and, in response to a plea from Gage, the officers were thereafter paid in cash.[41] Cash was also required for the bat, baggage, and forage allowance paid to officers, for the wages of civilians in the employ of the various departments, for the purchase and hire of wagons, horses, and ships, for the purchase of fresh food, forage, fuel, and construction materials, and for numerous lesser items, such as the secret service, aid to Loyalists, and the furnishing of an apartment for the accommodation of Prince William Henry on the occasion of his visit in 1781.[42] In 1777 rum procurement was transferred to the commissary general in America in the belief that he better than the government in London could ascertain the going price in the West Indies,[43] and thereafter the cost of rum was a major item in the American accounts. As the war progressed, inflation and shortage increased the price of just about everything the army needed. For instance, in 1778 firewood could be purchased at New York City for thirty-five shillings a cord, but by 1780 the demands of the army had resulted in the decimation of nearby forests; little wood was available to the British within fifty miles of the city, and the price accordingly went up to seventy-five shillings a cord and higher.[44]

The shortages of cash occurred for a variety of reasons. In 1775 neither Gage nor the Treasury were really aware of how expensive war could be. Gage, long accustomed to the stringent economy of peacetime, submitted cautious demands for £20,000 and £30,000 only when the need was urgent.[45] As a result the discount on bills rose to seventeen

---

[41] WO 1/2, 137, Gage to Barrington, 26 July 75; T 64/108, 1-2, 17-18, Howe to Robinson, 26 Nov, 31 Dec 75.

[42] AO 1/148/349, Accounts of Col. William Crosbie.

[43] Baker, 210.

[44] N-YHS, "Board of General Officers," 100-101.

[45] T 64/106, 3,4,5, Robinson to Gage, 22 June, 7 July, 8 July 75; *ibid.*, 14-16, Robinson to Howe, 1 Oct 75.

and a half percent, and he felt obliged to cut back on purchases of supplies. It was not until the end of September 1775 that he worked up enough nerve to ask for £100,000 all at once. The Treasury, equally shocked by the scale of expenditures, was as slow to respond as Gage was to demand. Hence, when in late September they learned that Gage had both requested a supply of £40,000 in specie and issued bills for a similar amount, they immediately assumed that the army was about to obtain a double supply of cash. Thus they informed Howe, who by that time had taken over as commander-in-chief, that the cash would not be sent out but, rather, kept in London to meet the bills when they were presented.[46] But what the Treasury did not know, and apparently could not guess, was that the bills issued by Gage had not produced cash. Specie had become so short that the remitters' agent in Boston could no longer obtain it in sizeable quantities.[47] Hence, when he received the commander-in-chief's warrants for large round sums, the agent could respond only by filling the military chest with bills of smaller denominations drawn on his principals in London, Harley and Drummond. These bills were accepted by the Boston merchant community, but only at large discounts.

It was probably this shortage of cash, along with Gage's ingrained inclination to economize, that led to considerable suffering in the army during 1775 for want of fresh food. It was not that fresh food was unavailable. High prices in Boston encouraged defiance of the Rebel blockade, and a trickle came into the city.[48] Rather, the army did not have the money to purchase it. As a result there was not even fresh meat available to make broth for the wounded of Bunker Hill. Like everyone else the wounded had to make

[46] BAHQP, 59, Robinson to Howe, 1 Oct 75.

[47] T 64/101, 73, Gage to Colin Drummond, 23 May 75; T 1/518, Gage to Robinson, 25 May 75.

[48] WO 36/1, Extracts of orders given to the British Army in America, 3, 4 Sept; 16, 20, 24, 25 Oct 75.

do with salt meat, which even the healthy often could not stomach.[49]

It can be asked, of course, why Gage and his successors, who also ran short of money at times, did not resort to issuing paper money and enforce its acceptance in all transactions, at least as a temporary measure. The answer in part is that this was outside the power of the commander-in-chief, but, more important, it was probably realized that such a resort could only lead to a diminution of supplies. Throughout the war civilians living outside the British enclaves were encouraged by the possibility of obtaining hard money or manufactured goods in exchange, to defy Rebel blockades and bring produce into the enclaves. This was an essential source of supply for the residents of Boston, New York, and Philadelphia. If forced to accept paper money of doubtful negotiability outside the British lines, these traders would have ceased operations. If this was Gage's line of thought, it was entirely valid. Three years later, in the summer of 1778, when the army prepared to move from Philadelphia to New York, Clinton estimated that he could not expect to obtain more than a few days' provisions during the march since it "lay through a devoured country inimical almost to a man."[50] The New Jersey countryside had indeed proved hostile during the winter of 1776-1777 and armed British foraging parties had ranged through it ever since, collecting, as they believed, every bit of food and forage and leaving behind only receipts redeemable at the commissary general office at headquarters. Yet when the army marched, there was an ample supply of cash on hand, and Wier determined to use it to pay for provisions. As a result the "inimical" people of New Jersey, despite the presence of Washington's army, flocked to the British with cattle, forage, and fresh provisions of all kinds:

[49] DeFonblanque, 140, 182; J. R. Alden, *General Gage in America* (Baton Rouge, 1948), 276.

[50] Add. Mss. 34,416, 153-159, "Notes of S[ir] H[enry] Clinton Relative to the Campaign of 1778."

the "devoured country," revived by the sight of gold, produced ten days' food for the army.[51]

The second shortage of cash occurred in 1778-1779. It began in the autumn of 1778 after the failure of supplies from England during the summer of that year necessitated large local purchases of food. These purchases, along with the expenses of moving the army from Philadelphia and re-establishing it at New York, quickly drained off £400,000 in specie requested that spring. By the end of October Clinton reported to the Treasury that the contractors' agents could no longer raise adequate supplies of cash for the army through the sale of bills.[52] Although Clinton repeated this warning to the government a number of times during the succeeding month, further shipments of specie did not arrive until April 4 the following year.[53] The extraordinary expenditures of the army during the last half of 1778 in part accounted for the shortage, but equally important was a failure in the accounting system. In early January 1779, just about the time that Clinton composed a letter to William Eden telling him of his distress for want of cash,[54] the Treasury was preparing a letter expressing surprise that Clinton should think the army was short. As was the case with food, it was convinced that he was well supplied. By its calculations, the army had drawn since the beginning of March 1775, £3,502,434.3.4, of which £853,485.10.1 was not yet accounted for and thus, presumably, was the balance remaining in the military chest.[55] Since the army at this time calculated that it in fact owed the cash contractors over £70,000, the difference between Treasury and army accounting amounted to over £900,000.

The huge discrepancy between the Treasury and army accountings was further demonstration of the problems that

51 T 64/114, 65-66, Wier to Robinson, 1 July 78.
52 T 64/109, 122, Clinton to Robinson, 22 Oct 78.
53 Uhlendorf, 260.
54 CP, Clinton to [Eden], 10 Jan 79.
55 T 64/107, 15-19, Robinson to Clinton, 19 Jan 79.

a lack of system and organization, and indeed simple communication, could occasion. For the discrepancy was an accounting problem, not the result of missing or misappropriated cash. It originated in the practice of issuing temporary warrants that had grown up during the war. These warrants, issued by the commander-in-chief on the deputy paymaster general in America, enabled the various department heads to draw round sums in cash to meet their departmental expenditures and were converted into final warrants credited to the army's accounts only when a detailed accounting of the expenditure of money was later presented to and approved by the commander-in-chief. Thus there was always a considerable amount of money out in temporary warrants, and it grew as the war progressed since Daniel Wier drew money on temporary warrants but considered himself accountable only to the Treasury. The problem was that while the deputy paymaster general reported to the paymaster general in London both the temporary and final warrants presented to him, he reported only the final warrants to the Treasury. Hence the Treasury's concept of the financial state of the army always differed from the reality by at least the amount of the outstanding temporary warrants.[56] Still the Treasury does not stand blameless. Not only had the army long since informed it that temporary warrants were in use, but when it received Clinton's plea for cash in December 1778, it called on the pay office and the cash contractors for their accounts of the army's financial position and was presented by the former with a list of outstanding temporary warrants. The Treasury received the list and even sent a copy of it along with its own accounting on the basis of final warrants to Clinton, but never bothered to combine the two.[57]

The accounting failure in 1779 would have been less objectionable had there not been a similar incident three

[56] BAHQP, 1,995, Clinton to Robinson, 11 May 79; *ibid.*, 1,996, Thomas Barrow to John Smith, 11 May 79.

[57] *Ibid.*; T 64/107, 15-19, enclosures Robinson to Clinton, 19 Jan 79.

years earlier. At that time—1776—the Treasury came to the conclusion, despite requests of the commander-in-chief for additional supplies of specie, that there was £790,776.6.0 in the military chest and accordingly held back shipments of cash to the army.[58] The discrepancy in this case was again the result of a massive failure in communications and administrative organization. It began with the failure of both the Treasury and the assistant deputy paymaster general in Boston, Thomas Apthorpe, to adapt to the wartime situation. Apthorpe had been accustomed in peacetime to submit his accounts but once a year and then only when all temporary warrants were cleared away. He continued in this practice until instructed by the pay office in London in 1776 to submit quarterly accounts along with lists of outstanding temporary warrants.[59] In the meantime, the Treasury, with colossal lack of common sense, added together the various sums paid into the military chest and, finding no account of expenditures, assumed that most of it was still there.[60]

The Treasury's action was also due to a growing suspicion that the financial affairs of the army were carried on with less than complete honesty. This suspicion was heightened by the fact that Thomas Apthorpe, besides being the senior paymaster actually with the army at that time, was also the Boston agent for the cash contractors.[61] As mentioned earlier, there was an extreme shortage of cash in Boston throughout most of 1775, and hence when the commander-in-chief issued warrants for money to meet the army's expenses, all that Apthorpe could do was provide

[58] T 64/106, 46-51, 64-66, Robinson to Howe, 24 June, 25 Nov 76.

[59] T 64/108, 69-71, Letter from Thomas Apthorpe, enclosed in Howe to Robinson, 6 Aug 76.

[60] T 64/106, 46-51, Robinson to Howe, 24 June 76.

[61] Apthorpe held the grade of assistant deputy paymaster; his immediate superior was the deputy paymaster at New York. The position of agent for Harley and Drummond he held jointly with Daniel Chamier, the commissary general.

bills drawn on Harley and Drummond. On the books, though, it appeared that the warrants were immediately honored in the normal manner; the Treasury, when it received records of these transactions, began to wonder why it was being asked to send out specie when it could be obtained so easily in Boston and why warrants were subject to huge discounts.[62] The suspicions thus aroused in the Treasury were heightened by its failure to understand the language of exchange in America. When a bill was drawn on London, its cash value was expressed not in terms of sterling or of Boston pounds but in terms of the percentage difference between the two. Normally a pound sterling was worth one and a third pounds Boston currency and a bill cashed at par was referred to as being "drawn at $33\frac{1}{3}\%$"; that is, a bill for £100 sterling drawn at $33\frac{1}{3}\%$ brought £133.6.8 Boston currency. A bill for the same amount "drawn at 20%" had been discounted by $13\frac{1}{3}\%$ and was worth only £120 Boston currency.[63] The Treasury apparently believed that the term "drawn at . . ." meant that the bill was discounted at the rate mentioned and it became particularly incensed when it learned at one point that bills were issued at $33\frac{1}{3}\%$ when there were ample reserves of cash in the military chest.[64] What in fact had happened was that, as a result of the arrival in Boston of large sums of cash in late 1775, bills on London could be sold in January 1776 at par or very little below. In order to conserve the cash in the military chest, Apthorpe had thus turned again to paying the army's expenses in bills and even sold some for cash in order to build up the reserves.[65]

The problem, then, was primarily one of communication and organization, and this was the responsibility of the Treasury. Yet Apthorpe and Chamier do not stand blame-

[62] T 64/106, 4-8, 46-51, Robinson to Howe, 9 Sept 75, 24 Jun 76.

[63] T 64/108, 69-71, Apthorpe to Treasury, 6 Aug 76.

[64] T 64/106, 29-44, Robinson to Howe, 1 May 76.

[65] T 64/108, 69-71, Apthorpe to Treasury, 6 Aug 76.

less. Funds for the army were provided under two account headings, "subsistence" and "extraordinary." Subsistence, as the term suggests, involved the normal pay, food, and quarters expenses of the army, and funds for this expense were voted in advance by Parliament on the basis of the army establishment. All other army expenses came under the extraordinary account. In wartime extraordinary expenses far exceeded those for subsistence, but unlike subsistence expenses, they were approved by Parliament only after the fact. It was very necessary then that extraordinary and subsistence expenditure be kept separate, but Apthorpe and Chamier, despite repeated orders from London, persistently confused the two.[66] For this reason, and because of their failure to send in regular accountings, the two were replaced. Thomas Barrow, a deputy paymaster general, superseded Apthorpe in 1776, and in the following year Harley and Drummond sent out two new men to act as their agents.[67]

As was the case with so many other supply failures, shortages of cash were not directly linked with operational problems. Even when specie supplies from Britain failed, cash could usually be obtained for bills in America, although at a discount that became larger as the shortage became more acute. Only in prolonged periods of shortage was it impossible to get cash at all, and even then most of the services of the army could be carried on with bills.

Yet repeated shortages were demoralizing for commanders, and this was particularly so with Clinton. Since they usually coincided with food shortages—cash reserves being exhausted by local purchases—cash shortages tended to support his conviction that he was being ignored and set up as the scapegoat for all the army's failures. In 1778, 1779, and 1780 his complaints to friends and officials at home linked shortages of cash with other logistical prob-

[66] T 64/106, 29-44, Robinson to Howe, 1 May 76.
[67] *Ibid.*; T 64/106, 64, Robinson to [Howe], 25 Nov 76.

lems and lack of reinforcements and naval support as reasons for his inactivity.[68]

Although the army could get by with heavily discounted bills, prolonged shortages of cash could also adversely affect the morale of soldiers and civilians alike. When all the deductions for uniforms, food, quarters, medical care, and pension were made, there was very little left of a soldier's pay. What was due he expected in cash and was likely to be very unhappy if it was not forthcoming. When delays in his pay were accompanied, as they usually were, with shortages of food and consequently diminished and poor quality rations, the desertion rate usually rose. This was particularly the case with German troops. They had little interest in the war and deserted in large numbers when times were hard.[69] Not surprisingly, then, when cash was short, the British were concerned to keep the fact from their German allies as long as possible.[70] Civilians who worked for the army suffered with the soldiers when cash was short, but probably the most serious repercussions were among the civilian population at large. It is not clear when the practice of paying for requisitioned goods with receipts redeemable at headquarters began or why. But whatever the reason for starting the practice, it was probably continued

[68] T 64/109, 122, Clinton to Robinson, 22 Oct 78; CP, Clinton to Eden, 10 Jan 79; Add. Mss., 34,416, 153-159, "Notes of S[ir] H[enry] Clinton Relative to the Campaign of 1778"; CP, Clinton to Eden, 2 July 79; Newcastle Papers, Clinton to Newcastle, 3 July 79; Clinton, *American Rebellion*, 126-127; CP, Clinton to Germain, 20 Aug 79; Newcastle Papers, NeC 2,623, Clinton to [Eden] 14 Aug 80; CP, Clinton to Germain, 30 Oct 80.

[69] E. J. Lowell, in his study *The Hessians* (2d ed., Port Washington, N.Y., 1965), estimated that of 29,867 Germans who served with the British some 5,000 deserted. One set of comparative figures is given by Ward (II, 585). Approximately 13,500 British regulars and 6,700 Germans made the march from Philadelphia to New York in 1778 and of these 136 British and 440 Germans deserted.

[70] CP, Clinton to [Eden], 10 Jan 79; T 1/549, 286-288, Prevost to Robinson, 7 Nov 79.

at least in part because quartermasters and commissaries found it immensely advantageous.[71] It may be conjectured that it began as a necessary measure in a period of cash shortage and continued in part for the same reason. Certainly the volume of goods the army was able to purchase during the march from Philadelphia to New York should have convinced it of the value of cash transactions. Perhaps it did, but through the remainder of 1778 and most of 1779 the army's cash reserves were almost non-existent, and another shortage occurred in 1780. The effect of deferred payments was well illustrated during Cornwallis' campaign in South Carolina in 1780. Cornwallis depended on Clinton for supplies of cash, but Clinton was short himself that summer.[72] Hence, whether or not he approved of the policy, Cornwallis had little choice but to use receipts redeemable in Charleston to pay for the food, forage, and horses that the army operating in the interior needed and that could be obtained only from the country people. Not only did the use of receipts open the way to numerous frauds, but the country people often could not get to Charleston to redeem the receipts they received and were forced to sell them to speculators at huge losses. As a result the very people on whom the army depended not only for supplies but also for aid and information often became, as a result of British requisitioning, if not pro-American, at least anti-British.[73]

[71] See *infra*, 180.

[72] PRO 30/11/4, 27-34, Balfour to Cornwallis, 5 Nov 80; Wickwire, *Cornwallis*, 140.

[73] Wickwire, *Cornwallis*, 235-236.

V

"How Men on Fixed and Moderate Salaries Could Better Their Fortunes."

In march 1782 a board of general officers convened at New York to consider two objections presented by the commissary of accounts, Major Duncan Drummond, to the accounts of Lt. Col. William Crosbie, the barrackmaster general. Drummond's objections pertained to the firewood supplied to the army by the barrack department. His commission directed him, among other things, to ensure that all the goods acquired by the army in America were purchased in the most economical manner, and he suggested that firewood, by far the largest item in the barrackmaster's accounts, had been excessively expensive. Crosbie claimed that the wood his department supplied cost less than the wood available on the open market at New York, but Drummond countered that this was true only if the first cost of the wood was considered; if the expense of maintaining wood yards and hiring ships and wagons for the collection and delivery of the wood were included, then the cost was considerably more than the open market price. He wished to know if Crosbie had ever attempted to reduce costs by letting contracts, subject to competitive bidding, to civilian firms. Drummond's second objection concerned the distribution of the wood. It had come to his attention, he noted, that the barrackmaster purchased wood by a measure called the "country cord" which was nine inches higher than the standard $4' \times 4' \times 8'$ cord, but dispensed it to the army in standard cords; Drummond wished to know how the extra nine inches, just over nine percent of all the wood purchased, was accounted for. The points raised by Drummond were not trivial. The army used as much as 70,000 cords of wood a year, and a difference of only a shilling a cord in the price amounted to £3,500. The difference between the country and standard cords amounted to 6,562 cords in 70,000, which had a value of £26,248 when the price of wood was four pounds a cord.

Crosbie's replies to these observations were that the hire of the wagons and ships could not be included in the cost of the wood since those vehicles were necessary for other services in the department as well as those connected with the collection and delivery of firewood and would have been on hire in any case. As for the wood itself, Crosbie maintained that the country cord was always loosely and irregularly stacked and when properly measured seldom exceeded four feet four inches in height. The remaining four inches' difference between the purchased and issued cords, he insisted, was taken up by losses of various sorts, such as through pilfering and by over-generous measurements in deliveries of lots smaller than a cord. Although Drummond protested, for obvious reasons, that both of these replies were inadequate, the board of general officers disagreed. Colonel Crosbie, it concluded, "has very fully and satisfactorily answered every objection stated by the Commissary of Accounts. . . ."[1]

The purpose of Drummond's objections to the barrack-master general's accounts was to bring about some reduction in the immense expenditures of the army in America, and he sought not so much to condemn Crosbie as to bring about changes in the methods by which the army procured the goods and services it required. The decision of the board of general officers frustrated that attempt for the time being by vindicating Crosbie and his methods. The board was to do the same thing again shortly afterwards when Drummond presented somewhat similar objections

[1] The minutes of this board of general officers are in T 64/112, 60-76. For details of the army's wood requirements see *supra*, 34.

to the accounts of the quartermaster general,[2] and another board the previous autumn had rejected a plan presented by Drummond for saving money by purchasing rather than hiring the ships and wagons required by the army.[3]

As will be shown, the various objections put forward by Drummond were reasonable and his suggestions sound. Why, then, were they rejected by these boards of senior officers? The reasons are not entirely clear, but it would seem that they were rejected at least in part because accepting them would have opened a Pandora's box for the army. For what Drummond was probing into was not just uneconomical procurement practices but large-scale corruption and profiteering in the army service departments. One can doubt the charges later made by the Loyalist Judge Thomas Jones in his *History of the Revolutionary War*[4] that the war was deliberately prolonged—and hence lost— in order that army favorites in high positions in the service departments might be enriched. But it is clear that many of the people in those positions, officers and civilians, came to see the war as little more than a chance to build fortunes for themselves at the expense of the public treasury, and that their actions contributed materially to the loss of the colonies.

In attempting to assess and understand charges of corruption, the investigator must, of course, bear several reservations in mind. First, it would be a strange war that did not present opportunities for illegal gain, and a strange

[2] T 64/112, 79-91.

[3] The records of this board are found in manuscript form in T 64/111. The New-York Historical Society printed another copy of the records in its 1916 *Collections* under the title "Minute Book of a Board of General Officers of the British Army in New York, 1781." The PRO manuscript is more complete in some details than the printed copy, but it is not well organized.

[4] Thomas Jones, *History of New York During the Revolutionary War* (ed. E. F. Delancey, New-York Historical Society, 1879), 365-366.

nation that did not produce people willing to take advantage of them. Even in peacetime institutions are never safe from embezzlement and the improper use of their facilities; in wartime, when screening of personnel is relaxed and regular checks and audits difficult if not impossible, the incidence of violations of trust is bound to rise. Hence it should come as no particular surprise to find that a commissary at Rhode Island used the facilities of the army pay office to transmit money to purchase a private stock of wine;[5] or that a few barrels in the commissary stores supposed to contain flour proved, when opened, to contain only floor sweepings;[6] or that general officers and their wives could obtain ample wood and drew unlimited quantities of "spermacitae" candles while the rest of the army, shivering from the cold, huddled around their tallow dips;[7] or even that a quartermaster general should try to claim as his own an elaborate barge built in the army shipyard by army carpenters with army material. In the scale of war such things are minor peculations.[8]

Secondly, one must beware of imposing irrelevant standards and confusing legitimate perquisites of office with criminal activity. In the 1770's not only was the British civil service still a long way from the almost painful honesty that characterized it in the late nineteenth century, but the government, in order to compensate for low salaries, often allowed office holders to profit from the transactions for which they were responsible. Hence the commissary general long had the right to what was called the "fifth quarter" of livestock purchased by the department and slaughtered for the troops. This consisted of the head, hide, and tallow,

[5] N-YHS, Wier Letter Book, Wier to Jonathan Clarke, 21 Nov 79.

[6] BAHQP, 5,164, 13 July 82.

[7] M. L. Brown (ed.), *Baroness von Riedesel and the American Revolution* (Chapel Hill, 1965), 100; WO 60/33, box 2, Paumier to Watson, concerning candles and wood, n.d.: *ibid.*, "Generals and officers who received Spermacitar [sic] candles. . . ," n.d.

[8] WO 60/27, Memorial of Captain Lewis, 27 Aug 82.

and usually was one fifth of the value of the carcass.[9] Very probably he also received a percentage on the soft bread baked for the army. The army bakeries produced two kinds of bread: a very hard, very dry "biscuit" for use as field rations and a soft yeast bread. Both were issued in one-pound loaves but neither required exactly one pound of flour. The "biscuit" required more than a pound, and Wier regularly included in his returns a "deficiency in baking flour into hard bread."[10] Soft bread, on the other hand, required less than a pound of flour, the bakers giving nine pounds of bread for seven of flour. Nowhere, however, does Wier account for this overage.[11] It would seem also that the commissaries were permitted to dispose of, for their own advantage, the barrels, casks, and bags in which the various provisions were delivered; certainly there is no record of them ever being returned or otherwise brought to account. This would also apply, probably, to the brine in which meat was preserved. Salt was in short supply in colonial America, and it is unlikely that the brine was wasted. Bat, baggage, and forage money was a perquisite of all officers. It was an allowance of five shillings a day, paid for the period an officer was on campaign, supposedly to compensate him for the cost of maintaining a horse and transporting or storing his baggage. During the American war, though, officers could expect to receive this allowance for half the year at least no matter what type of service they were on, and staff officers received it year round.[12]

It is also the case that an abuse can grow so gradually and over such a period of time that the recipients of its benefits come to accept it as a right. Such was the case with rum. At the beginning of the war rum was issued only on

[9] PRO 30/11/2, Patrick Ferguson to Cornwallis, 24 July 80.

[10] See for example T 64/114, 180, Return of Stores in New York, 30 Apr to 31 May 79.

[11] WO 36/1, Army Orders, 4 Dec 75.

[12] Alnwick Castle Mss., John McKinnon to Percy, 22 Jan 78; Mackenzie Papers, "Comparative View of the Expenses in the Secretary's Office" [1782].

special occasions, as a reward, to stiffen men's courage before battle or to purify doubtful water when the army was
in the field; by 1777 the soldiers had come to regard a daily
ration as their right. Such also was the case with food rations for the headquarters staff. Although usually rations
were provided only for enlisted men, the cost and difficulty
of obtaining food in America made it necessary to allow
everyone this privilege; senior officers were allowed to draw
extra rations for their "families" and servants. For each
ration drawn, the pay of the individual officer involved was
supposed to be subject to the same regular stoppage of four
pence half penny that was applied to the pay of an enlisted
man. As it turned out, stoppages were never levied on staff
and general officers. Throughout the war they continued
to draw rations—probably as often for resale on the civilian
market as for their own use—as an extra emolument.[13] By
1781 Col. Tredwell Watson, a member of Clinton's staff,
was so convinced that he had a right to whatever rations
he felt necessary that when a commissary refused him a few
extra rations to provide for a guest in his household, he
complained bitterly and indignantly to Clinton.[14] When in
1782 Sir Guy Carleton, the new commander-in-chief, and
Brook Watson, the new commissary general, descended on
the army like avenging angels and ended this practice,
among others, the commissary general reported that the
change was received with reluctance and bad temper by the
officers, who "from past indulgences verily believed emoluments arising from public trust to be legally their private
due. . . ."[15]

But the irregularities to which the present chapter is
directed do not fall within any of the above categories.
There is no question that the individuals and departments
involved knew of the illegality or at least the impropriety

[13] T 29/52, 2 Oct 82; Mackenzie, 225.
[14] CP, Col. Watson to Clinton, 14 July 81.
[15] Shelburne Papers, vol. 69, 81-88, Watson to Richard Burke, 17
Aug 82.

of their practices for their actions were condemned by their peers and in some cases even by their own words. The latter was the case with Col. Crosbie, barrackmaster general. In his response to Drummond's query about the disposition of the wood that represented the difference between the four-foot nine-inch "country cords" purchased by his department and the four-foot cords issued, Col. Crosbie replied that it was eaten up by poor stacking, unavoidable overages on part-cord issues, and pilfering. His explanation would perhaps have stood had not Brook Watson, exercising a part of his commissary general's commission that Daniel Wier had allowed to remain dormant, taken over the army's firewood business. In his first report to the Treasury, Watson noted that because of the difference in the size of the purchased and issued cords he was able to save almost one-sixth on expenditures for firewood. From this and from an unexplained reduction in issues, Watson estimated an annual saving to the crown of £55,000.[16] Whether Crosbie profited personally is not clear, but certainly someone did, and it is difficult to believe that the barrackmaster himself did not know of it. And if Judge Jones is to be believed, that was not the only way those in the barrack department could profit from firewood. According to him, fortunes were made in the department through the exploitation of wood lots on abandoned Rebel estates. This wood was free except for cutting expenses, but instead of being brought to the credit of the government, it was appropriated by the barrackmasters and sold to the army at the current civilian price.[17]

Another practice, in which it would appear Major Gen. James Robertson was involved while he was barrackmaster general at Boston, concerned exchange. In the fall and winter of 1775 an acute shortage of cash existed, so much so that army bills drawn on London could only be sold at a discount of at least fifteen percent, and people leaving the city were forbidden on pain of confiscation of the excess to

[16] *Ibid.*   [17] Jones, 337-339.

take more than five pounds in specie with them.[18] In this situation anyone who had cash could turn a nice profit by purchasing the bills that the paymaster was forced to issue to pay the army's expenses. The bills could then be sent to England for exchange into cash, which was then returned to Boston to purchase more bills if the situation still warranted. Obviously, however, few people had cash or the exchange rate would not have been what it was, but among those who did were the heads of army departments through whom what cash the government had sent out was spent.

The Treasury became aware very quickly that this opportunity for profit was being taken and, without proof of where the money involved came from, suspected the customs office.[19] However, it is unlikely that much customs money was involved since the port of Boston had been closed for some time and revenue would at best be small. A more likely candidate was the barrackmaster general's office through which most of the army's expenditures were made at that time. Robertson's involvement was indeed asserted by Captain Francis Hutcheson, late of General Haldimand's staff and one of the "in group" at headquarters. "General Robertson is quite the young man," he wrote to Haldimand, "gives balls and routs, which he may do, exchange will pay for all. He has six thousand pounds sterling cash arrived in the Centurion for bills he sent home last August at 15 pct, and has now sent it back again in bills at 10 pct—the money for which he will have out again by the last of April, which will clear him fifteen hundred pounds sterling. These bills are originally got from the Paymaster General, for warrants he had on him for his Barrack Department."[20] Hutcheson went on to state that although Robertson earlier looked forward to com-

[18] T 64/108, 17-18, Howe to Robinson, 31 Dec 75; BAHQP, 72, Proclamation by Howe, 28 Oct 75.

[19] T 64/106, 29-44, Robinson to Howe, 1 May 76.

[20] Add. Mss. 21,680, Hutcheson to Haldimand, 25 Jan 76; J. Shy, *Toward Lexington* (Princeton, 1965), 358.

manding a regiment he had lately become less enthusiastic about it since it would mean losing the barrackmaster's post. This charge is certainly not inconsistent with Robertson's character. He was one of the rare officers who had come up through the ranks and had in the process acquired a reputation for greed.[21]

Perhaps the most intriguing case of embezzlement during the war concerns Captain John Montressor. Montressor was chief engineer with the army in America from 1774 until his retirement from the army in 1778. In that capacity he was responsible for all the money issued to and spent by the engineer department and when he returned home had to submit his final accounts to the audit office. Had he been able to submit them immediately on his return, they might well have been accepted. As it was, he was not able to prepare them until 1782, and by that time the audit office had begun to examine army accounts with unprecedented care. As a result, of the £233,449.13.11 in expenses that Montressor claimed, £50,639.7.5 was challenged. Called before the auditors, Montressor admitted that he had forged some of the receipts submitted as proof of expenditures and increased the amount of others by changing the figures or adding items. He also admitted to having obtained signatures on otherwise blank receipts and inserting the amount later.[22]

Montressor later called that interview a "court of inquisition" and addressed a long memorial to the Treasury that attempted to explain the irregularities to which he had admitted. In the first place, he pleaded, although the warrants for cash for departmental expenses were made out in his name, he had been under the impression that the paymaster of the works for the engineer department was the responsible accountant; his responsibility, he thought, was only to build the works and ensure that purchases were made "in the most advantageous manner to the public." It

21 Willcox, *Portrait of a General*, 453.
22 AO 1/2531/663, Accounts of John Montressor.

was not until the paymaster returned to England in 1780, he asserted, that he learned his true situation. The paymaster of the works, however, died shortly after his return. For reasons that he does not explain, Montressor was unable to obtain the engineer department vouchers from his estate and had to draw up his accounts largely from duplicate receipts provided him during the war. Some of these receipts, he claimed, were lost when an armed schooner on which he kept his papers was captured in the Delaware River in 1778. Finally, in explaining expenditures of over £25,000 incurred in building fortifications at Philadelphia that the auditors objected to, he claimed that the receipts were inadequate because the material involved had been purchased from Loyalists living outside the British lines. To protect these people from possible Rebel reprisals should any records be captured, no receipts were signed and no detailed record of the transaction kept. The purchases, he said, were made by Pierre Nichol, a draftsman in the department who knew the country. Unfortunately, Nichol had since died.[23]

Montressor's memorial is to a degree convincing, if for no other reason than that it as well as his accounts and his interview with the auditors demonstrates an ingenuous quality that it is difficult to associate with a grand embezzler. Certainly his family believed Montressor, as did the historian J. C. Webster, who wrote a brief biography of him.[24] However (contrary to Webster's account) the auditors did not. When Montressor died in 1799, they turned to collect the outstanding sum from his estate and his heirs. The audit office accounts list the repayments. The last for £5,476 was made in 1825. Nevertheless, the audit office records are not in themselves entirely satisfactory. The loss of

[23] N-YHS, "Montressor Journals," 534-541. I have also drawn many of the details of Montressor's career from G. D. Scull's introduction to this volume.

[24] J. C. Webster, "The Life of John Montressor," *Proceedings and Transactions of the Royal Society of Canada*, series 3, vol. 22, sec. II.

the war and the rumors of embezzlement produced a mild "witch hunt" atmosphere in the 1780's of which Montressor might have been the innocent if rather stupid victim.

However, there is a considerable body of circumstantial evidence that supports the auditors' decision. In 1798, when Montressor's pleas were finally rejected, and just before his death, a number of his friends wrote to Lord Cornwallis, a wartime friend and then Lord Lieutenant of Ireland, requesting his intercession with the government. Cornwallis did write to Pitt attesting to Montressor's good character, but the implications of his letter were most damaging. "I hope I can state without impropriety," he wrote, "that Montressor is a man of very amiable private character, that in his official situation he only followed the inviting examples of the times, and that I think him an object of as much lenity as the nature of his case will admit."[25] Further, Montressor's actions were not such as to inspire belief. If his accounts were as confused and incomplete as he claimed, why did he not state this in the beginning? Also, his accounts as originally submitted stated that he had spent £233,449.13.11 but had received from the paymaster general only £231,244.14.11 and that the government therefore owed him £2,204.19. One can wonder at the precise detail derived from such scrambled accounts. One must also wonder at his sudden retirement at the age of forty-two—albeit after twenty-eight years' service—and his situation in Britain thereafter. There is no indication that Montressor should have been a wealthy man. He spent almost his entire career in America and lost his home and substantial land holdings as a result of the Revolution. For this loss, by his own admission, he was never compensated. His father worked his way up to Lieutenant Colonel of Engineers and died in 1776, but there is no evidence that he left any considerable estate for division among his children. Montressor's continual complaints about lack of promotion and

25 PRO 30/8/327, 205-206, Cornwallis to Pitt, 14 June 1799.

lack of recognition also indicate a slim pocketbook. Yet on his return to England, Montressor obviously had wealth. He purchased a colonel's commission just before his retirement from the army and established two residences, at Belmont in Kent and Portland Place, London. He spent 1785 and 1786 in Europe and placed his two eldest sons in military school there.[26] An exoneration of Montressor would have to account for his wealth.

The commissariat was the department most replete with established perquisites. It was also the center of considerable extra-legal activity associated with its main task of collecting and distributing food and forage. Perhaps the least damaging practice was the involvement of some commissaries in private trade. The narrow perimeters of the British areas of control made it inevitable that there would be food problems for civilians as well as soldiers, and it is not surprising that commissaries, whose jobs inevitably gave them inside information on both areas of shortage and sources of supply, could not resist the temptation to indulge in some private trade. The serious conflict of interest that could result was obvious and is made clear in a letter from Wier to William Butler, the assistant commissary who accompanied Colonel Campbell's expedition to Georgia in late 1778. In an attempt to build up a supply of rice to substitute for flour at New York, two army victuallers were sent to Butler to be loaded with that commodity. In due course the ships returned to New York, but their cargo was not all intended for the public stores. Wier wrote immediately to Butler: "The two victuallers are safe arrived; these vessels were sent by the orders of the commander-in-chief for the express purpose of bringing rice for the use of the troops. I was therefore very sorry that you should be so far off your guard as to put on board a quantity on any other account. Had I suffered this to have been landed & sold at public auction or private sale, it would [have] given room

[26] N-YHS, "Montressor Journals," 3-8; Webster, "John Montressor."

for the most disagreeable suspicions & reflections on myself and the whole department. I have therefore taken the rice for use of the troops and you will be paid for it at the same rate with the rest."[27]

The disturbing part of this letter is the phrase "so far off your guard." It carries the implication not only that Wier would not normally have condemned such a transaction even though it involved the misuse of government ships, but that he was aware that these actions were a breach of trust; Wier condemned Butler's lack of finesse not his action. Butler was shortly afterwards replaced as chief commissary with the army in Georgia by deputy commissary Peter Paumier, but Wier carefully pointed out that this was not because he doubted Butler's ability but because the growing size of the force demanded a more senior officer. The change apparently did not seriously affect Butler's private operations. Both Judge Thomas Jones and an anonymous correspondent of Carleton's asserted that when he retired to England in 1781 Butler took a small fortune with him estimated by Jones at £40,000.[28]

A more vicious practice in the commissary department was revealed in 1782 when a board of officers was convened in Charleston to investigate a charge laid by Captain John McKinnon, the local deputy quartermaster general, against the local commissary general's office run by John Morrison. McKinnon charged that commissaries were using short measures for issuing rations. The board reported that the department was indeed using a measure one quarter less than the standard (Winchester) bushel and that even then "the Deputy Commissary's [measure] falls short very near one pint in the peck. . . ." Morrison, disregarding the short-

27 N-YHS, Wier Letter Book, Wier to Butler, 5 May 79.

28 Jones, 336; BAHQP, 4,647, [?] to Carleton, 24 May 82. This letter is not anonymous; rather, the signature portion of it was at some stage cut off. Although the grammar, composition, and spelling in this letter leave much to be desired, the script is clear and practiced, indicating that the writer was perhaps a junior clerk.

age in the measure he did use, argued that wine measure was the proper one, but when the matter was referred to the commissary general's office in New York, Brook Watson replied that "it has ever been the custom in my department to issue the several articles of dry provisions by the Winchester bushel. . . ."[29]

Another practice in the commissary department, this time involving hay, was reported less formally by Ambrose Searle. Searle received his information from Captain Henry Chads, the army shipping agent, and said that it was later confirmed by Joseph Galloway and others. When the army foraged, it was regular practice to give receipts to Loyalists and others not obviously Rebels for hay taken for the use of the army. The receipts could then be presented at the commissary paymaster's office at headquarters for payment. According to Chads, however, when farmers presented themselves for payment, they were required to sign blank receipts for the cash received—that is, receipts without either a sum of money or quantity of hay entered—and those who declined to do so were refused payment.[30] Neither Searle nor Thomas Jones, who told a very similar story in his *History*,[31] did anything more than hint strongly what the signed but otherwise blank receipts were used for, and the commissariat was never taken officially to task for the practice. Nevertheless, John Montressor's accounts reveal a similar practice and suggest a use. Receipts of his totalling £10,600 were rejected by the auditors because, as Montressor admitted, the amounts in the receipts were not all paid to the persons who signed them.[32]

Although no action was taken in the matter of hay, abuses in the collection of supplies, especially by the commissary department, led to the only action taken under

[29] WO 60/24, packet 25, "inquiry into a complaint of short measure. . . ," 6 May 1782; BAHQP, 4,575, 4,622, Edward Hall to John Smith, 8 May 82, Brook Watson to Morris [Maurice] Morgan, 16 May 82.

[30] Searle, 293.   [31] Jones, 343-344.   [32] AO 1/2531/663.

either Howe or Clinton to prevent profiteering: the institution of the office of commissary of captures. As mentioned earlier in this study, that office was established by Clinton during the Charleston campaign.[33] The task of the commissary was to move with the army on campaigns and take possession of overrun Rebel property, particularly cattle. The office resulted from a report submitted to Clinton sometime in 1779 by Major John André asserting that the existing practice of giving units a reward of one dollar (4/8 sterling) a head for Rebel cattle turned over to the commissariat was unsatisfactory since many units not unnaturally preferred a good meal to a dollar. The result was a very unequal division of highly desirable fresh meat. André's report, however, went much further than this. Without making accusations against specific persons, he suggested that the system gave commissaries "full power to embezzle" and "great temptation to do it." The commissaries, he indicated, not infrequently paid the modest reward for cattle and other provisions from their own pockets and then sold them to the army or elsewhere for their true value: "this was one solution of the question 'how men on fixed and moderate salaries could better their fortunes.' "[34]

The commissary of captures office proved its worth. During the Charleston campaign some 1,000,000 rations of meat alone were collected and distributed, and Clinton ordered that the office be revived every time the army took to the field. However, it is clear also that the commissaries of captures by no means ended the opportunities for profiteering in the commissary general's department. Lord Cornwallis was one of the few senior officers in the army who sincerely deplored profiteering and when he became commander in the South took the opportunity to attack it. His attacks give some idea of the methods used by the commissaries. For instance, an order issued by him in December

[33] *Supra*, Ch. II, 86-88.

[34] CP, "André, on plundering with proposed regulations," filed at the end of 1779.

1780 indicated that the department applied to the purchasing of provisions something like the same practices reported by Searle in respect to hay. It is suggested also that when fresh food was very cheap the commissaries purchased it on their own and substituted it for salt provisions. Presumably, then, the more expensive salt provisions thus saved could be "sold" back to the army.[35]

Cornwallis recognized also that the system of issuing receipts to farmers for provisions commandeered could, if not properly controlled, lead in another way to huge profits for the commissaries. As he explained in a memo to Clinton, many receipts were never presented for payment and commissaries pocketed the money saved. He also noted that at Wilmington he confiscated a number of receipts in the hands of the commissary department. Those receipts, normally used by regiments to acknowledge salt rations turned over to them by the commissaries, had in fact been given for fresh food taken without payment from the countryside.[36]

For three of the army service departments, then, there is a very strong if somewhat circumstantial evidence of profiteering and corruption. For the fourth department—that of the quartermaster general—the evidence is much more concrete, and points to what can only be called an attack on the public treasury. Appropriately, the vehicle for the attack was the army's transport services and particularly the wagon service.

The wagon service was established in the spring of 1777[37] after the events of the previous winter proved the impracticability and even danger of attempting to supply the army's transport needs with wagons hired on a casual as-needed basis from local farmers. By Howe's orders the quartermaster general was thereafter to maintain on long-

[35] *Commons Journals*, vol. XXXVIII, 1109, "Orders by Earl Cornwallis, Wynnesborough, 23d December 1780."
[36] PRO 30/11/74, "Memorandum of Earl Cornwallis. . . ," [1781].
[37] *Supra*, 24-25.

term hire a wagon service prepared for any emergency and sufficient to meet all the needs of the army. The wagon train was ready to take the field for the 1777 campaign. The train remained as initially established until the late spring of 1782 and although varying in size from time to time averaged 730 wagons and 2,100 horses for the army based at New York alone. In addition, there was a small train at Rhode Island as long as that post lasted and when the Carolina adventure began a train was established there which averaged 134 wagons and 591 horses. The hire of these wagons at New York and Rhode Island amounted to approximately £185,000 New York currency a year and, when the Southern train was established and Rhode Island abandoned, to about £195,000. Although the quartermaster was supposed to supply all of their needs as well, in practice the other service departments employed some wagons themselves, the hire of which came collectively to about £25,000 a year. Thus the cost of the land transport of the army from 1777 to 1782 amounted on the average to about £220,000 per year in New York currency; in sterling approximately £128,000.[38]

£128,000 is a considerable sum, even in today's devalued and depreciated pounds. In the eighteenth century it amounted to a sizeable fortune, and it is not too surprising that those in a position to do so looked for a way to share in it. The method found was revealed to the public in 1781-1782 when the commissioners appointed by Parliament to investigate the handling of public funds turned their attention to army expenditures in North America. The commissioners presented their report—their seventh— to Parliament in June 1782[39] and revealed therein that the largest part of the wagons hired by the army in North

[38] The total cost of wagon hire from the beginning of January 1777 to the end of May 1782 was £642,192.8.6 sterling.

[39] "Seventh Report of the Commissioners appointed to examine the Public Accounts of the Kingdom," *Commons Journals*, vol. XXXVIII, 1106 *et seq.*, hereafter "Seventh Report."

America were owned by officers in the various service departments and most of them by the very officers in the quartermaster general's department responsible for the hiring. The wagons were hired by the department at the daily rate of eleven shillings and ninepence sterling for a four-horse wagon with a driver and six shillings and ninepence sterling for a two-horse wagon with driver. Both drivers and horses received army rations although the drivers' wages were paid by the proprietors. The upkeep of the wagons and shoeing of horses largely fell on the army, which was also responsible for replacing or compensating the owners for horses and wagons destroyed or captured in the service and horses that died of a number of diseases. By agreement there was to be three months' notice by either party of termination of employment. The Commissioners of Public Accounts found these terms to be, at the very least, generous, since the owners did virtually nothing but supply the original wagons and horses. They estimated that the owner of fifty four-horse wagons would have his investment back in five months and thereafter receive a clear income of £9,855.8.4 per annum.[40]

The wagon service, then, could be very lucrative, and from at least 1776 officers of all ranks and in all departments—from William Robertson, a steward at the hospital who rented a single cart and horse, through Captain D'Aubant, an Engineer who owned eleven two-horse wagons and three one-horse carts[41]—began to share in the profits. By far the greatest share, however, one quarter each, went to the quartermaster general and his two senior deputies. From 1777 to 1779 these were Sir William Erskine, Lt. Col. William Shirreff, and Major Henry Bruen. Erskine and Shirreff returned to England in 1779 and were replaced by Major Lord William Cathcart as quartermaster general and Captain Archibald Robertson. Cathcart's appointment, however, was only temporary, and he was succeeded by

40 *Ibid.*, 1,070-1,071.   41 WO 60/32.

Major General William Dalrymple in March 1780. Those who left office sold out their interest to their successor. When a wagon train was established to serve the army in South Carolina, it was formed around the nucleus of the wagons and horses captured when Charleston fell. These vehicles were sold, on Clinton's order, to Dalrymple, Bruen, and Robertson and the ownership of the train as eventually established was in approximately the same proportion as that at New York.[42]

But while the profits that accrued to the owners of the wagons were in the range of profiteering by the standards of any age, this fact alone is not sufficient to condemn the service or the men who ran it. Profiteering does seem to be a concomitant of war and, however much deplored, has seldom been considered a crime. Nor was it in the eighteenth century even necessarily an abuse of position for the officers of the quartermaster general's department to be owners of the wagons. Erskine excused his ownership on the grounds that "it had ever been the practice in America since General Braddock's time,"[43] and even the Commissioners of Public Accounts were very cautious in their criticism. Their statement that army officers owned the wagons hired by the QMG was not accompanied by any automatic condemnation or assumption of guilt. Rather, the commissioners went to great pains to point out the dichotomy in the position of a quartermaster general who owned wagons. "Trust and interest," they explained, "draw opposite ways; his trust obliges him to be frugal for the Public . . . but his interest leads him not to spare the public purse." Only when this had been made perfectly clear was it concluded that "in such a contest it is not uncharitable to suppose that the public interest will frequently be sacrificed to private emolument."[44]

---

[42] Add. Mss. 30,030, 452-457, "Narrative of General Dalrymple's proceedings upon his appointment of Quarter Master General," n.d.

[43] Clinton, *American Rebellion*, 559.

[44] "Seventh Report," 1069.

That there was some degree of impropriety involved in the officer-ownership of the wagons is clear from the actions of the officers themselves. They went to some lengths to conceal their ownership and even, when defending the system of hiring wagons before a board of general officers in New York in 1781, did not reveal their proprietorial interest in the service. The more considerable owners employed agents: James Frazer of New York, for instance, acted for Captain D'Aubant.[45] The three senior quartermasters employed the partnership of Winthrop and Kemble throughout the war.[46] The small proprietors set up their drivers as owners. They signed weekly for the full amount of hire due but in fact received only their wages, the remainder being kept on account for the owner.[47]

The evidence that public interest did give way to private emolument does not rest on the fact of officer-ownership or the size of profits, however. It involves, rather, the methods the various quartermasters took to establish the principle of a hired train and the methods used to ensure that profits would be high. When Erskine excused his ownership of the wagons hired by his department by explaining that this was the way things had always been in North America, his state-

[45] WO 60/32.

[46] There is no record of a partnership of this name in New York before the war, so it is possible that it was set up specifically to handle the quartermasters' share of the wagon business. Winthrop and Kemble were probably also agents for the ships that Shirreff admitted the quartermasters had an "interest" in. In the only summary of shipping on hire in the various departments that gives the owners' names, Winthrop and Kemble are listed as the owners of 15 of the 44 vessels hired by the QMG department. (WO 60/33, Return of vessels in his Majesty's Service, 12 June 1782.) The list also gives one small vessel owned by Sir Henry Clinton, and of the twenty ships in the employ of the commissary department eight were owned by deputy commissaries. In other places Winthrop and Kemble also appear as owners of privateers, rum contractors, and suppliers of building materials, but whether they were acting in their own interest or the quartermasters' in these cases is not clear.

[47] "Seventh Report," 1088.

ment, although he probably did not realize it, was not entirely true. There had been an experiment in public ownership of the land transport of the army in 1757 when Lord Loudoun, commander-in-chief at that stage of the Seven Years' War in North America, authorized the expenditure of £25,000 to purchase a train of 50 wagons to be used in the transport of provisions. The experiment was a success, but apparently the train was not maintained, and by 1775 the lesson had been lost.[48] In 1776, however, in response to a letter from General Howe—then still at Boston—stating that he was entirely without land transport for the coming campaign, the Treasury purchased a wagon train and dispatched it to meet the army at New York.[49] The train was placed by the Treasury under the supervision of Francis Rush Clark Esq., who was armed with a commission appointing him "Inspector and Superintendent of the Provisions Train of Horses and Waggons attending our army in North America. . . ." The history of Clark's charge is most material to the story of the army wagon service. For, if Clark is to be believed, his train was deliberately and systematically destroyed in order to discredit the idea of public ownership of army transport. Clark's charges, along with his experiences in North America, are contained in a number of letters he wrote while in North America and in a manuscript he prepared entitled "A Plain Unadorned Narrative of Observations & Occurrences Respecting His Majestys Provient Train and the Carriage of the Army."[50]

Clark's wagon train did not fare well from the very beginning. Although assembled in May of 1776, it did not sail until July or arrive in New York until November 17. The long, hot voyage took the lives of 367 of the 845 horses and 59 more died shortly after disembarkation. Although badly

[48] Pargellis, 297-298.

[49] CO 5/92, Howe to Dartmouth, 2 Dec 75; T 64/108, Howe to Robinson, 1 Dec 75.

[50] Clark Papers. The volume of the papers is not large, and they deal almost entirely with the wagon train.

in need of a period of recuperation, the remaining horses were immediately plunged into the operations then underway in New Jersey, and before the end of the winter, 114 more horses had died. By the end of 1777 Clark had only 101 animals left.[51] While the losses the train experienced were not necessarily abnormal—given the condition of the horses and the rigor of the service in which they were engaged—the conditions under which Clark claimed he had to operate were anything but normal. On the excuse that he lacked formal instructions from the Treasury, Clark's train was not given the separate service status implied in his commission, but rather was shuttled back and forth between the departments of the commissary general and the quartermaster general with neither really accepting responsibility for it. Debts he contracted to keep the train in operation went unpaid because he did not have access to funds, and for the same reason he could not purchase replacement horses.[52] During operations in the field, he complained that his men, horses, and equipment were continually harassed and abused by officers of the quartermaster general's department to the extent of being refused forage and shelter even when both were available. Further, Clark continued, the efficiency of his train was the subject of continuous unjustified complaints by these same officers, and his wagons criticized as being too heavy for North American roads and made of shoddy materials.[53] In sum, the situation Clark described was one of competition rather than cooperation between his train and the wagons hired and operated by the quartermaster general's department. The contest was hardly an equal one. Clark was not familiar with army routine and lacked access to headquarters to register his complaints personally. Nevertheless, he did not give up his charge without some struggle. He wrote letters

[51] WO 60/32, "Return of Horses embarked June 1776. . . ."

[52] PRO 30/55, vol. 30, Memorial to General Carleton by Clark, 14 Jan 83.

[53] Clark Papers, "Narrative."

explaining his situation to Howe, Cornwallis, Clinton, the Treasury, and even to the commissary general, Daniel Wier, whose commission made him theoretically responsible for army transport.[54] Howe and Clinton gave Clark absolutely no support, and the Treasury apparently did not even answer his letter. Daniel Wier replied that the quartermaster people were determined to have control of the wagon service and he was not prepared to stand in their way.[55] Wier's rejection ended Clark's hopes. By 1778 his wagons lay rotting in the wagon yards at New York, and his last few horses, with the exception of a pair of matched greys employed in drawing General Clinton's carriage, had been apportioned out among the various service departments. Clark himself became an assistant in the commissary department.

As a final note on Clark's story, it should be added that in 1778 he drew up and submitted to both the commander-in-chief and the Treasury a calculation of costs in the wagon service in which he concluded that the government could purchase and maintain a train sufficient to serve the entire army for a sum that over two years would amount to less than half the cost of a similar hired train. But, as with his complaints, his calculations came to nothing.[56]

Clark's story, of course, cannot be accepted unchallenged. He emerges from his correspondence as a weak and rather ineffective person, given more to complaints than action;

54 Clark Papers, Clark to Howe, 9 July 77; Clark to Wier, 10 Nov 77; Clark to Cornwallis, 14 Feb 78; Clark to Clinton, 26 Mar 78; Clark to Erskine, 17 Apr 78.

55 Clark Papers, "Narrative"; Wier to Clark, 8 Dec 77.

56 Clark Papers, Clark to Robinson, 15 Dec 78. Clark sent his proposal and, apparently, a copy of his "Narrative" to the Treasury via his patron John Strutt, member of Parliament for Maldon and ancestor of the present owner of Clark's papers. John Robinson acknowledged receipt of the papers in a letter to Strutt of 27 March 1779 and promised to consider them. There is no evidence that the matter was ever brought before the Treasury Board and certainly no action was taken by it.

it is difficult to believe that any organization under his control would be very effective. The army would probably have had a cheaper wagon service had he been in charge but not a more useful one. Nevertheless, there is in his story a ring of truth, in part because it is difficult to believe that he had the imagination to invent it but more because of the external corroboration it receives. In the first place, the particular villains of Clark's *Narrative* were Erskine and Bruen, both of whom became, even if they were not so in the winter of 1776, major owners of the wagons. Clark's charge that he could not get the funds to support his train also receives support. For most of the time from his arrival in North America to 31 March 1778, Clark was attached to the QMG, but departmental accounts show that in that year and a half he received only £5,151, barely sufficient to pay the wages of the crew he brought with him from England.[57] Thereafter, as he claimed in a memorial submitted to Carleton in 1783, he was shunted between the quartermaster general and the commissary and was unable to obtain further funds.[58] Finally, it is true that the "failure" of Clark's train was used as an argument against government ownership of the wagons. Major Bruen, during the course of the inquiry into the wagon service in 1781, stated that when Howe ordered the reorganization of the service in 1777, the idea of government ownership was rejected because of the example given by Clark's train. Bruen credited Howe with stating that the train, with its heavy losses of horses and its wagons unfit for North American service, had proved to be merely a waste of the £100,000 that it had cost and that continued government ownership would "lead to such expenses as could never be ascertained."[59]

What finally condemns the various quartermasters, though, is their own words in defense of the system of private ownership before the board of general officers in 1781. This board was assembled by Clinton in August of that

[57] AO 1/337/1348.   [58] PRO 30/55, vol. 30.
[59] N-YHS, "Board of General Officers," 75.

year to consider a proposal by Duncan Drummond to reduce army expenditures in the area of transportation by
purchasing the wagons, horses, and ships then hired. All
the vessels and vehicles, Drummond believed, "might be
purchased considerably within one years hire of the present
cost and establishment."[60] The hearing did not go well for
Drummond. He made his presentation concerning wagons
and ships, but, for reasons that are not clear, it was pref-
aced, indeed overshadowed, by a long comparison of army
expenses for comparable periods under Howe and Clinton.
The comparison concluded that Clinton's expenses were
considerably the greater. The board, not unnaturally, made
the investigation of this charge its major focus, and the
weeks of hearings that followed were concerned more with
presentations by the various army departments proving that
the additional expenditures had been justified than with
the question of wagons and ships. Further, Drummond's
comparison of the cost of hired and government-owned
vehicles proved to be very poorly drawn up, such basic
factors as maintenance costs having been omitted. After a
number of hearings in which Robertson, Bruen, and Dalrymple attacked the idea from every angle, Drummond was
finally forced to withdraw his original comparison and submit a far more coherent and comprehensive one. The withdrawal of the original comparison was all the opportunity
that Clinton, who had become disturbed by the direction
of the investigation, needed.[61] He dissolved the board and
reported to the Treasury that the investigation had been
ended because the "projects and plans" that had led to its
being assembled were now withdrawn by Drummond "from
his [Drummond's] acknowledged conviction of their
impropriety."[62]

[60] *Ibid.*, 1-2, Drummond, as Commissary of Accounts, could not be
ignored as Clark had been.

[61] Willcox, *Portrait of a General*, 448-449.

[62] N-YHS, "Board of General Officers," 209-220; CP, Clinton to Robinson, 8 Dec 81.

Drummond's attempt to reform the service, then, failed, as had Clark's before him.[63] Nevertheless, for the historian it is the arguments presented by the quartermasters against Drummond's plans that are important. Considered only in the light of the material presented to the board, these arguments appear valid; considered in the light of later evidence, they are revealed as hypocrisy and lies. First of all, both Sir William Erskine, in his testimony before the commissioners of public accounts, and General Dalrymple, in a later narrative of his experiences as quartermaster general, admitted that they and their senior deputies had been the owners of the wagons hired by the army. Yet in their submissions to the board of general officers, Bruen, Robertson, and Dalrymple consciously concealed this fact, speaking of the proprietors always in the third person and referring to meetings and discussions with them. Their most damaging statement in this respect was the assertion of their conviction that only with a hired train could the public be well served. "There is no man conversant in business or that is capable of judging of human nature," they wrote, "who can suppose that a contract held by the publick can or will be executed with that economy care and attention as when the interest of individuals are immediately concerned. . . ."[64] Under any other circumstances this would have been an acceptable (although debatable) position. As it was, it was sheer hypocrisy, for it meant in effect that these men could not be induced by either their regular pay or by their extra allowance for staff duties to organize an efficient wagon service. Only the profits accruing from ownership could so stimulate them.

The quartermasters also argued, in defense of the exist-

[63] Neither man, however, had any reason for self-reproach. Lord Cornwallis attempted to reform the quartermaster general's wagon service in the South, but even his considerable power as commander-in-chief in that area was not sufficient for the job. His struggle is eloquently related in Wickwire, *Cornwallis*, 232-235.

[64] N-YHS, "Board of General Officers," 197.

ing system, that the owners of the wagons, far from receiving enormous profits, drew only a modest thirteen percent per annum return on their investment of £60,879.4.5. Thus, they stated, it would be seven years, not less than one year as Drummond supposed, before a train purchased by government would pay for itself.[65] Had this indeed been the case, then the quartermaster and his two deputies would have shared at most £7,914 a year. While it is probably true that the profits did not run as high as the commissioners of public accounts asserted, on the other hand, the figures given by the quartermasters were outright lies. This is established by the papers of Staats Morris Dyckman.[66] Dyckman was a Loyalist resident of New York who was taken on as a clerk in the quartermaster general's department in 1776. He was apparently employed on accounts, for when Erskine returned to England in 1779 he took Dyckman with him to guide the accounts of his period as QMG through the audit office. The experience served him well, for thereafter he was employed by Cathcart and Dalrymple for the same task. The first two accounts went through with ease, but Dalrymple's, submitted in 1783 in the wake of the Report of the commissioners of public accounts, were subjected to intense scrutiny and not finally passed until 1803. The story of the trials and tribulations of Dalrymple's accounts is a fascinating one, but it does not belong here. Suffice it to say that the long delay was in part a form of official harassment. After the revelations of the commissioners of public accounts, Dalrymple's were the only quartermaster department accounts still open and the auditors were determined

[65] *Ibid.*, 201.

[66] The Dyckman Papers are in two groups. One, about twenty documents, is in the New-York Historical Society labeled "Papers relating to Gen. Dalrymple's period as Q.M.G." The bulk of the papers, however, is still in private hands, and although the New-York Historical Society has a microfilm copy of them, they are not open to the public. The papers are not catalogued or organized. The two groups of the papers will be distinguished here as "Dalrymple Papers," and "Dyckman Papers."

to take out the public's vengeance on him.[67] At first they attempted to disallow all expenditures for transportation on the rather specious grounds that Dalrymple could not produce formal authorization from the commander-in-chief for making them. When Dalrymple admitted that he, Bruen, and Robertson had in fact owned three quarters of the wagons, they then sought to disallow an amount equal to the profit made on the ownership. It was entirely due to Dyckman's skill as an accountant and ambassador that the profits were finally computed at just over £33,000.[68]

But in the course of his long defense of the accounts, Dyckman carried on a voluminous correspondence not only with Dalrymple but also with Bruen, Robertson, Shirreff, and Sir William Erskine's heir, a younger Sir William Erskine, and came into possession of a number of the quartermaster department papers. These letters and papers constitute a damning indictment of the quartermasters and, indeed, of Dyckman himself, who was not above threatening to expose the whole affair when it appeared at several points that he was not going to receive the payment for his services he believed had been promised.[69] In the first place, although they do not give an exact account of the total profit made by the quartermasters, they do give a very good idea of it; and it is far above the thirteen percent per

[67] Dyckman Papers, Comptrollers of Accounts to Treasury, 18 May 85. The auditors sought in the end to obtain the return of the excess profits. This attempt to readjust a contract was not without precedent. A public outcry developed in 1777 because it was believed that Richard Atkinson, a London merchant, had profited excessively on army rum contracts during the early years of the war. After numerous hearings, £9,171.10.8 was deducted from the original contract price of £154,096.16.6. (Baker, 165-170.)

[68] *Ibid.* "Statement of the first cost and expense of the Quarter Master General's train of waggons and horses. . . ," n.d. but after Jan 1801.

[69] Dalrymple Papers, 11 Mar [1800]; Dyckman Papers, Dyckman to Shirreff, n.d. [probably 1800]; Dyckman to Erskine, 3 Dec 1800; Dyckman to French, 3 Nov 1800; Robertson to Dyckman, 15 Dec 1800.

annum put forward to the board of general officers or the
£33,067.11.2 computed for the benefit of the auditors. In
one letter to a Mr. French, one of the executors of Henry
Bruen's estate, Dyckman stated that the total wagon hire
during Dalrymple's incumbency as quartermaster general
was £303,757 and noted that three quarters of this was clear
profit and that the ships the quartermasters owned and also
hired out to the army were "almost equally productive."[70]
Dyckman's general statement of profits is backed up by the
one instance where specific profits are noted in the papers.
This is an account sheet entitled "Major Gen. Dalrymple
in account with Col. Bruen as joint proprietors of the
Horses, Waggons, Vessels &ca" which gives the profit on
horses and vessels at Charleston owned by the quartermaster in the first and second quarters of 1782 as £4,358.13.6
and £5,310.19.9 respectively.[71] Since the establishment at
New York was approximately six times that at Charleston,
profits there in the neighborhood of £29,000 per quarter
are indicated. In all probability, however, the profits at
New York were even greater since Cornwallis, before he
marched off to meet his fate at Yorktown, instituted a number of reforms in all the service departments that cut down
on the opportunities for such profits.

More demonstrable evidence of the profits that came the
way of the quartermasters is found in the improvement in
the fortunes of these men. This is most evident in the case
of the three deputy quartermasters, Shirreff, Bruen, and
Robertson. All three were career officers, having joined the
army in the 1750's or the early 1760's, and their slow promotions and unfashionable regiments indicate only moder-

[70] *Ibid.*, Dyckman to French, 11 Sept 1802.
[71] Dyckman Papers, "South Carolina Account," n.d. On an undated
sheet in the Dalrymple papers entitled "An account of several payments and disbursements made by General Dalrymple . . ." one entry
reads: "paid Lord Cathcart upon his quitting the Department the
same having been out of Genl D's share of the first quarters profits . . .
£3000."

ate means at the best.[72] Yet all three retired during or immediately after the war and purchased large estates. Shirreff, who left with Erskine in 1779, very quickly turned up in possession of a mansion and lands at Old Alresford, near Southampton, where Admiral Rodney soon became a neighbor.[73] Bruen set up a new, successful line in the Irish gentry with the purchase of the estate of Oak Park in county Carlow after his retirement in 1783,[74] and Robertson, who left the army about the same time, was able to come up with £35,000 to purchase the 20,000-acre estate of Lawyers in Ayrshire, Scotland.[75] Of the quartermaster generals themselves, less can be said. Erskine and Cathcart were men of family who left and returned to ancestral estates. Dalrymple's fortunes, however, do demonstrate noticeable improvement. According to Bruen, when he took office in 1780, Dalrymple, although he was the younger brother of the 5th Earl of Stair, did not even have the money to purchase the quartermasters general's share in the "investments" from his predecessor and he (Bruen) loaned him the necessary funds interest free.[76] After the war, however, when he

[72] Promotion dates were as follows:

	Lieut.	*Capt.*	*Major*	*Lt. Col.*	*Regiments*
Bruen	1761	1768	1777	1782	63rd, 15th
Robertson	1763	1775	1780		Engineers
Shirreff	1755	1765	1768	1776	47th

[73] See his will, Somerset House, vol. Heseltine, 355; *Universal British Directory* (1791), vol. 2.

[74] Sir J. B. Burke, *Burke's Genealogical and Heraldic History of the Landed Gentry* (London, 1939), 2,549. According to Mrs. F. D. Thompson, the owner of the Dyckman Papers, the present generation of Bruens admit that their "fortune and estate was derived from the American War."

[75] Lydenburg, Introduction. Robertson, as did Shirreff, purchased a colonelcy just before retiring on half-pay. Both received automatic promotions through the general officer ranks but neither ever returned to active service.

[76] Dyckman Papers, Bruen to Wm. Adam, 3 Oct 85. Adam was apparently legal advisor to the quartermasters during the long negotiations with the audit office.

too retired, Dalrymple was able to stand for Parliament, establish a home on Portland Place, and travel extensively in France and Italy.[77] It is worth noting also that Dalrymple, Robertson, and Bruen's executors paid Dyckman almost £10,000 for the last few years alone of his services in getting the accounts passed.[78]

One more question remains to be answered with respect to the quartermaster general's transport services: how were the profits achieved? The answer seems to be that virtually all the running expenses of the wagon train were a charge on government. This was certainly the case until June 1779, for both Erskine and Shirreff admitted during their examination before the commissioners of public accounts that horses and wagons lost in the service were replaced at the expense of the public, who also bore the cost of keeping the wagons in repair, shoeing the horses, and providing rations for men and animals.[79] When Dalrymple, Bruen, and Robertson made their submissions before the board of general officers, however, the most telling point they were able to make against Drummond's comparison of the costs of public and privately owned trains was that he had not included maintenance costs in his estimates, and that these costs were borne by the owners.[80] Thereafter they produced a letter from Winthrop and Kemble that purported to be an informal agreement for the supply of wagons and horses. By the terms laid out in the letter the government was responsible for replacing equipment destroyed or captured by the enemy or lost in transport and horses that died of

[77] Dalrymple won a contested election for the Scottish seat of Wigtown Burghs in 1784. He ran in his brother's interest and voted with the opposition. He did not seek reelection in 1790. (Sir L. Namier and J. Brooke [eds.] *History of Parliament, 1754-1790,* London, 1964; Dalrymple Papers, "An account of several payments and disbursements . . . ," n.d. [probably 1804]).

[78] Dyckman Papers, "List of money received from the quartermasters," n.d. (probably 1803).

[79] "Seventh Report," appendices 16 and 18.

[80] N-YHS, "Board of General Officers," 78 *et seq.*

the disease called the glanders. It also stated that the maintenance of the train was to be the responsibility of the proprietors, "being nonetheless assisted by the artificers of the quartermaster general department at all times when not otherwise employed. . . ."[81] Although dated April 17, 1777, it seems likely that this letter was not in fact written until at least 1781. This is indicated by two points. First, there is a direct contradiction between the letter and Erskine's and Shirreff's testimony before the commissioners of public accounts on the matter of who was to bear the costs of maintenance. Secondly, according to Dyckman, the practice of charging the government for horses that died of the glanders did not begin until he returned to New York in 1780 and reported that Erskine's and Cathcart's accounts had gone through the audit office with ridiculous ease.[82]

Two possible reasons for the forgery present themselves. First, having made the bald assertion before the board of general officers that the costs of maintenance in the wagon train were borne by the owners, it then became necessary to provide within that general context a way that most of the expenses could still be charged to government: hence the provisions for the replacement by government of equipment lost and horses dying of glanders as well as the provision respecting the assistance of quartermaster department artificers. Secondly, when the second board of general officers was convened in March 1782 to consider Drummond's objections to the quartermaster's accounts, Drummond stated that his main objection was that he could not properly check the accounts because the quartermaster would not produce the wagon contract that alone would permit him to determine what expenses with respect to the wagon train were allowable.[83] Significantly, it was at this time that

[81] T 64/112, 81-84.

[82] Dyckman Papers, Dyckman to French, 27 Nov 1802, also in undated notes in which Dyckman lists his "services" in respect to the accounts.

[83] T 64/112, 94 et seq.

the Winthrop and Kemble letter made its first official appearance.

Thus, having been forced to say that the train was maintained by the owners, the quartermasters were stuck with that, and Dyckman's papers make it clear that his most signal accomplishment was the adjustment of the department accounts so that they appeared to support that claim.[84]

As a final note it might be added that Dyckman's papers also give some hints to other ways in which a quartermaster could improve his fortune. There are in the papers, for instance, a large number of receipts connected with the replacement of horses lost to the enemy in the Carolinas. They suggest that while horses could be purchased for seven or eight pounds sterling, the quartermaster regularly charged the government fifteen pounds, the maximum allowable, for horses lost from the train.[85] Dyckman also hints very strongly that the wagon drivers, supposedly paid by the owners, were carried on the department payroll as laborers at least part of the time.[86]

The question of profiteering and corruption is relevant to this study in several ways. First of all, of course, it speaks most eloquently to the problem of efficiency discussed earlier. It also proves to be relevant to morale and to the atti-

[84] Dyckman Papers, Dyckman to Shirreff, n.d. (probably 1780); undated notes of Dyckman's listing ways he had saved money for the accountants; partial letter, Dyckman to [Shirreff], 26 Mar 1802; fragment in Dyckman's hand that lists various payments for horses he had managed to get accepted by the auditors and concluded: "Here is £14,336 in six months charged for horses expressly worn out and expended in the service, an undoubted charge against the proprietors"; Dalrymple Papers, sheet entitled "Carolina Accounts," n.d.

[85] See also PRO 30/11/82 (Cornwallis Papers), 30-31, 46-47, Cornwallis to Balfour, 16 Nov, 30 Nov 82.

[86] Dyckman Papers, Dyckman to Shirreff, n.d. (probably 1800). See also Mackenzie, 424; after recounting a number of abuses in the wagon service in Rhode Island, Mackenzie notes that "it also weakens the Regiments as many soldiers are employed as drivers."

tude towards the war in England. On the point of efficiency, only for the wagon service is there any real evidence. At first glance it is ambiguous. Sir Henry Clinton praised the wagon service without stint,[87] and when called on for testimonials of the services rendered to their departments by the quartermaster general's wagon service, the barrackmaster general, chief engineer, and commissary general readily obliged.[88] These paeans of praise deserve close scrutiny, however. Clinton's was made after the war, when he sought to justify his conduct in the light of the report of the commissioners of public accounts. It is in the form of a lengthy digression in his narrative of the Revolution and is patently an attempt to make efficiency override questions of economy. The testimonials of the heads of the service departments can be taken as sincere, but they referred to garrison transportation at New York. Much more revealing are assessments of the efficiency of the train during operations in the field. Until the winter of 1777 the quartermaster general's department supplied the wagons needed by the artillery. After the operations in Pennsylvania that autumn, however, Major General James Pattison, the senior artillery officer, decided that the artillery should purchase a wagon train for its own use. The reasons he gave for his actions are most pertinent. The artillery, as part of the ordnance office, was a separate accounting unit from the rest of the army and thus was charged by the quartermaster general for the wagons used; Pattison was convinced that he would save money by buying rather than hiring the wagons and horses he needed. But he expected more than economy to result, for he had found that the wagons he had from the quartermaster general "were in so bad a condition as not to be worth repairing."[89]

General Cornwallis, when campaigning in the South, also found the quartermaster's wagon train less than satis-

[87] Clinton, *American Rebellion*, 242.
[88] N-YHS, "Board of General Officers," 204, 205-206, 250-251.
[89] RAI, Ms. 7, 33-34, Pattison to Board of Ordnance, 22 Jan 78.

factory. He testified before the commissioners of public accounts that during operations in 1780 "upon several occasions the wagons and horses employed in the public service were found to be in bad condition and unable to perform the service required." His private correspondence for the period reveals a growing dissatisfaction with the wagon service that finally led him to order his own staff to purchase horses and wagons with government funds. These horses, he claimed, could draw four times as much as those supplied by the quartermaster although they cost no more.[90] When his general dissatisfaction with the army service departments finally led to the General Order of 23 December 1780, mentioned earlier, much of the ire expressed there was directed at the quartermaster general's train: "The Quarter Master must absolutely be restricted from charging more for waggons than he has actually paid, for which he must produce his vouchers; and he is not to charge for hire of horses and waggons purchased; nor is he to purchase either horses or waggons but upon government account. If the necessity of the service should oblige him to hire waggons in the country, either to attend the army, or to carry supplies to different posts, he is to pay the proprietors the full price allowed by government for the hire of such waggons, for which the receipts of the proprietors will be his vouchers."[91]

The size of the wagon train came under criticism during the war also. General James Robertson, commanding at New York in 1780 while Clinton was in South Carolina, attempted to reduce the train there, and General Leslie attempted the same thing at Charleston after Cornwallis

[90] PRO 30/11/3, 88-108, 29 Aug 80; PRO 30/11/79, 45-46, 47-48, Cornwallis to Balfour, 27 & 31 Aug 80; PRO 30/11/80, 1-4, Cornwallis to Balfour, 3 Sept 80; PRO 30/11/82, 30-31, 46-47, Cornwallis to Balfour, 12 & 16 Nov 80.

[91] "Seventh Report," 1109. For a fuller account of Cornwallis' reasons for dissatisfaction with the wagon service see Wickwire, *Cornwallis*, 232-235.

moved into Virginia; both claimed that the number of wagons was ridiculous for the size of the force to be served. In both cases, however, the deputy quartermaster involved refused to make any reduction, on the ground that the size of the train had been set by the commander-in-chief and only he could authorize any change. When appealed to, Clinton supported the quartermasters.[92] The size of the train was, of course, very much Clinton's prerogative, although he probably took the advice of his quartermasters on this, and he was certainly better off with one too large than too small. Nevertheless, there are reasonable limits to the size of safety factors. Despite Clinton's assertion that a commander-in-chief could not be interested in both economy and winning battles,[93] he does have a duty to be frugal with his country's resources, especially when frugality is urged on him repeatedly by a worried government. And in the size of the wagon train there is strong indication that economy was thrown entirely to the winds.

The indication comes from a comparison of the train that served the army at New York in the last six months of 1782 that, under Brook Watson's reform administration, was owned by the army, and any other six months when the quartermasters owned and operated the wagon service. The same comparison completely vindicates Clark's and Drummond's attempts to bring about government ownership of the train. Certainly the last six months of 1782 cannot be compared exactly with any other six months in the war: Carleton was under orders to end the fighting, and this no doubt provided the opportunity for considerable retrenchment in services. Nevertheless, the war was still on, and Carleton, apprehensive of a strong American attack, still had to maintain the defensive perimeter of New York.[94]

[92] N-YHS, "Board o fGeneral Officers," 224-225; BAHQP, 4, 772, Leslie to Carleton, 11 June 82.

[93] Willcox, *Portrait of a General*, 449.

[94] BAHQP, 5,446, 5,594, 5,770, Carleton to Secretary of State, 25 Aug, 13 Sept, 1 Oct 82.

There were also as many men at New York as there had been at any time since 1779. But, whatever the differences, they would have to be extreme to account for the differences in the wagon figures. Between 1776 and 1782 expenses for wagon hire in the New York area never fell below £90,000 (New York currency) for any six-month period, and the number of wagons and horses was never less than 523 and 1,515 respectively. In the period from 1 July to 31 December 1782 the total expenditure in the new wagon master general's department was £55,441.11, and this included £35,880 for the purchase of 240 wagons, 914 horses, and some miscellaneous equipment. In the same period £6,206.16.6 was also paid out for casual wagon hire that would at most have obtained the service of 68 wagons and 136 horses for the whole period.[95] Thus the reformed wagon service was carried on with one third less equipment than had ever been required before and at two thirds the cost, although that cost included the purchase of a considerable train.

Field Marshal Lord Bernard Montgomery has estimated that the morale of the armies involved is the single most important factor in determining the outcome of battles and wars. If his assessment is correct, then corruption and profiteering contributed significantly to Britain's failure in the War of the American Revolution. Morale, of course, is an intangible, difficult to identify in specific situations and to analyze. Nevertheless it is possible to make assessments based on the actions and statements of those involved. Eric Robson, in his brilliant analysis of the Revolution, found evidence of declining morale in the reluctance of many officers, often the best ones, to serve in America and in criticism of senior commanders and their conduct of the war on the part of those who did serve.[96] Robson did not look into outbursts against corruption and profiteering, but on no point are the criticisms more persistent or more bit-

[95] WO 60/19; WO 36/3.   [96] Robson, 121-152.

ter. For despite Clinton's public assertions that the utmost economy was constantly practiced, it was apparent to most people in the army that fortunes were being made in the army services. Indeed, Clinton privately admitted this himself.[97] In the summer of 1777 Ambrose Searle confided in his diary his belief that "certain persons" were "by various and shameful tricks" raising the expenses of government "for their own aggrandizement. . . ."[98] As the years went by, other diarists and letter writers drew connections between corruption and profiteering and the unsatisfactory course of the war. Francis Rush Clark wrote in 1779 to his patron, John Strutt, deploring the lack of energy shown by the army and expressed a fear that the cupidity he had seen so clearly demonstrated was a contributing cause of that failing.[99] Captain James Parker and Major Charles Cochrane also drew connections between embezzlement and the course of events. Parker, who lived in America for some time before the war, drew his conclusion in American terms. "I am afraid," he wrote, "this business will end in the total ruin of all the Loyal subjects at last." Cochrane was a professional soldier, and his concern, expressed in a letter to Colonel Charles Stuart, was more for his profession: "I most seriously wish I could flatter myself into a belief that I might describe our situation here as having even the prospect of being more respectable, military or of publick utility, than in truth I see there is any appearance of. . . . The profession of a soldier has long been (and is so still) absorbed in the powerful pursuits of fortune, contracts and dissipation, that if any one has a wish of serving for his honour in endeavouring to effectuate it, he will meet so many obstacles thrown in the way by Great Officers & people whose interest 'tis to continue things in the same channel."[100]

[97] CP, Clinton to Lincoln, 30 Dec 81.
[98] Searle, 242.
[99] Clark Papers, Clark to Strutt, 10 Jan 79.
[100] Stuart, 112, Major Charles Cochrane to Stuart, 19 Aug 81.

Lieutenant William Hale saw things from a much more basic light, and his view probably reflected that of many common soldiers. Complaining in a letter to his father of the price of necessities, he went on: ". . . from this Great Britain may judge of the vast sums lavished on Commissaries, Quarter Masters etc. and the consequent distress of those whose blood and toils are held as nothing in the parliamentary scale of supplies."[101] Such an attitude on the part of the common soldiers would not only be destructive of morale but would provide an easy rationalization for the many in the war who gave way to the temptation to plunder. It is probable that Lord Cornwallis' General Order of December 1780 condemning fraud and embezzlement in the service departments was meant as a public declaration that the evils that were common knowledge were at last to be brought under control.

It was not just Britons who were dismayed by the corruption. Chief Justice Frederick Smyth of New Jersey, on hearing that Colonel Stuart had publicly attacked the commissary and quartermaster departments, wrote him a pompous but nonetheless deeply felt letter of commendation: "In conscious virtue bold pursue your stroke, may justice give force and vigor to your endeavours to bring to light and shame wretches grown great on the spoils of their country."[102] It is quite understandable that Judge Thomas Jones, observing both the inactivity of the army and the corruption it harbored, should have come to the conclusion that the war was deliberately prolonged in order to enrich army favorites; that the war had been converted from an attack on the American Rebels to an assault on the British Treasury.[103] Indeed, Jones was not the only one to come to such a conclusion. Admiral Sir George Rodney, after a long stay at New York with his fleet in 1780, wrote a private letter to Germain condemning almost every aspect of the

101 Wilkins, 235, Lieut. William John Hale to his father, 20 Jan 78.
102 Stuart, 106, Smyth to Stuart, 20 May 80.
103 Jones, 128, 365-366.

conduct of the army under Clinton. Professor Willcox has shown that Rodney was not above changing the record a bit to make it appear that he wanted to organize some action that summer but had been blocked by Clinton's sloth, when such was not the case. But, still, his comments on the situation at New York are, in the light of Jones' charge, most interesting:

". . . I behold her [England's] treasures squandered, her arms inactive, and her honour lost, and by the very men entrusted with the most important and honourable confidence of their Sovereign and his ministers, paying not the least regard to the suffering of their country, but retard[ing] the completion and extinction of the rebellion to make the fortunes of a long train of leeches, who suck the blood of the state, and whose interest prompts them to promote the continuance of the war, such as quartermasters, and their deputies *ad infinitum*, barrack masters and their deputies *ad infinitum*, commissaries and their deputies *ad infinitum*, all of which make princely fortunes, and laugh in their sleeves at the generals who permit it, and by every means in their power continue to discountenance every active measure, and, instead of having an idea of speedily concluding this unhappy war, their common discourse turns upon what may occur in the two or three ensuing campaigns."[104]

Nor was it just morale that suffered at the hands of the army service departments. There are indications that the wagons and horses that the quartermasters claimed represented an investment of over £60,000 were in fact virtually confiscated from their original American owners. Before the establishment of the permanent wagon train in 1777, horses and wagons were either hired or impressed from local farmers. In either case justices of the peace evaluated the equipment for repayment by the army in case of loss, and a daily rental was paid. In December 1776, however, a representative of the quartermaster general's department visited a

---

[104] HMC, Stopford-Sackville Mss., Rodney to Germain, 22 Dec 80.

number of farmers on Long Island whose wagons and horses had been taken into the service and offered them money that he said was the value of the equipment and was being paid on order of the commander-in-chief. The sums involved were much less than the appraised value of the horses and wagons, but the farmers were induced to take the money and sign receipts for it nevertheless because the representative, a Mr. Cowenhoven, assured them that they would still receive their rental. They found, however, as they pleaded in a memorial to General Howe, that shortly after they signed the receipts the rental ceased.[105]

In the South equally pernicious practices existed that in the end virtually deprived Cornwallis of horses although the country abounded in them. Horses that were the property of Rebels could be taken without ceremony, but the needs of the army often led to the impressment of animals owned by Loyalists. When such animals were taken, the owners were given certificates that, when presented in Charleston, entitled them to reimbursement. The receipts, however, listed the property taken and not its value, and when and if the owner was able, without a horse, to get to Charleston he often found that his reimbursement was in no way equal to his loss.[106]

Finally, the effect of profiteering and corruption in the army services on the attitude towards the war in England must be considered. Certainly there was knowledge of the army's problems in Britain. Although reports like Clark's and Rodney's were suppressed by the government, stories of profiteering based on letters such as those mentioned above and on reports of such returned soldiers as Lt. Col. Stuart circulated.[107] They were probably the basis of the commissioners of public accounts' note of "rumors of im-

105 Clark Papers, a copy of the memorial was sent by Clark to Strutt, 21 Dec 78.
106 Wickwire, *Cornwallis*, 236.
107 Stuart returned home with his regiment, the 26th, in 1779. The public attack on the service departments commended by Smyth was thus probably made in Britain.

positions, and of much wealth acquired during a short service upon slender appointments. . . ."[108] Nevertheless, the effect of the stories from North America are difficult to assess because they become a part of a swelling tide of criticism of the cost of the war and of the North government's conduct of it.

There had always, of course, been a minority in Parliament that criticized the North government's American policy, but not until 1777 and Burgoyne's disastrous defeat at Saratoga was this hard-core opposition joined by a more amorphous dissatisfied element. By late 1779, four years of unsuccessful war and increasing taxation led to an opposition of dangerous strength in Parliament and a diffused dissatisfaction throughout the country. In December of that year what was to become the Association Movement took shape. Organized originally by the Reverend Christopher Wyvill among the gentry of Yorkshire, the movement quickly spread to the London area.[109] The aims of the association were threefold: reform of representation, parliaments of shorter duration than the current seven years, and "economical reform." On the last of these aims the Yorkshire Petition, drawn up in late 1779 by 7,000 of the wealthiest and most influential of that county's freeholders, was most explicit:

"Alarmed at the diminished resources and growing burthens of this country, and convinced that rigid frugality is now indispensibly necessary in every department of the state, your petitioners observe with grief, that, notwithstanding the calamitous and impoverished condition of the nation, much public money has been improvidently squandered, and that many individuals enjoy sinecure places, efficient places with exhorbitant emoluments, and pensions unmerited by public service, to a large and still increasing

[108] "Seventh Report," 1069.

[109] Ian R. Christie, *Wilkes, Wyvill and Reform: The Parliamentary Reform Movement in British Politics, 1760-1785* (London, 1962), 68 *et seq.*

amount; whence the crown has acquired a great and unconstitutional influence, which, if not check'd, may soon prove fatal to the liberties of this country."[110]

The parliamentary opposition, led by such men as Edmund Burke, the Marquis of Rockingham, the Earl of Shelburne, Charles James Fox, and Colonel Isaac Barré, did not see eye to eye with the association on all these aims, but they and the Tory backbenchers who had long supported North were agreed on the need for economical reform and the reduction of Crown influence in Parliament via patronage. With the moral influence of the association behind it, the parliamentary opposition swelled in numbers and launched a new attack on the government in early 1780. Not yet strong enough to force legislation, it nevertheless made significant advances. Very early in the year it persuaded parliament to demand a full account of the army commissariat (through which a large part of the extraordinary expenditures of the army were made), its size and the salaries paid, and records of all the money issued to it.[111] In March, to head off a more dangerous proposal for a select committee of Parliament, the government was forced to establish the commission to examine the public accounts. Then, in April, although a bill to reduce substantially the Civil List was lost, Parliament passed Dunning's famous resolution that the power of the Crown had increased, was increasing, and "ought to be diminished."[112]

Unfortunately for the anti-government forces, the pressure for reform that they could bring was substantially reduced in the late spring of 1780 by the Gordon Riots, problems of opposition organization, and the arrival of the

---

[110] C. Wyvill, *Political Papers, chiefly respecting the attempt of the county of York and other Considerable Districts . . . to effect a reformation of the Parliament of Great Britain* (London, 1794-1808), "Petition of the Gentlemen, Clergy, and Freeholders of the County of York," 30 December 1779.

[111] T 64/107, 52, Grey Cooper to Clinton, 15 Feb 80.

[112] Christie, *Wilkes, Wyvill and Reform*, 96-97.

news of Clinton's capture of Charleston. The movement was still dangerous enough to cause Charles Jenkinson to write to Clinton in the summer of 1780, expressing his great concern that economy always be attended to since "every session of Parliament complaints are made of the amount of the army extraordinaries . . . ,"[113] but the successes of the early part of the year could not be expanded and in the general election of that year the opposition was unable to increase its strength. Even when, in early 1781, the commissioners of public accounts presented their sixth report and were free for a new assignment, the opposition could not direct it to the field of inquiry it desired. Barré, among others, had long sought an investigation of army contracting and contractors in Britain. The contractors, he said in a speech in 1778, were "known to be animals of a greedy nature, always craving and never satisfied, their appetites for dishonest lucre and foul gain were as insatiable as their consciences were easily satisfied."[114] North, however, aware that the opposition sought to expose contractor corruption and attribute it to the government, was able to play upon the general desire for economical reform and divert the investigation to army expenditures and accounting practices in America. This Barré opposed. The army in America was too far away from the government, politically, and further, although he believed that there were "secret impositions and frauds" in the American accounts, he was sure that no satisfactory investigation of them could be made from Britain.[115] Barré's point was well taken. When the commissioners presented their Seventh Report they hinted at reports of fraud in America but stuck to the position that they would "admit no charge against persons abroad, who have no opportunity of being heard in their

---

[113] BAHQP, 2,896, Charles Jenkinson to Clinton, 6 July 80.

[114] Quoted in Baker, 242.

[115] J. Debrett (ed.), *Parliamentary Register* (London, 1781), 1781, vol. III, "Commons" 456.

own defense."[116] In any case, although the Seventh Report did reveal exorbitant expenses and profits in at least the army's transportation services, the report was not issued until after the news of Cornwallis' surrender at Yorktown brought the fall of the North government.

Did the enormous corruption and profiteering in the army in America have, then, no effect on politics in Britain, play no part in North's fall? It would be naive to believe so. The independent country gentlemen who held the balance of power in Parliament were never particularly enamoured with the North administration. Yet they had little trust in the opposition politicians either. They felt the heavy and growing burden of war taxation and saw more and more clearly the rationale of the Association demands for economical reforms, but they supported North because they supported the King whose policies North carried out and because defeat at the hands of the American Rebels was almost unthinkable. They would continue to support North as long as things went reasonably well. As the first few months of 1780 indicated, however, there was an end to their tether. For the next two years Parliament was in a delicate balance. On the one side the independents heard the voice of North urging support for the King's American policy. On the other side they heard the opposition condemning the war and promising an end to corruption and profligacy in government. What the independents wanted was to support the King, to gain victory—or at least avoid the disgrace of defeat—and to achieve economic reform, in that order. As long as victory was possible they continued to support North. When Yorktown seemed to end that possibility they ousted him and opted for the economical reforms that the "impositions and frauds" in America had helped to make one of the major issues of the day.

[116] "Seventh Report," 1066, 1069-1070, 1072.

VI

The Northern War

To this point only marginal reference has been made to one very significant area of operations during the American Revolution: Canada and the northwest.[1] It has been necessary to exclude this area from the main study because, first, Canada was, after 1775, an entirely separate command; Sir Guy Carleton and his successor Frederick Haldimand were responsible directly to the government in London, not to the commander-in-chief in the Thirteen Colonies. This meant that although the army in Canada depended for logistical support on the same departments and organizations in Britain as served the army to the south (and suffered similarly from their failures) its logistical departments were entirely separate. And those departments demonstrated some significant difference from their counterparts to the south. Further, the logistical problems encountered by the army in Canada were often very different from those which afflicted the army in the Thirteen Colonies. In part this was because Canada, unlike the Thirteen Colonies, was completely under British control after the middle of 1776 and in part because the geographical setting of operations was significantly different.

The distinctions between the logistical organization of the army in the Thirteen Colonies and that in Canada were not so much in terms of offices as in the functions of offices. The core of the difference lay in the functions of the commissary general's department. In the first year of the Revo-

[1] This area is more properly known as the Province of Quebec, but at the time and since it has been popularly known as Canada. I shall follow the popular convention.

lution the commissariat in Canada was still subsidiary to the commissary office at Gage's headquarters.[2] Following the almost total destruction of the British forces in Canada in 1775, however, the old organization was cut away. Nathaniel Day was sent out with Burgoyne's relief force in 1776 with a commission as commissary general to the forces in Canada, a commission identical to that given to Chamier and Wier. It gave him charge of all North American procurement for the army and authority to operate all the army's transport services.[3] In the southern army, as noted, the influence of barrackmasters and quartermasters was too strong for the commissaries: procurement and the operation of transport services were split up among the various departments, to become a way to fortune for a host of officers. The situation there did not change until 1782, when Carleton took over as commander-in-chief and supported Brook Watson in the reform of the service departments. In Canada, probably due to Carleton's support, Day's office immediately became the comprehensive department that it was intended to be.

It was probably also due to Carleton's influence and close supervision that the army service departments began on a note of honesty unknown in the southern army.[4] Within a year of the establishment of the departments, officers in

[2] The Commissary in Canada before the war was John Christopher Roberts. However, he employed George Allsopp as a substitute, who in turn employed Adam Cunningham to do the actual work. (Gage Papers, Allsopp to Gage, 26 Oct 72.)

[3] Day's instructions from the Treasury are in T 64/104, 1-3.

[4] Carleton demonstrated his honesty as an administrator when as governor of the Province of Quebec in the decade before the Revolution he refused to countenance fee-taking and dishonesty in the customs service. (O. M. Dickerson, *The Navigation Acts and the American Revolution* [Philadelphia, 1951.]) His honesty did have limits, though: the army's transport service remained under Colonel Thomas Carleton, the quartermaster general and Sir Guy's brother, until Haldimand took over as commander-in-chief. (T 64/103, 128-130, Day to Gauchee, 1 May 77; T 1/547, 363-368, Day to Robinson, 28 Apr 78.)

them were forbidden the traditional indulgence of acting as agents for civilian firms and a relief fund for widows and children was set up with the profits from the "fifth quarter" and the sale of empty provisions containers.[5] The administrative honesty continued under Haldimand. Indeed, so convinced was he that his departments were without corruption that when he read the seventh report of the commissioners of public accounts he requested that the government send an inspection commission to investigate the public accounts of the army in Canada.[6]

Logistical problems in Canada began immediately on the arrival of the relief force in 1776, and to a very large extent explain the failings of the campaign of that year. That campaign is of particular interest since it has become an established interpretation that a more vigorous prosecution of it could have resulted in the complete destruction of the American force that occupied Canada the previous winter and ensured the success of Burgoyne's expedition in 1777.[7] It is worth noting the origin and exact nature of these criticisms. They came initially from the pen of Lt. Col. Gabriel Christie. Christie came to Canada with Burgoyne's force and vented the criticisms in a long letter to Germain in October 1776 that focused on three points. First, he claimed that Carleton could have captured the entire Rebel force in Canada. In June of that year the Americans began a retreat up the Richelieu River from Sorel on the St. Lawrence. Carleton dispatched half his force to follow them but took the remainder by water farther up the St. Lawrence and then by land across the peninsula formed by the Riche-

[5] T 1/525, 282-283, Day to Robinson, 13 July 76; Add. Mss. 21,851, Orders, 29 Dec 76; T 64/103, 95, Orders, 4 Apr 77; T 64/103, 46-49, Day to Robinson, 22 Aug 77. One of the assistant commissaries was forced to choose between retaining his commissary commission and his civilian agency; he chose the latter.

[6] T 1/588, 133-134, Haldimand to Sheridan, 25 Oct 83.

[7] A. L. Burt, *Guy Carleton, Lord Dorchester, 1724-1804* (Ottawa, 1960).

lieu and the St. Lawrence, to St. John. Had he moved quickly, Christie claimed, Carleton could have arrived at St. John before the Americans and thus trapped them between the two superior British forces. Instead Carleton delayed inexcusably and the Americans slipped away down Lake Champlain, taking all the shipping on the lake with them. Christie's second criticism was that Carleton then delayed overlong in chasing the Americans down the lake. He did not get away until early October and then failed to take Ticonderoga or even to keep Crown Point, which was taken, as a base for operations the following year. Finally, Christie claimed that the logistical services of the army were in complete disorganization.[8]

Two background points must be made. First, Christie and Carleton hated each other. Christie was a deputy quartermaster in Quebec following the Seven Years' War and was one of the principals in the bitter dispute between Governor Murray and the army in 1764-1765. At that time Murray objected to Christie's operations as quartermaster because they involved considerable coercion of the Canadians and because Christie used his official position to further his private business interests.[9] There is no record of a clash between Carleton and Christie before 1776 but that one did occur is clear from references by both Germain and Burgoyne. It was probably a result of Carleton's uncompromising attitude towards officials who mixed public and private business. In any case, the events of 1776 provided ample scope for the development of animosity on Christie's part. Christie was in England when the war broke out and there obtained an appointment as quartermaster general to Burgoyne's force. When the army landed in Quebec, however, it immediately came under Carleton's command. He, exercising a prerogative of the commander-in-chief, had already appointed his younger brother, Major Thomas Carleton, to be quartermaster and was determined not to

[8] Germain Papers, vol. 5, Christie to Germain, 26 Oct 76.

[9] A. L. Burt, *The Old Province of Quebec* (Toronto, 1933), 116-118.

employ Christie in any capacity. Christie's anger overflowed in a number of letters to Germain and although without an official position, he went with the army on the campaign "watching and minuting every transaction, & perhaps commenting too much on them in conversation." Christie's criticisms, then must be seen as those of a disappointed, angry, and vindictive man.[10]

The second point is that no one, other than Christie, found serious fault with Carleton's conduct of the campaign. Neither in personal or official letters during and after the campaign did such people as Generals Burgoyne and Phillips voice criticisms.[11] Nor is there serious criticism in any of the journals kept by junior officers.[12]

Logistics, of course, do not explain all the problems of the campaign. The failure to trap the Americans on the Richelieu, criticized by Christie, was much more a case of bad luck than logistical failure. The bad luck was of a kind familiar to everyone in the eighteenth century: failure of the wind. The force under Burgoyne, ordered to follow the Americans up the Richelieu, was disembarked at Sorel on Friday, June 14, and marched out the following morning.

[10] Germain Papers, Burgoyne to Germain, 22 June 76; HMC, Stopford-Sackville Mss., Germain to Burgoyne, 23 Aug 76; WO 4/273, 166, Barrington to Carleton, 16 Aug 76. Christie owned several seigneuries on the upper Richelieu and a large house at St. John. His assessment of Carleton's tactical abilities might well have been influenced by the fact that the Americans burned his house when they evacuated St. John.

[11] Newcastle Papers, NeC 2,327, Phillips to Newcastle, 22 June 76; Germain Papers, Burgoyne to Germain, 22 June 76; CP, Burgoyne to Clinton, 7 Nov 76. See also CO 5/125, 60-61, Capt. Douglas to Philip Stevens, 26 June 76.

[12] Add. Mss. 32,413, "Diary of William Digby of the Campaigns with the Northern Army, 1776-77, entitled 'Some Account of the American War between Great Britain and her Colonies' by Wm. Digby, Lieut. 53rd Regt."; New York Public Library, "Journal by an officer—probably of the 47th Regt of Foot—at Boston in 1775-6 and then in Canada, 1776-9"; James Murray Hadden, *A Journal Kept in Canada and upon Burgoyne's Campaign in 1776 and 1777* (ed. H. Rogers, Albany, 1884).

The remainder of the army, according to plan, was to proceed a further fifty miles up river, disembark at La Prairie, and march fifteen miles to St. John. It was a good plan and might well have succeeded had not the wind dropped shortly after the fleet left Sorel. On Sunday, June 15, Carleton finally gave up his plan and disembarked at Vercheres, not fifteen miles from St. John but fifteen miles from Sorel. On the following day, Monday, when the Americans were clearing the rapids at Chambly, Carleton moved only eight miles to Varennes. In the next two days, the force covered the remaining forty-odd miles, arriving in St. John on Wednesday.[13] That, of course, was the day after the Americans cleared the town, but the point to note is that the march that Carleton's force made was as long as that made by the Americans or by Burgoyne's force—some fifty miles. Further, although he did not begin his march until Monday morning, two and a half days after the Americans left Sorel and two days after Burgoyne started out, he arrived at St. John only one day after the others.

While fifty miles in three days is not particularly good marching time even at the slow pace of an eighteenth-century army, under the circumstances it was a very respectable effort. Carleton's troops were not in good physical shape. Most had been confined on board crowded troop transports for several months and needed at least a few days to regain their land legs and toughen up their feet.[14] Carleton was probably wise to march his force only eight miles the first day: Burgoyne pushed his soldiers some twenty miles in the first twenty-four hours and as a result had to spend the next day resting.[15] Also, once on shore, the soldiers' diet of salt provisions was supplemented by fresh food—often green fruit stolen from roadside orchards—for the first time in months and the result was an outbreak of

---

[13] *Ibid.*, these journals lay out very clearly the stages of the marches.

[14] Carleton, in his orders of June 17, specifically directs his men to "clean and oil their feet and shoes." (Hadden, 185.)

[15] Add. Mss. 32,413, "Diary of William Digby. . . ," 16 June 76.

the "flux" which inevitably slowed the army down.[16] Finally, there was need for caution. With the advantage of hindsight and thus the knowledge that the American force was in an advanced state of disintegration it is easy to demand that Carleton should have thrown caution to the winds. But from Carleton's point of view the situation was somewhat different. The American army numbered close to 8,000 and however contemptuous the British might have been of American fighting qualities at the beginning of the Revolution there was ample reason for respect by 1776. Carleton's rate of progress was a nice balance between due caution and speed.[17]

The logistical problems of the campaign, although they did not affect the movements described above, began some time earlier and had their most serious effect in the summer and autumn. They began, in fact, when the Treasury victualler *Swift* caught fire and sank in the English channel in March. The *Swift* was one of four supply ships that, with five naval vessels and the 29th Regiment, were sent out as harbingers of Burgoyne's force. Their orders directed them to be at the mouth of the St. Lawrence, ready to move up to the relief of Quebec, as soon as the ice in the river broke up. The supply ships were to bring with them, along with quantities of coal, rum and stores, provisions for 3,000 men for three months. Unfortunately no record exists of the ladings of the various supply ships, but if the cargo of the *Elizabeth*, the ship sent a few weeks later "to replace her cargo [the *Swift*'s] with something equally serviceable," then the *Swift* must have carried almost all of the provisions.[18] Thus the initial force that reached Quebec

[16] Mellish Papers, [Dr. John Hays] to Charles Mellish, 29 Sept 76.

[17] General Phillips, in a private assessment of the campaign had no reservations at all when he attributed the American escape to the failure of the wind. (Newcastle Papers, NeC 2,327, Phillips to Newcastle, 22 June 76.)

[18] Add. Mss. 21,697, 130-132, Germain to Carleton, 17 Feb 76; Add. Mss. 21,687, Mure, Son & Atkinson to Carleton, 28 Apr 76.

and turned the planned withdrawal of the American besiegers into a rout was more a moral than a real reinforcement. Provisions in Quebec were low and the countryside
around the city had long since been stripped of food by
the besiegers.[19] While it may be doubted that the cautious
Carleton even thought of pursuing the retreating Americans before the arrival of the main force, it is unlikely that
he could have done so for want of reserves of provisions.

The provisions' situation should have been relieved when
the main fleet arrived in late May. Troop transports were
usually provided with three to four months' food for the
troops on board, and arrangements had been made with
Mure, Son & Atkinson for the shipment, in quarterly lots,
of a year's provisions for 12,000 men.[20] The fleet also
brought Nathaniel Day, the newly appointed commissary
general, who had been informed by the Treasury that he
could probably purchase a large part of the army's provisions needs in the province.[21]

But the supply situation, thus apparently well in hand,
was in fact precarious in the extreme. Day, although he
developed in later years into a competent commissary, was
a neophite. Further, he had only joined the force a few days
before it sailed and the deputies and assistants appointed
with him did not arrive until later in the summer.[22] Thus
Day, without experience or assistance, was plunged immediately into the most difficult tasks a commissary could face,
those of establishing depots and supplying an army on the
move. Of course these tasks did not fall entirely to the commissary general. When the army was on the move the
quartermaster general bore as much responsibility for the
organization and distribution of supplies as did the com-

[19] WO 1/2, 250-251, Allan Maclean to Barrington, 20 Nov 75.

[20] Add. Mss. 21,687, 263-269, Mure, Son & Atkinson to Carleton,
28 Apr 76.

[21] AO 16/10, 44, Robinson to Carleton, 20 June 76.

[22] T 64/102, 31, Robinson to Day, 30 Mar 76; T 64/103, 36-38, Day
to Robinson, 12 June 77; T 1/547, 363-368, Day to Robinson, 28 Apr 78.

missary. Lt. Col. Christie had apparently prepared some plans for the logistical organization of the campaign while the force assembled in Britain, but when he found on arrival in Canada that his place had been usurped he became decidedly unhelpful. But, in any case, the plans could not have been very sound if they collapsed, as they did, in his absence.

When the army arrived in Quebec, then, it had little in the way of logistical organization and the result was several months of chaos. As the fleet moved up river from Quebec city and the troops disembarked at various places, dictated by the tactical necessity and the draught of the transports, masters of vessels, without instructions and probably anxious to leave the hazardous river navigation, allowed the troops to take what they would from the ships stores and deposited the remainder at the nearest convenient point on the shore. The army's provisions and stores were scattered from Deschambault to Montreal and, since no one had thought to provide provisions' tents or tarpaulins, they often lay in the open, exposed to the weather and the depredations of local inhabitants.[23] It is not possible to determine exactly the losses that were occasioned, but the result was that by the end of June, at the latest, the provisions Burgoyne's army brought with it were virtually exhausted.[24]

Even this situation would not seriously have affected operations had not two alternative sources of supply also failed. In the first place, the continuing supply of provisions from Mure, Son & Atkinson did not, for reasons that are not clear, begin to arrive until September. The victuallers that appeared that month brought only some twenty

[23] T 64/103, 36-38, Day to Robinson, 12 June 77; Add. Mss. 21,706, 25-33, Robinson to Carleton, 26 Mar 77; T 64/103, 1, Day to Robinson, 22 Sept 76.

[24] From the opening of the campaign in May to September 2 the army received from victuallers and troopships provisions for 12,000 men for 47 days. (T 64/102, 29, General State of . . . Provisions. . . .)

days' provisions for 12,000. In October a further seventy-five days' provisions for the same number arrived, but by the end of that month the campaign season was definitely over. That would have been the end of deliveries for the year had not 1776 been an unusually mild winter. As a result the St. Lawrence remained free of ice until well into December, permitting victuallers to get up to Quebec with a further six months' provisions.[25] But figuring provisions on the basis of 12,000 men gives an inaccurate picture of the army's possible reserves. The contract with Mure, Son & Atkinson was for that number and that was the approximate size of the regular army force in Canada by the end of September. But the army in Canada fed far more than its establishment of effectives. Indians and French Canadian militia units assembled for the assault down Lake Champlain had to be provided for as did several thousand civilians employed or impressed to staff the service departments and man the extensive communications lines within the province. Most of the latter were employed in transporting stores and knocked-down boats from Sorel to St. John, where the fleet that was later to challenge Arnold's small navy and transport the army to the south end of Lake Champlain was assembled. In all, Day estimated later, he fed not 12,000 but 20,000 that summer and autumn.[26] At that rate the provisions that arrived in September were sufficient for only twelve days, those in October for forty days and those in November and December for four months.

And even the provisions that did arrive, both with Burgoyne's fleet and later, were inadequate in terms of quality. The bread and flour Day received were as bad as that provided for the army at New York and were often packed in

25 T 1/520, 200-201, Carleton to Robinson, 10 Aug 76; T 64/102, 19, "Return of Stores and Provisions Received. . . ."

26 T 1/520, 200-201, Carleton to Robinson, 10 Aug 76; T 64/103, 36-38, Day to Robinson, 12 June 77.

inadequate barrels or in tierces, a container far too large for the army's purposes and too fragile to withstand frequent handling or overland journeys.[27]

The second alternative source of supply was the Province of Quebec itself. Although never a great food-producing area, Quebec could in years of good harvest supply considerable quantities of provisions. Indeed, from June 1776 to January 1777, Day made local purchases to the extent of over £70,000 to make up for deficiencies in the deliveries from Britain.[28] But as a source of supply for the British army in 1776 Quebec had drawbacks. Until the new crop was harvested, food was somewhat scarce, particularly in the areas close to Quebec and Montreal, due to the earlier demands of the American army.[29] Second, no adequate organization existed for collecting food on the scale required by the army, or for preserving it in a form suitable for use on campaign. In this situation Day had to become, as he put it, "purveyor general" to the army, continuously riding about the countryside purchasing provisions or persuading people to bring them into the army, and even arranging for the construction of mills capable of producing flour suitable for the army's purposes.[30] As a result, although Day was able to make up the deficiencies in the supplies from Britain with local purchases he was unable to build up a reserve of provisions sufficient for a campaign.

The failure of provisions in the summer and autumn of 1776 meant the failure of the more ambitious parts of the campaign. Although Canada was retaken, the army could

[27] T 64/102, 2, Day to Robinson, 26 Oct 76.

[28] T 64/102, 22-27, Day to Robinson, 20 June 77. In total, between May 25 and Dec 24 he purchased 4,329,345 lbs. of flour and bread and 2,980,867 lbs. of meat—sufficient for 20,000 men for about six months. (T 64/102, 29, General State of . . . Provisions. . . .)

[29] Newcastle Papers, NeC 2,327, Phillips to Newcastle, 22 June 76.

[30] T 64/102, 3-5, 22-27, Day to Robinson, 15 May, 20 June 77; T 64/103, 46-49, Day to Robinson, 22 Aug 77. Day reported that the flour produced in the local mills was so coarse that surplus grain was usually exported whole.

not move across Lake Champlain because it was not sent and could not collect a reserve of provisions. Critics at the time and since have blamed the failure of the campaign (and, indeed, the failure of the following year's campaign) on Carleton's long pause to build an excessively large fleet on Lake Champlain.[31] That the fleet was excessively large was demonstrated by the decisiveness of the battle of Valcour Island, but it is apparent that without provisions' reserves Carleton had little choice but to prepare well for the future since he could not act at the moment.

This is not to say that there was not an element of perhaps excessive caution involved in Carleton's activities during the summer. But that caution apparently had more to do with the morale of the British force and an apprehension that the Americans might attempt to return than with a reluctance to advance. Without provisions Carleton not only could not attack but would be in a poor defensive position if the Americans attempted to return; he could not be sure of the strength of the American force, since it had retreated along its line of communications, and was concerned that the logistical weakness of his force should not be known lest it provoke an attack. Hence the army was fed on the fresh provisions that Day, by dint of tremendous effort, provided and the shortage of reserves kept a secret. As Day reported, "the supply [of fresh provisions] became constant and general to all quarters where the troops were stationed [so] that no person could tell but that the magazines were filled with salt provisions, except the generals and a few of my department."[32] In the meantime, to deter the Americans and to keep up the morale of the British, offensive preparations went ahead at full tilt even though they were more than adequate for the situation.

Carleton finally launched his attack on October 4 and

[31] In addition to the works already noted above, see HMC, Carlisle Mss., vol. III, 188-189, Hans Stanley to Francis 10th Earl of Huntingdon, 18 Dec 76.

[32] T 64/103, 36-38, Day to Robinson, 12 June 77.

defeated Arnold's fleet at Valcour Island a week later. From this victory he went on to Crown Point, which the Americans evacuated and destroyed on his approach. But there the campaign ended. Carleton believed that Ticonderoga could not be taken without a siege and he had neither the provisions nor the weather for such an undertaking. Nor could he even establish a base at Crown Point. Again the impossibility of supplying such a base with provisions to last it through the winter was a factor, but equally important was a shortage of quartermaster stores and barrack equipment. A large quantity of this material had been ordered out in August but was delayed so long that the ships missed their passage up the St. Lawrence despite the late arrival of winter and ended up at New York.[33] Without these stores Carleton had difficulty even constructing positions and barracks in Canada. Vital posts at Isle aux Noix and St. John were not finished until December and he had no hope of constructing an adequate position at Crown Point. As he pointed out later "the corps left there must have been inevitably lost. . . ."[34]

That the failure to establish a base at the south of Lake Champlain in 1776 had serious consequences was attested to by Sir Henry Clinton. In a long analysis of the war written in 1782 he identified various critical points in the war that in sum, he believed, explained why Britain lost. One of the earliest was "losing the fruits of summer's labour and autumn's victory on the lakes in '76. . . ." Clinton did not explain further, but his thinking might have paralleled Germain's, who believed that the failure to hold Crown

[33] T 1/537, 118-119, Carleton to North, 24 May 77; Add. Mss. 21,689, Mure, Son & Atkinson to Carleton, 3 Sept 76; T 64/106, 67-71, Robinson to Howe, 14 Jan 77; T 64/108, 103-105, Howe to Robinson, 5 Apr 77. See also Mellish Papers, Dr. John Hays to Mellish, 16 Apr 77.

[34] T 1/537, 118-119, Carleton to North, 24 May 77. The Americans felt the same way. The commander at Ticonderoga estimated that it would take 10,000 men several months to rebuild the fort there. (Ward, I, 385.)

Point freed a large part of the Rebel forces in northern New York. They were then transferred to New Jersey, where they gave Washington the strength necessary for his successful attack on Trenton and Princeton. Germain held Carleton responsible for all this, as have historians since, but Clinton saw things in a different light. He attributed the failure to take possession of the south end of Lake Champlain to "want of provisions and materials to establish the troops there."[35]

1777 was the year of Burgoyne's campaign. Historians have generally seen his defeat as a triumph of American arms, but it is better classified as a disaster of British planning. No campaign of the war better illustrated the logistical problems of operations in America or the consequences of failure to understand them. The logistical preparations for this campaign commenced in January when Nathaniel Day began to stockpile provisions at St. John at the head of navigation on the Richelieu River. When Burgoyne, who had spent the winter of 1776-1777 in England, arrived back in Canada on May 7, the provisioning was complete.[36] The army, after spending a comfortable winter, was already assembling and the fleet was ready to carry it and the provisions to the south end of Lake Champlain. Burgoyne brought a considerable quantity of equipment with him, but by early June most of it too had been transported to St. John and the loading of ships there had begun.[37] On May 28 the "magnificent armament" sailed.

There was only one flaw in the army's preparations: land transportation. In January, when Day began to assemble stores, he noted in a memorandum to Carleton that no pro-

[35] Alnwick Castle Mss. LII, Clinton to Percy, 2 May 82; Germain Papers, Germain to Carleton, 26 Mar 77.

[36] T 64/103, 55-59.

[37] T 64/103, 154, Day to deputy commissary at St. John, 31 May 77.

vision had been made for the transportation of the army when it got to the other end of Lake Champlain.[38] The memorandum passed unnoticed, and not until early in June, when General Phillips brought up the question with respect to the artillery, did anyone apparently consider land transport again. Then, in a flurry of activity, contracts were let with Jacob Jordan, a Montreal merchant, for the hire of 400 horses for the artillery and 500 two-horse carts with drivers for the army.[39] But it was too late. Perhaps if there had been a long siege of Ticonderoga, as everyone expected, the train would have been ready when the time for the overland movement to the Hudson and then to Albany came. As it was, the American army evacuated Ticonderoga immediately and if it was to be brought to battle pursuit had to be immediate and close. But the wagon train, which came overland from St. John, did not begin to arrive until mid-July and then was woefully short in numbers.[40] Without horses and wagons to transport supplies and artillery, first across the portage from Lake Champlain to Lake George and then from Lake George to Fort Edward on the Hudson, such pursuit was impossible. Although the Americans evacuated Ticonderoga on July 6, Burgoyne, who decided to march the main body of the army from Skenesboro to Fort Edward, leaving the supplies to go by Lake George, did not leave Skenesboro until July 23 or take possession of Fort Edward on the Hudson until early in August. There the army stalled. Only 180 of the contracted wagons had arrived and over the abominable road from Fort George to Fort Edward they could do little more than keep the army in day-to-day supply. Even to do that the horses had to be driven to the point of collapse.[41] Not until Septem-

[38] T 64/103, 55, Memorandum 26 Jan 77.

[39] Lieutenant General John Burgoyne, *A State of the Expedition from Canada* (London, 1780), xxviii-x:x.

[40] *Ibid.*, xxi, Burgoyne to Germain, 20 Aug 77.

[41] *Ibid.*, 41-42, evidence of Captain Money.

ber 13 was a reserve of supplies, including provisions for thirty days, collected and the army able to move on. It was in order to obtain more horses and an easier supply of provisions that Burgoyne detached Colonel Baume on his disastrous attempt on the American supply depot at Bennington. By the time Burgoyne was ready to move, the American forces, demoralized by the retreat from Ticonderoga, had recovered. When he crossed the Hudson and thus cut off his communications with Canada, they closed in around him.

The great logistical problem of Burgoyne's campaign, then, was transportation. But, in fact, behind that was a whole series of fundamental failings. These began with the incredible failure even to consider the problem of land transportation until three weeks before the army departed. This resulted from a combination of errors. First, it was apparently, and incorrectly, assumed by Burgoyne that at least part of the transportation needs of the army could be met by *corvees*—legal labor services due to the state—on the French Canadian peasants.[42] More important, Burgoyne seems to have assumed that he would have no trouble obtaining all the horses and wagons he required from the Americans once he landed south of the lakes. For, even when he did finally let the contract for wagons, it was only for 500, barely enough to carry fourteen days' supplies, although it was planned to carry thirty days' provisions at all times.[43] As it turned out, Burgoyne was entirely wrong. Although the wagonmaster with the army had instructions to hire or purchase as many vehicles as he could find, only

[42] *Ibid.*, xxx, Burgoyne to Carleton, 7 June 77.

[43] *Ibid.* In response to a request from Burgoyne, Day prepared a chart showing the number of wagons required for provisions for forces of various sizes for various lengths of time. According to it an army of 10,000 required 1,125 carts, each capable of carrying 800 pounds, to carry 30 days' provisions. (*Ibid.*, xxx, Burgoyne to Day, 4 June 77; *ibid.*, appendix Aa.)

thirty oxcarts were added to the train for the move from Fort George to Fort Edward.[44]

The assumption that the army could obtain many of the vehicles it needed from the Americans was a fundamental error, apparently resulting from bad intelligence. As a letter to Lord Rochford in 1775 indicated, Burgoyne had some awareness of the problems that an army in America would meet when attempting to move through hostile territory.[45] Yet for this campaign he was prepared "to trust to the resources of the expedition" for most of the horses and wagons and all of the oats and hay he required.[46] His trust was not well placed. Much of the area through which the army passed was so sparsely settled that under the best of circumstances it would have been difficult to obtain anything from it. Further, the people of the area proved to be anything but friendly. As a result the required horses and wagons, as well as horses for the German Dragoons with the expedition, were never acquired, and forage for the horses with the army was in perpetually short supply;[47] at Fort Edward the total supply of oats, a most necessary part of the diet of working horses, amounted to a wagon load— less than 800 pounds.[48]

On this problem of transportation, two more points deserve consideration. First there is a question concerning the size of the artillery train that accompanied the army. After the failure of the expedition, critics, who recognized the part played in it by transportation problems took Bur-

---

[44] *Ibid.*, Evidence of Captain Money. By the middle of August the figure was 50 ox carts. (*Ibid.*, xxi, Burgoyne to Germain, 20 Aug 77.)

[45] *Supra*, 62-63.

[46] Burgoyne, xxx, Burgoyne to Carleton, 7 June 77.

[47] *Ibid.*, 53, Evidence of Captain, The Earl of Harrington; DeFonbalanque, 262; Newcastle Papers, NeC. 2,810, Phillips to Newcastle, 10 July 77; Hadden, *Journal*, 107-108; Add. Mss. 32,413, "Diary of William Digby," 64, 70, 79.

[48] Burgoyne, 70, evidence of Capt. Bloomfield, Lieut. Digby ("Diary," 79) states that by the end of September horses were dying from a combination of overwork and lack of grain.

goyne to task for taking with him an artillery train far larger than the situation demanded. The train was indeed huge, consisting of two twenty-four pounders, four twelve-pounders, eighteen six-pounders, six three-pounders, and twelve mortars of various sizes.[49] Burgoyne defended its presence on the grounds that it was necessary for the reduction of the defensive works that the Americans were so adept at throwing up, and claimed that it never interfered with the transportation of provisions. The first point can be doubted, especially as it applies to the period after the fall of Ticonderoga; the second point was pure evasion. It was probably true, as Burgoyne led many witnesses before the parliamentary inquiry into the expedition to admit, that the provisions' train was never required to assist the artillery.[50] But that was not the point. What was important was that from the beginning of the expedition the artillery employed 400 horses that not only ate up large parts of the supplies of hay and oats, but might have been used to carry provisions or even to mount the German Dragoons.

The second point concerns the discipline of the army. As noted earlier,[51] eighteenth-century officers were notorious for the quantities of personal luggage they insisted on carrying with them on campaign. Foreseeing that this might cause problems, Burgoyne ordered officers to strip their baggage to a bare minimum even before the army left Canada.[52] At Skenesboro widespread disobedience made it necessary to repeat the order and to enjoin officers against purchasing horses for their own use and against appropriating provisions' carts to carry personal baggage. These orders likewise fell on deaf ears, as did threats that private vehicles and horses would be expropriated and private goods found on government vehicles burned.[53] One German officer wrote with an air of pride-of-accomplishment that although the army was desperately short of transport, he had acquired

[49] *Ibid.*, 9.
[50] *Ibid.*, 42, 68, 78.
[51] *Supra*, 57-58.
[52] Burgoyne, 72.
[53] *Ibid.*, 40, 73; O'Callahan, 27, 37; Hadden, 310, 312.

two horses for himself "and fortune will probably provide a third."[54] At Fort Edward it was discovered that government horses and wagons were being hidden in the woods and brought out only for use in transporting private goods, and as late as September 14 Burgoyne had to issue another General Order condemning the "enormous mismanagement . . . in respect to the King's carts."[55]

The whole concept of the campaign of 1776 from Canada has been criticized by almost every historian who has written about the Revolution. Whether or not it was a strategic blunder is not in the purview of this study to decide. That it was filled with tactical blunders there is no question, and fundamental among them were those related to logistics.

Military histories of the American Revolution tend largely to ignore the northern theatre of operations after 1777. There is good reason for this. After the campaign of 1775-1776 the Americans did not again attempt to draw Canada into the Revolution, and after 1777 the British mounted no further serious operations from that base. Yet, it was not intended by the British that the north should be so quiet. Although no grand operations were planned, Germain took very seriously a suggestion by Lt. Gov. Henry Hamilton of Detroit that Indians and Loyalist frontiersmen could be used effectively to harass the frontier areas of the rebellious colonies. He thus issued instructions to Carleton in 1777 to do all that he could to implement Hamilton's plan. Raids were to be mounted from the so-called "upper posts"— Oswegatchie, Niagara, Detroit, and Michilimackinac— bases in 1777 for some 1,000 British regulars. Their purpose was "to divide the attention of the Rebels and oblige them to collect a considerable force to oppose him [Hamilton], which cannot fail of weakening their main army, and facilitating the operations directed to be carried on against them

54 Pettengill, 83.
55 O'Callahan, orders of 27 Aug and 14 Sept 77.

on their quarters. . . ."[56] Further, a force of approximately 6,000 regulars was maintained in the old settled area of the St. Lawrence itself. That force was primarily defensive, but it also posed a threat to the northern flank of the rebellious colonies and on at least one occasion (1779) it was proposed that it should mount a diversionary raid from Canada in support of the army at New York.

In none of these intended roles was the northern force notably successful and in large part the reason was logistics. It had been hoped that the army in Canada could obtain the food it needed locally, but that proved from the beginning to be impossible. At best the army could count on obtaining about half the flour it needed from Canada and even that was not a very satisfactory supply; the wheat was of such poor quality and the milling facilities so crude that the flour could not be stored for any length of time. Crop failures in 1779 and 1780 added to the problems.[57]

Thus virtually all of the supplies the army required had to come from Britain. This was recognized by the Treasury. Yet in every year from 1778 to 1781 the army suffered critical shortages of supplies. In 1778 the problem was primarily one of numbers. The Treasury contracts for that year were for only 7,000, the number of regulars in Canada, but the army was in fact feeding 11,000. The difference was accounted for by employees of the army departments, Loyalists and refugees, Indian contingents, and prisoners of war, of whose presence on the ration lists Day had warned the Treasury only in general terms.[58] American privateers that swarmed in the Gulf of St. Lawrence added to the problem by taking a number of ships, including several victuallers. A problem peculiar to the supply of Canada turned up that year also. The St. Lawrence River was closed by ice for at

[56] BAHQP, 462, Germain to Carleton, 26 Mar 77.

[57] T 64/115, 26-28, 80-82, Haldimand to Robinson, 24 Oct 78, 13 Sept 79; Add. Mss. 21,715, 10, Haldimand to Robinson, 31 Oct 80.

[58] T 64/104, 14-15, Robinson to Day, 18 Apr 78; T 1/547, 370-371, Day to Robinson, 18 July 78.

least five months of the year and even in the late fall passage up the river was extremely precarious due to frequent severe storms. If ships from Britain were to be sure of making their passage to Quebec, they had to leave by the end of July at the latest. Because they were dispatched too late in the year some of the 1778 victuallers ended up at Halifax rather than Quebec.[59]

As a result of the various problems with deliveries in 1778 the army in Canada was short of provisions over the winter of 1778-1779. General Haldimand, who had taken over as governor and commander-in-chief in June 1778, requested that the contracts for 1779 be for at least 15,000 men and that the first fleet sail as early as possible in that year. The Treasury agreed to his request. In December the Canada contractors were ordered to provide nine months' supply for 3,021 men at the upper posts, plus six months' supply for 10,360 in Canada by the end of January 1779, and Gordon was directed to dispatch them by March 20. A similar quantity was ordered delivered by May 1 and dispatched by July 5.[60] But the supply was delayed at every turn. Because of shipping problems and late deliveries by contractors, the first convoy of 1779 left Cork on April 30 instead of March 20, and did not arrive in Quebec until late July. Further, of the thirteen ships in the convoy one was wrecked and two fell victim to American privateers. The second convoy, because of delays in loading, did not leave Britain until August 17 (instead of July 5) nor arrive in Canada until October 3.[61]

Despite the arrival of the two convoys in 1779, the provisions' situation in Canada at the end of that year was not

[59] T 64/115, 66-67, Haldimand to Robinson, 21 Nov 78; Add. Mss. 21,713, Germain to Haldimand, 16 Apr 79.

[60] T 64/115, 26-28, Haldimand to Robinson, 24 Oct 78; T 64/104, 18-19, Robinson to Day, 22 Dec 78.

[61] BAHQP, 2,128, 2,234, Haldimand to Clinton, 19 July, 29 Aug 79; T 64/115, 128, Haldimand to Robinson, 4 Oct 79.

bright. Not only had three victuallers in the first convoy been lost, but the numbers being fed in Canada were growing steadily. The additions to the ration rolls were partly refugees from the Thirteen Colonies and partly recruits for the Loyalist units serving in the upper country, but most were Indians. In 1779 General John Sullivan made a punitive expedition against the villages of Britain's Iroquois allies. The success of that expedition drove thousands of Indian refugees into the British posts at Niagara and Detroit, where, if they were not to die of starvation, they had to be fed from army stores. As a result Haldimand had to send rations for over 6,000 instead of the predicted 3,000 to those posts. Thus again in the fall of 1779 Haldimand had to request an increase in the size of the contracts and early shipment of the 1780 provisions.[62] Again he was disappointed.

In response to Haldimand's requests, the contracts for 1780 were increased to provide for 15,000 men for eighteen months and the contractors directed to deliver the first half of the provisions by February 14.[63] The contractors could not live up to the delivery date, however, and even when the provisions were assembled convoys proved incredibly difficult to organize. Four victuallers were finally dispatched with a fleet of merchant ships in May, and seven more victuallers, carrying the remainder of the first half of the year's provisions, left Britain on June 5. They took the northern route around Newfoundland, losing one ship in the process, and did not arrive in Quebec until the beginning of September.[64] Difficulties in obtaining escort vessels delayed the departure of the convoy with the second half

[62] T 64/112, 80-82, Haldimand to Robinson, 13 Sept 79.

[63] T 29/48, 29 July 79; T 29/49, 28 Apr 80; T 1/560, 75-79, Knox to Robinson, 25 Apr 80.

[64] Add. Mss. 21,704, 30, Germain to Haldimand, 8 Apr 80; Add. Mss. 21,714, 108-109, Haldimand to Germain, 12 Sept 80; T 1/563, 322-323, 327-328, Day to Robinson, 25 Oct, 24 Nov 78.

of the year's provisions until August 24. It immediately encountered heavy gales that dispersed it all over the North Atlantic. Not a single ship arrived at Quebec.[65]

The disaster of 1780 brought about a thorough review of Canadian provisioning and in the end detailed plans for the 1781 provisions were coordinated between the Treasury, the Navy Board, and Germain's office.[66] In early April Germain wrote confidently to Haldimand that "so large a supply of provisions will now be sent out from England and Ireland that I trust you will never again be in distress or exposed to difficulties."[67] The year 1781 did see the end of provisioning problems in Canada, but even with all the planning, the provisions for that year did not arrive until August 22.

The provisions' failures of 1778-1781 had a serious effect on the northern war during those years. The main force in Canada was without stores of provisions for a good part of the campaign season each year. It could be maintained at those times only by scattering it throughout the whole settled countryside in detachments small enough to live off local resources, leaving only small forces in the main defensive works. Had a serious attack materialized, Haldimand complained, he could not have repulsed it because without reserves of preserved food he could not hold his force together. In 1779, when the first provisions' fleet did not arrive until late July, it appeared that very situation might develop. In the fall of 1778 Admiral d'Estaing issued a proclamation, circulated widely in Quebec, calling the French Canadians back to their old loyalty and 1779 seemed to portend both an attack from without and an uprising from within. Yet Haldimand was as powerless to deal with

[65] Add. Mss. 21,704, 84, 96-102, Germain to Haldimand, 20 Mar, 12 Apr 81.

[66] CO 5/258, 122-123; T 29/49, 20 Sept 80; T 64/201, Germain to Treasury, 21 July 80.

[67] Add. Mss. 21,704, 96-102, Germain to Haldimand, 12 Apr 81.

an attack as he was to mount a diversionary raid that he had promised Clinton as an aid to the latter's operations on the Hudson. "I was under the necessity to continue the troops in quarters dispersed all over the province," he wrote later to Clinton, "that they might be more easily supplied with fresh provisions, to save what little remained of the salt, it having been reduced to a few days provisions when the victuallers arrived."[68] The shortages of provisions also frustrated Haldimand's plans to raise corps of Loyalists and French Canadians to aid in the defense of the province.[69]

But the most serious effects of the shortages were felt on operations in the upper country. The regular supply of the forces there was particularly critical. Although there were some settlers at Niagara and Detroit, and more were encouraged during the war to clear land and raise crops, the produce of the area was never sufficient to feed the forces assembled there.[70] Virtually all supplies had to be brought from Montreal, a long and difficult task. Most of the transportation was by water, but at several points along the St. Lawrence and again at Niagara the supplies had to be portaged around rapids and falls. The trip never took less than six weeks and to move a year's provisions required the services of a fleet of ships on lakes Ontario and Erie, an armada of batteaux for the St. Lawrence section, and a small army of sailors and batteauxmen.

Very early in the war a pattern for the supply of the upper posts was established. Provisions were collected at Montreal in the fall and repacked in containers suitable for the trip up-country. Over the winter sleighs moved them

68 BAHQP, 2,129, 2,234, Haldimand to Clinton, 19 July, 29 Aug 79; Add. Mss. 21,714, 34-35, 41-43, 54-57, 172-175, 18 June, 13 Sept, 14 Sept 79, 25 Oct 80.

69 Add. Mss. 21,714, 44, 92-94, Haldimand to Germain, 13 Sept 79, 12 July 80.

70 Add. Mss. 21,714, 110-112, Haldimand to Germain, 25 Oct 80; T 1/578, 50-51, Haldimand to Germain, 23 Oct 81.

around the long rapids at Lachine to storage depots at Coteau du Lac and The Cedars. When the ice broke up in the spring they were moved on to the upper posts.[71]

In 1777 and 1778 the supply for the upper posts was, apparently, adequate and operations against the American frontier proceeded with bloody success. But a crisis was building. There were sufficient provisions for 1778 only because some supplies sent out for Burgoyne's force in 1777 had not been needed. Provisions for only 7,000 were sent out from Britain in 1778 and that was not sufficient for both the army in Canada and the forces at the upper posts. Thus in the spring of 1779 only a portion of the provisions required for the upper posts was ready at Coteau du Lac and The Cedars. The remainder would have to be sent up as provisions arrived from Britain during the summer and fall. Moreover, the demand for provisions increased tremendously in that year. Although Governor Hamilton was himself captured at Vincennes in February 1779, his activities had drawn in progressively larger numbers of Indian warriors who often brought their wives and children with them. Then in the summer General Sullivan began his campaign against the Iroquois, and refugees from the devastated villages began to stream into the upper posts. By late summer the demand for rations had jumped to well over 6,000 a day. Yet not until early fall could new supplies be got to the posts. Without provisions Haldimand could not even send out the troop reinforcements the situation demanded. Further, British influence with the Indians was based in considerable part on their ability to support them. When supplies ran short, as they did in 1779, the Indians inclined to neutrality. It seemed to Haldimand, with good reason, that the whole upper country might be lost.[72] That

[71] Add. Mss. 21,714, 30-31, Haldimand to North, 18 June 79; Add. Mss. 21,715, 10, Haldimand to Robinson, 31 Oct 80.

[72] BAHQP, 2,016, 2,234, 2,252, Haldimand to Clinton, 26 May, 29 Aug, 4 Sept 79; T 64/115, 80-82, Haldimand to Robinson, 13 Sept 79, Add. Mss. 21,714, 44, Haldimand to Germain, 13 Sept 79.

might, indeed, have happened had not Sullivan, also afflicted with logistical problems, been late in launching his campaign. He was stopped short of Niagara not by the British or the Indians but by the approach of winter.

With the arrival of the second fleet from Britain in October 1779 the outlook for the upper posts for 1780 was somewhat improved. Yet the contracts for 1779 were made for volumes insufficient to meet the rate of consumption in Canada. That and the loss of three victuallers that year meant that no more provisions could be sent up-country than were sufficient to maintain the situation. It was not even possible to counter George Rogers Clark's diminutive force in the Illinois country and Haldimand had to give up the idea of establishing a base at the mouth of the Oswego River.[73]

The history of the idea of a post on the Oswego is a history in miniature of the provisions' situation in Canada. The Oswego River is the easiest communications route between Lake Ontario and the Mohawk River and had been the site of earlier forts. An American base there could have been supported from the extensive settlements on the Mohawk River and used to harass the British supply route to the upper posts. To forestall this possibility, and to establish a base for operations against the Mohawk settlements, Haldimand wanted to etablish a post there himself. He had the troops available but never the provisions. In every year from 1778 to 1781 he expressed his intention to establish the base and in every year his intention was frustrated by lack of provisions.[74]

Because of the failure of the second provisions' fleet in 1780, 1781 was another year of stalemate in the upper country. By 1782, when the situation finally did improve, the

[73] Add. Mss. 21,714, 92-94, 108-109, 110-112, Haldimand to Germain, 12 July, 17 Sept, 25 Oct 80.

[74] Add. Mss. 21,714, 57-58, 132, Haldimand to Germain, 25 Sept 79, 25 Oct 80. Haldimand finally did get his post established at Oswego in late 1781.

war was effectively over. All British commanders in North America received instructions early that year to cease offensive operations.

The last years of the war in the north were, for many reasons, anti-climactic. The extension of the war with the entry of France meant that fewer resources were available for operations in North America and that Canada, with its largely French population, was a less secure base than was the case earlier. Further, after 1778 the whole focus of the war began to shift southwards. Nevertheless, there were enormous opportunities for Britain on the frontier. The Indians, for whom the American pioneer settlers were always the enemy, were natural allies. And the St. Lawrence-Great Lakes transportation route, for all its problems, was still a better entry to the interior than any controlled by the Americans. Sullivan and Clark, by dint of enormous effort, achieved successes for the Americans but they could be neither consolidated nor followed up. The best the Rebels could hope for on the frontier was a stalemate. Britain and her Indian allies held the potential for victory, as Haldimand realized, but persistent shortages of supplies prevented that potential from becoming reality.

CONCLUSION

IN A SUMMATION OF THE LOGISTICAL PROBLEMS OF THE British army in America, one point stands out as crucial: the inability of the army to obtain any dependable supply of provisions in North America. In Canada this was because the population was small and agriculture miserably inefficient. In the Thirteen Colonies it was the result of the widespread and relatively efficient Whig organization. As seen from Britain, at least in the first few years, this was a war against a rebel faction rather than against the people of the Colonies generally. It was a war not essentially different from the dynastic wars of eighteenth-century Europe, fought by professional armies who expected and respected the neutrality of civilians. It proved instead to be a popular war, a war in which the people were involved. And there was little doubt which side the majority of the people favored. The easy disposition of most of the established governments in the colonies in 1775 and the speedy defeat of the few attempts by Loyalists to re-establish the old governments demonstrated the complete ascendance of the Whigs. Most ardent Loyalists fled to British bases or British ships in the first year. Many of those who remained were purged the following years, as the steady flow of refugees into the British bases testifies. The military effect of this Whig dominance was immense. It meant that Britain could control little more than those areas actually occupied in strength by the army and only as long as they were so occupied. As the size of the army varied, so did the area it could occupy. When a large part of General Clinton's force was detached to the West Indies in 1778, Philadelphia had to be abandoned. The army was a ship; where it moved in power it commanded, but around it was the hostile sea, parting in front but closing in behind, and always probing for signs of weakness. Whereas a defeated American army could melt back into the countryside from whence it came, a British force so circumstanced was likely to be totally lost. Its only hope was to fall back on a fortified port. If the navy was not there with its usually overwhelming power, the army might still be lost, as Yorktown demonstrated. A British army without lines of communication with the sea was, by a continuous *petite guerre* as well as by the natural processes of attrition, bound to weaken while the American force opposing it grew stronger. This was the painful lesson of Burgoyne's campaign of 1777. Advancing from Canada with his "magnificent armament," Burgoyne deliberately restricted and then cut his lines of communication with his base. He expected his march to Albany and New York to be a triumphant progress with all the army needed available for the taking. Since there were only 4,000 dispirited and disorganized American regulars opposing him, his action was not as irresponsible as some critics have supposed. But he found a population openly hostile and the countryside stripped in his path. Disease and skirmishes took their irreplaceable toll while the mass citizen army that was to overwhelm his hungry, limping force collected around the nucleus of the American regulars.[1]

In logistical terms Whig control and the general hostility of the American people meant that the British army could not expect supplies from any area it did not occupy. And the winter of 1776-1777 indicated very clearly just how much territory an army that at its greatest numbered 55,000 men but averaged only 35,000 could occupy. Howe, convinced that the American army was not only inferior but also deteriorating, confidently established posts across New Jersey to control that province. Washington thereupon demonstrated that even if he could not defeat the British

[1] Burgoyne, 13-15; Preston, et al., 174.

army as a whole, he was quite capable of destroying it piece-meal. Thereafter the army confined itself to more limited areas, leaving the countryside and its products to the enemy. But even if a larger army had been available to the British, it is doubtful that it could have been supplied from America. The area that the army did control was small, but while a larger army could control a larger area, it would also need more supplies and hence a still larger area: sufficiency was an ever-receding horizon.

The inability to obtain supplies in America meant that dependence had to be on Britain. And that in turn imposed fundamental limitations on the operations. An army that was out of touch with the sea could operate freely only for so long as the supplies it could carry with it lasted. When they ran out, the army had to move continually in search of new supplies or starve. Thus it could not hold territory. And since it had to march, it could not force an American army to battle; the Americans could choose to fight or not, and when they did fight, it was on their own terms. This is what both Burgoyne and Cornwallis discovered. Burgoyne met total disaster, and Cornwallis only narrowly avoided it. Two months on the march in North Carolina without adequate supplies seriously weakened his army, and its last strength was dissipated at the battle of Guilford Court House. Cornwallis won the battle, but as Charles James Fox pointed out, "another such victory would ruin the British Army."[2]

In the first two years of the war, this logistical imperative was generally not understood. Howe worked under the assumption that driving the American army from the field of battle in any area would return that area to loyalty to the crown or at least to neutrality, thus giving the army the required logistical base—hence the continued assumptions throughout those years that the necessity of supply from Britain was only temporary.

In 1778, in part as a result of the earlier experiences and

2 Quoted in Wickwire, *Cornwallis*, 311.

in part as a result of the withdrawal of some of the British force due to the entry of France into the war, there was a change in British thinking as to the way that the war would have to be conducted. It was decided that the Loyalists would have to be brought in as an auxiliary military force on the side of the crown. This expedient had been rejected earlier, in part because it was believed that the regular force was quite adequate to the suppression of the Rebellion, and in part because it was felt that the setting of American against American could only retard the return to conditions of tranquility. The new situation seemed to make it necessary. As seen by Germain, the new strategy was to use the regular army to regain an area then leave it to be defended by Loyalist corps with only small regular army garrisons in support. This was the course of action Cornwallis followed, and it ended in disaster. It might be argued that the strategy could have succeeded. Certainly there were more Loyalists in the South than anywhere else in the colonies. That it did not succeed was due to a number of factors, and one of them was logistics. First, there was the inability of the British to supply adequate arms and equipment for a Loyalist force. A second logistical factor, more subtle and difficult to evaluate, was the effect on the Americans of British foraging for fresh provisions and hay. The foraging operations were never gentle affairs. Although most senior officers recognized the need to carry out these operations with a minimum of disruption and distress to the civilian population, the plundering tendencies of the British and German regulars were almost impossible to restrain as the repeated injunctions against that practice in army general orders testify. The number of Americans, in the South and elsewhere, who were driven from loyalty to neutrality, or neutrality to opposition, can never be known, but it was surely large.[3] And their numbers were swelled by those who

[3] Willcox *(Portrait of a General*, 350), suggests that this was one result of Leslie's operations in Virginia in 1780. See also Wickwire, *Cornwallis*, 25-28.

were victims of the corrupt practices of commissaries, quartermasters, and barrackmasters.

Clinton rejected the strategy of using Loyalists and regular army detachments to hold large areas of the colonies. He saw in the defeats of the winter of 1776-1777 the danger of detachments, and in the fate of Burgoyne's expedition the danger of attempting to depend on the loyalty, or even the neutrality, of the Americans. The only strategy he thought to be viable was that pursued by Howe. He sought, by striking at strategic points, to bring the American army to decisive battle and through its destruction bring the colonies to submission. But to carry out that plan he needed large and dependable reserves of supplies. They were seldom available to him.

Why Clinton and his predecessors did not have the supplies necessary for their campaigns is the basic logistical question of the war. The answer to that question lies fundamentally in the inability of the British administration to respond adequately to the challenges of the war. The American war demanded of the administration a level of initiative, efficiency, and cooperation never before required of it. It could not meet these demands, at least not before Britain lost the will to continue the struggle.

The problems began at the highest level, that of interdepartmental cooperation. They were in no small part due to the fact that the heads of departments, with the exception of the Secretary at War, were also members of the cabinet and not unwilling to carry disagreements on cabinet decisions into obstruction of the Secretary of State's executive plans. In this respect the Admiralty was probably the most guilty department of all. Germain once complained that if the First Lord of the Admiralty approved operations decided on by the cabinet, ships were always available; if he disapproved, none could be found.[4] The logistical problems that the Admiralty helped produce, while perhaps not quite so basic, were nevertheless signifi-

---

[4] Mackesy, 20.

cant. That department, for instance, was given the task of enforcing the embargo placed by Parliament on trade with the rebellious colonies and for this purpose instituted a licensing system for all ships sailing from Britain to America. Given the extent of smuggling, this was not unreasonable. However, in June 1776 Robert Gordon, the commissary at Cork, informed the Treasury that Admiralty agents there insisted that army victuallers be licensed and that applications be accompanied by exact cargo manifests. As the ships involved were loaded at Cork and applications had to be made in London, sailings could be delayed for weeks or months.[5] Although food shortages plagued the army and shipping was at a premium, the best the Treasury could work out with the Admiralty was a compromise: ships were still to be licensed for each voyage, but the cargo manifests could be made up at Cork.[6]

As irritating as the problem of licenses, and perhaps the most galling of the navy's practices, was that of pressing seamen from army victuallers. Low pay, harsh discipline, and vile living conditions made recruiting a perpetual problem for the navy. Captains anxious to have their complements full and their ships ready were forced to raid civilian ships, including those employed in the Treasury victualling service, for the men they needed. The Treasury complained steadily about this practice, but it never entirely ceased. As late as 1779, indiscriminate navy press raids were still carried out. One such raid virtually immobilized a victualling fleet assembled at Cork and led the Lords Commissioners of the Treasury to warn the Admiralty that unless it disciplined its officers "it will be utterly impossible for the [Treasury] Board to supply H.M. troops. . . ."[7] To be fair, it must be pointed out that the Admiralty did issue orders against the pressing of men from army victuallers. But,

[5] AO 16/10, 33-34, Robinson to Knox, Robinson to Stephens, 16 June 76.

[6] *Ibid.*, 49, Robinson to Gordon, 29 July 76.

[7] T 29/48, Treasury Board Minutes, 5 Feb 79.

equally, it should be noted that naval captains faced with the choice of a reprimand for disobeying this order or for failing to keep their ships' complements up to strength often chose the former. Such was the case even when the Navy Board took over the army victualling service. Thus when a Cork fleet arrived in New York in 1780, press gangs from Admiral Rodney's fleet, then in port, pressed virtually every able-bodied man on it. Only the most urgent personal pleas from Clinton returned the men to their ships and the fleet to Cork.[8] In this case the situation ended happily, but it was not always so. H.M.S. *Diomede* escorted the victualler *Hercules* to Charleston in 1782. Then, following what was by then time-honored practice, stripped her of most of her crew just off Charleston bar. As a result the *Hercules* went aground trying to work into the harbor, and part of her cargo was lost.[9]

As long as the Howe brothers, general and admiral, were in command in America, cooperation between the army and navy on actual operations was generally good. When they retired, however, relations between the services deteriorated, with often disastrous results. The running battles between Sir Henry Clinton and most of the admirals assigned to the American station have been amply chronicled elsewhere,[10] but it is worth noting again that the by-product (and also a cause) of these disputes was the frequent failure of naval protection of army supply and communication routes in America. In 1779, for instance, for want of a naval escort, a fleet of nine supply ships had to be dispatched to the army in Georgia with no other convoy than a privateer. Seven of the ships fell victim when the fleet was attacked by a small American force.[11] In succeeding years even communications between New York and outlying posts on Long Island were endangered, and the army had frequent occa-

8 CP, Clinton to Rodney, 12, 13, Nov 80.
9 T 64/119, Paumier to Watson, 5 Oct 82.
10 Willcox, *Portrait of a General*, passim.
11 Mellish Papers, Dr. Hays to Mellish, 4 May 79.

sion to complain bitterly of the lack of escorts for ships carrying rice from the south to New York and for empty victuallers returning from New York to Cork.[12]

The Board of Ordnance could be equally exasperating in its conduct. It did not have the same selfish disregard for objectives other than its own that was behind most of the problems with the Admiralty and its captains, but its procedures were slow and cumbersome and produced, inevitably, delays and shortages. On it the arming of naval ships and victuallers depended, but ships regularly lay idle for months waiting for the Board to act on requisitions. Lord Sandwich, the First Lord of the Admiralty, found the delay on at least one occasion "mortifying beyond imagination."[13] And when Clinton sent General Dalrymple home in the fall of 1780 to discuss with the government a number of important questions about the conduct of the war, he instructed him specifically to go into the question of ordnance supplies: "Our Artillery stores are delayed too long. G[eneral] Pattison [senior Artillery officer in America] told me he had made a requisition last March to a very considerable amount. We hear nothing of it, we have no small arms and are so much in want of powder that I scarcely dare fire a salute or permit the troops to practice. Pray trace these neglects to their source and complain *loudly* of them."[14]

By the following May the demand for small arms was still not satisfied, and an expedition to the Chesapeake was supplied with a few extra muskets only by disarming the New York City militia.[15] Even when providing for its own, the ordnance department could be incredibly lax. Almost despairing of his troops' receiving their regular clothing

---

[12] Add. Mss. 34,416, 311-12, Clinton to Eden 3 Apr 79; CP, Clinton to [?], 3 Apr 79, Robinson to Clinton 23 Jan 81, Balfour to Clinton, 1 Dec. 81. See also ch. II, 73, ch. III, 97-98, 132-133.

[13] Mackesy, 18.

[14] CP, Clinton to Dalrymple, 30 Oct 80.

[15] *Ibid.*, Clinton to Germain, 13 May 81.

allowance in 1778, General Pattison was driven to write to his superiors in London "I presume if we are to continue here it is not intended to be in a state of nakedness."[16] But his problems were mild compared with those of the artillery detachment in Halifax. In 1778 it had been three years without a clothing issue.[17]

But the main problem of logistical administration did not lie in want of cooperation between government departments. It lay, rather, in the departments themselves, or at least within areas of clear administrative authority and responsibility. General Pattison put his finger on it when he noted in a letter to the Board of Ordnance complaining of clothing shortages that "want of method and a regular system must necessarily create intricacies and confusion. . . ."[18] No better capsule illustration of the problem is available than a letter from Secretary at War Charles Jenkinson to Clinton in 1779, four years after the war began. Jenkinson complained that the War Office had never received regular and accurate returns of the army in America. He was thus unable to give "His Majesty and Parliament that accurate information respecting the troops in America which is from time to time expected and required from me."[19]

The inefficiency both men were pointing to was characteristic of eighteenth-century British administrations. It was not that they were necessarily inefficient with respect to their traditional tasks. Rather, they were anything but adaptable when it came to new tasks and highly unlikely to approach them with "method and a regular system." The root of the problem lay in both the administrators and the administrative philosophy. In this enlightened age we at least like to believe that people are hired and promoted because of their competence. Such was not the case in the eighteenth century. The engrossing needs of the patronage

[16] RAI, Ms. 7, 146, Pattison to Gen. Cleveland, 17 Sept 78.
[17] *Ibid.*, 86, Pattison to Board of Ordnance, March 78.
[18] *Ibid.*, Ms. 7, 59-60, Pattison to Board of Ordnance, 3 Mar 78.
[19] WO 4/274, 187-188, Jenkinson to Clinton, 5 Apr 79.

system had reached into every level of administration to the extent that, as J.E.D. Binney pointed out with respect to the Treasury, "no clerk entered . . . without the influence of a patron behind him."[20] The concomitants of this, at least in the lower ranks of the administration, were promotion by seniority alone and extreme laxity of disicpline; the result, abounding incompetence and inefficiency to which even the competent and efficient eventually succumbed.[21]

In the upper ranks of the administration—and indeed of the army itself—the problem of patronage was compounded by that of amateurism, the idea that the educated gentleman, the "well-rounded man," could handle any task he set his hand to. Thus "gentlemen" became army officers and administrators without the least hint of specialized training.[22] At best this meant a period of on-the-job training that could be painful for the army; at worst it meant incompetence and disaster. During the war of the American Revolution, Britain's military forces, particularly the army, faced tasks of unprecedented magnitude and complexity. To support them required an administration of unprecedented efficiency, capable of adaptation and innovation. It was not forthcoming. The system, while not rejecting the efficient, coddled the inefficient, and, as is the wont of such systems,

[20] J.E.D. Binney, *British Public Administration and Finance, 1774-1792* (Oxford, 1958), 181.

[21] This whole analysis of the nature of British administration in the eighteenth century, while confirmed by my own investigations, is drawn from a number of monographs, the most important of which are: Baker, Mackesy, Binney and F. B. Wickwire, *British Subministers and Colonial America 1763-1783* (Princeton, 1966).

[22] The career of William Lord Cathcart in America demonstrates the system at its worst. He joined the army in 1777 as cornet of dragoons and quickly became one of Clinton's aides de camp. He obtained promotion to captain in the same year, to major in 1778, and lt. col. in 1781. In 1779, straight from Clinton's "family," he took over, temporarily, the job of quartermaster general. When he was not confirmed in the office permanently and did not get the job of adjutant general, he returned to England. (CP, Clinton to Lincoln, Apr 80, Cathcart to Clinton 15 Mar 80.)

only slowly and reluctantly broke the bonds of precedent to meet the new challenges thrown up to it.

Nowhere was the problem of organization and competence more apparent than in the Treasury and its associated army department, the commissary general's office. These departments bore the major burden of logistical responsibility during the war. Since long before the American war, of course, the Treasury had been involved in army logistics. However, its task had been largely the administration of contracts; it had little contact with the reality of supply. The American war not only increased the magnitude of the Treasury's task but brought it into direct involvement in supply. It had not merely to let contracts but search out sources for new kinds of supplies, arrange for storage and transportation, and worry about quality, quantity, and delivery dates. To be sure, supplies still came from contractors, and most of the rest of the work was done by Treasury commissaries such as Robert Gordon at Cork and the various commissary generals in America. But there remained with the Treasury the vital task of overall direction and coordination. Insofar as one existed at all, it was the nerve center of army logistics. Yet there was no apparent feeling in the Treasury that a special situation existed that required an expansion of the number of people in the office, or even that people with technical competence in either the commissary or commercial aspects of the task were needed. As a result the department not only was understaffed but maintained a degree of naivete with respect to the various commercial transactions and technical problems in which it became involved that was inevitably detrimental to the welfare of the army. These shortcomings of the department were manifested in a number of situations. In the first four years of the war the army experienced a series of provisions crises that, if not entirely the fault of the Treasury, could in many cases have been anticipated and more competently dealt with by a better prepared department.[23] It was not, of

---

[23] A full analysis of these crises is contained in ch. III.

course, necessarily a failing of the department that problems occurred; under the circumstances some were inevitable. Rather, the failing of the department lay in its continued inability to cope with them. Nothing illustrates this better than the problem of sub-standard provisions. Army complaints about the quality of the provisions shipped from Britain began with the arrival of the first victuallers in 1775 and continued, convoy after convoy, year after year. It was not until 1779 that commissaries could report the quality generally acceptable and not until the Navy Board took over the task of inspection and shipping in the following year that complaints from the army were reduced to an acceptable level. There was considerable controversy as to whether responsibility for bad provisions lay with the contractors, shipping, or methods of inspection and storage at Cork and in America, but the point here is not one of responsibility but that for three and a half years the Treasury was unable to find a solution to the problem.[24] Similarly, the Treasury seemed unable or unwilling to force its contractors to comply with delivery dates agreed to in contracts and the army suffered accordingly. Again, it was not until the Navy Board took over that this problem was eventually solved.[25] Further, the Treasury could even be unsure of what it expected of its own appointees. It was usual for the recipient of a commission to receive formal instruction to set precisely the bounds of his authority, to establish his relationship to other officers, and to guide him in the performance of his duties. When Wier took office as commissary general, however, apparently all he was offered by way of instructions from the Treasury were copies of recent correspondence between that department and the army. Five years later when Brook Watson took office, he received no more assistance.[26] This failing in the case of the commissary general is perhaps understandable since he held two commissions and was responsible to two masters, but the same

24 *Ibid.*   25 T 29/49, 4 Nov. 79; Baker, 43-50.
26 T 29/52, 1 Apr 82.

failing in the case of Duncan Drummond, the commissary of accounts, was inexcusable. Drummond was appointed to office in early 1779, but a year later was still without instructions. He finally took up his duties without them, but for want of the formal authority that the instructions would have provided, the one chance for an independent inspection of the commissary general's accounts was lost.[27]

The relation of the evidence that indicates the Treasury's inability to handle the task that fell to it could go on indefinitely, but one more case—the problem of adapting supply to the needs of the army—will suffice at this point. Since before the war provisions were contracted for annually by the Treasury in terms of whole rations that included meat, bread (or flour) and small species—butter, pease, oatmeal, and rice. When the troops were actually on campaign, however, the small species were seldom issued, and as a result commissaries in America began to report, as early as 1777, embarrassingly large surpluses of these items. At times they overflowed the inadequate warehousing facilities of New York, and ships desperately needed elsewhere were detained to accommodate them. Suggestions for changes or adjustments in the contracts to eliminate these surpluses were made by the commissaries in 1777, 1778, and 1781,[28] but it was not until the fall of the latter year that the Treasury even began to act.[29] Even so, the Navy Board took up the

[27] BAHQP, 2,964, Drummond to Captain Smith, 14 Aug 80; CP, Drummond to Robinson, 30 Mar 81. Wier considered himself responsible to the Treasury only and refused to open his accounts to Drummond. By the time that Drummond procured a letter from the Treasury giving him specific authorization to inspect commissary accounts, Wier was on his death bed. He died a short time later, and his accounts were packed up by his executors and shipped to England. Drummond never got at them.

[28] HSP, Wier Letter Book, Wier to Robinson, 20 May, 8 June, 12 July, 25 Oct 77; T 64/114, 20-22, 5 May 78; T 1/577, 294-295, Morrison to Robinson, 12 Mar 82; T 1/569, 29, Morrison to Robinson, 2 July 81; T 1/570, 205-206, Townsend to Robinson, 23 Mar 82.

[29] T 64/119, 43, Robinson to Wier, 4 Sept 81.

same complaint in 1782.[30] Similarly, in 1779 Peter Paumier, the deputy commissary general in the South, suggested that butter be eliminated from the rations for the troops there since it quickly melted and turned rancid in the heat. Again no action resulted.[31] Further, when the troops were in the field the lack of small species was compensated for by an extra three ounces of pork per day. Although the Treasury was informed of this practice very early, no attempt was made to compensate for it in ration contracting.[32] Throughout the war the army continued to accumulate huge stocks of "small species" that, if they did not rot first, came into use only on those occasions when supplies of bread and meat failed. And the Treasury was continually bewildered by the rate at which the army used up its meat rations.

The commissary general's department, because it was so much a product of the war, demonstrates far more change and adaptation than the Treasury, but, nevertheless, its problems were basically the same. It did not get off to a good start in the war at all. The first commissary general, Daniel Chamier, was a patronage appointment, owing his position to the influence of his brother Anthony with Lord Barrington.[33] Appointed in 1773, Chamier was satisfactory as a peacetime commissary, but less than adequate as a wartime commissary general. His inadequate procedures for accounting for provisions used and in store were in large measure responsible for provisions' crises in 1776 and 1778.[34] His department's lack of organization made a tactical error involved when the army moved from Long Island to Throg's Neck in October 1776 more serious than it needed to be.[35] After giving him an early vote of confidence,

30 WO 60/24, Commissioners of the Navy to Treasury, 12 July 82; Add. Mss., 22,707, 92, Navy Board to Treasury, 16 July 82.

31 T 64/120, 1-2, Paumier to Robinson, 20 June 79; Baker, 34-37.

32 HSP, Wier Letter Book, Wier to Robinson, 20 May 77.

33 *London Evening Post*, 15 June 76.

34 See ch. III, 113-121.

35 Clinton, *The American Rebellion*, 49.

Howe came to trust Chamier so little that he conducted all the important correspondence with the Treasury about provisioning himself. Chamier was replaced in 1777 for a number of reasons, among which were probably age and health as well as incompetence, but the same influence that got him his first appointment then secured him the position of commissary of accounts. As it proved, he was unable to handle it either.

Daniel Wier, Chamier's successor, was a much more judicious appointment. A senior commissary with the army in Germany during the Seven Years' War, he then became involved in trade with both East and West Indies and so had considerable experience behind him.[36] In the appointment of deputy and assistant commissaries, however, the old failing was still apparent. Of the six people appointed to these positions by royal warrant in 1776, only one, Peter Paumier, can be positively identified as a man of previous experience. John Morrison, although recently a major in the East India Company service, had as his chief qualification that he was an "old acquaintance" of North. James Christie and James Brindley were Loyalists who fled early to England and qualified for commissions via the King's sympathy.[37] When, during the war, further appointments were made, those originating in America tended to be much more rational than those coming from London. Howe in 1776 named Gregory Townsend, Frederick William Hecht, William Butler, and Anthony Knecht, all of whom were experienced in army commissariat duties, to be assistant commissaries.[38] But from London came such appointments as Abijah Willard,

[36] BAHQP, 1,449, Memorial to Anthony Knecht, 5 Mar 79; Minute Books of the West India Committee, vol. I, 4 Mar 77; *New Complete Guide to All Persons Who Have Any Concern With the City of London* (London, 1772).

[37] BAHQP, 165-166, North to Howe, 26 Apr 76; T 64/106, 26-28, Robinson to Howe, 12 Apr 76; T 64/113, 166.

[38] BAHQP, 1,449, Memorial to Anthony Knecht, 5 Mar 79; T 64/108, 47-49, Memorials of William Butler, F. W. Hecht, and Gregory Townsend.

a dispossessed member of the Massachusetts Council,[39] and Francis Rush Clark, the erstwhile Commissary of His Majesty's Provisions Train. Clark's papers reveal him as one of the most miserable examples of the evils of the patronage system. His only virtue was that he came in time to recognize his own incompetence. In the sometimes vicious intrigues of army headquarters, command of the wagon service soon slipped out of his grasp, and he ended up the war as assistant commissary of forage at Charleston, a position much more suited to his abilities.[40] But Clark's case stands out; it was not easy to demote or get rid of incompetents. John Morrison was removed as chief commissary at Rhode Island on the complaint of the officer commanding there, only to be appointed later to the same position at Charleston despite the objection of one senior military officer that he was "by no means equal to the business."[41] And the competence of both Hecht and Butler was seriously questioned at times by their fellow commissaries.[42] A letter from Nathaniel Day, the commissary general with the army in Canada, to his deputy John Drummond at Quebec illustrates well the depths that incompetence could reach and the despair that it could inspire in others. "I cannot help being very unhappy," Day wrote, "seeing at this critical time the provisions of the field stopped by sending in lieu pease for garrison consumption, notwithstanding I gave you such clear and positive directions to forward flour, bread, beef & pork, and if these directions are not tended to, destruction must fall upon my department, as it must be the means of ruining the army in the field. Send forthwith

[39] T 27/33, 445, Robinson to Clinton, 7 Jan 81.

[40] Francis Rush Clark Papers.

[41] N-YHS, Wier Letter Book, Wier to Butler, 5 May 79; PRO 30/11/70, 26-29, Balfour to Cornwallis, 2 Dec 81.

[42] N-YHS, Wier Letter Book, Wier to Butler, 5 May 79, Wier to Paumier, 10 Aug 79; PRO 30/11/3, 173, Geo. Turnbull to Cornwallis, 2 Oct 80; T 29/51, 18 Mar 82.

flour, bread, beef & pork to Sorell. I want no pease nor small species; the pease you have sent is become a burthen as the unloading and lodging take up time. . . ."[43] Despite their failings, however, Drummond, Hecht, and Butler remained permanent fixtures of the establishment.

However, the problem in neither the commissariat nor the Treasury lay in incompetent personnel alone. It lay also in the failure of both organizations to recognize the implications of the situations they faced. The Treasury was aware that the army depended on supplies sent from Britain. It also recognized that it was responsible for both ordering them and ensuring that they were delivered on time and in good condition. But it was a department cast by time and tradition in a passive mold and the task that fell to it required active, even ruthless, executive supervision. This was not merely beyond its competence but also its comprehension. It brought to contracting invaluable experience and, however much it groaned about costs, never skimped on quantity or quality. But all its other activities were marked by indecision and an unwillingness to use authority, as was the case with bad provisions and late deliveries. It was not until the Navy Board was persuaded in 1779 to take over the active aspects of the Treasury's task that the logistical problems of the army were put on the way to solution. The commissary general's department under Wier, although considerably more effective than it had been under Chamier, demonstrated the same failing. Wier received his commissary training with the army in Europe during the Seven Years' War, where it had been possible to supply the army through the organization of local supplies. As commissary general in America he was most competent at this task. There was little that could be done towards feeding the army from America that he did not do. Indeed, on at least one occasion when supplies from Britain failed, Clinton credited the salvation of the army to his ability to

[43] T 1/534, 146-147, Day to Drummond, 12 May 77.

glean food from the countryside.[44] But despite these occasions, the army did depend basically on Britain and that dependence demanded a very different set of skills. It demanded the development of an efficient system for the reception and unloading of supply ships to ensure the quick turn-around of scarce shipping. It demanded a good warehousing and distribution system so that supplies that came from Britain in quantities sometimes sufficient to feed the army for six months could be dealt with easily and with a minimum of wastage. Most of all, it meant an efficient system of accounting so that the state of provisions could be ascertained at any time and future needs accurately determined. Yet in none of these tasks did Wier really succeed. Complaints from Britain that supply ships were delayed overlong in North America began in 1776 and went on without interruption until 1782.[45] At least in part the delays complained of resulted from poor unloading facilities and lack of warehousing, which meant that ships had to be used as warehouses.[46] One of the reasons for Chamier's removal was his persistent failure to provide adequate reports of provisions on hand and of the numbers being fed, but six months after Wier's appointment the Treasury had occasion to complain of his returns also and over a year later, in January 1779, was still complaining. It was not until April 1779 that Robinson professed himself satisfied with the returns, but on a number of occasions thereafter had nevertheless to chide Wier for neglecting to provide, with each return, an estimate of how long provisions on hand would last.[47] In part this failing can be attributed to depu-

[44] Newcastle Papers, NeC. 2,623, Clinton to [William Eden], 14 Aug 80.

[45] For example: T 64/106, 29-44, Robinson to Howe, 1 May 76; T 64/119, 10-11, 9 Jan 78; CP, Robinson to Clinton, 29 July 80; T 64/107, 80, Rose to Carleton, 26 Sept 82.

[46] HSP, Wier Letter Book, Wier to Robinson, 25 Oct 77; T 64/107, 65, Robinson to Clinton, 26 July 81.

[47] T 64/119, Robinson to Wier, 26 Sept 77, 25 Nov 77, 6 Dec 77, 9 Jan 78, 3 Sept 78, 31 Oct 78, 19 Jan 79, 6 Apr 79, 6 Aug 79, 3 Mar 81.

ties and assistants who, Wier complained, persistently failed to turn in the regular and accurate returns that were indispensable to adequate accounting. Wier probably did not have the power to discipline his subordinates in any serious way—and therein lay part of the problem—but also there is no indication that he ever sought to do so, or, more important, that he ever sought to introduce new procedures that would at least in part have alleviated the problem. One possible solution would have been to introduce standardized forms for all routine procedures, but there is no indication that Wier ever attempted such a reform. Indeed, his own returns submitted to the Treasury displayed an undesirable degree of individuality in organization, content, and size. It was not until 1780 that any sort of standardization appeared and the use of printed forms began.[48] Only in the same year, too, was the requirement made that all formations, military and civilian, with the army submit weekly reports of their ration strengths. The main purpose of the reports was to allow accurate accounting of the stoppages to be assessed against each unit for rations drawn, but they also served other purposes. They allowed more accurate and regular accountings of the numbers fed and tended to eliminate the double rationing that occurred when a detachment drew rations at its point of duty while its regiment continued to draw for full strength.[49] For neither of these reforms, however, could Wier take credit. Printed forms appeared first at the lower levels of the department and were not generally used in the commissary general's office until Brook Watson took over in 1782. The reporting requirement came as a result of a general economy drive, not from any commissariat initiative. Wier had attempted to introduce a system of weekly returns in 1778, but when it failed—for reasons not entirely within his control—he never renewed the effort.

Any assessment of the efficiency of the army logistical sys-

[48] T 1/568.
[49] Mackenzie Papers, General Order, 5 Apr 80.

tem must take into consideration one more factor: communications. No large organization can function coherently without efficient communications. The more complex the organization and the more complex the methods it seeks to use, the greater the dependence on them. It is, indeed, communications that determine the size of the organization, the complexity of the operations that it can undertake, and the area over which it can operate. Communications in turn, of course, depend on the means available. In our age of electronic marvels, supersonic aeroplanes, and ships whose size is measured in hundreds of thousands of tons, worldwide organizations are possible. In the eighteenth century, dependence lay on wind-driven ships and horse-drawn vehicles and the possibilities were distinctly limited. A simple exchange of messages between America and Britain required at least three months, and twice that time was not unusual. These were hardly ideal conditions for the conduct of extended operations, and there are strong indications that the British army in America was operating at the extreme edge of its communications possibilities, and hence of its ability to act as a coordinated unit. This was certainly the case with operations organized from Europe, as the disaster to Burgoyne indicates, and both Howe and Clinton were right to reject further attempts to dictate tactics from London. But this could also be the case within the American theatre of operations itself. Cornwallis has been criticized for setting up a virtually independent command in the South in 1781, and Clinton for allowing him to do so, but in communications terms that outcome was almost inevitable. Cornwallis summed up the problem when he commented on "the delay and difficulties in conveying letters, and the impossibility of waiting for answers."[50]

The logistical limitations posed by the communications context were, if anything, more severe. From 1775 to 1783 the basic dependence of the army for food and material lay upon Britain. For the army to survive and operate, an effi-

[50] Wickwire, *Cornwallis*, 325.

cient communications route of unprecedented length in time and distance had to be established; it was years before this was accomplished. Perhaps the situation would have been better had a logistical system adaptable to the wartime problems existed at the start of the war. However, not only did an organization have to be developed, but, as indicated earlier in this chapter, it had to be done within an administration framework that was anything but adaptable. Indeed, the administrative approach to the problem of communications could be as unimaginative as it was to the other aspects of logistics. Thomas Hutchison noted this when he visited the offices of the American Secretary in 1776. "I was surprised," he later wrote in his diary, "to see Mr. P[ownall] and Mr. K[nox] looking over the letter book to see by what vessels the orders went. In my business as a merchant I never wrote a letter of consequence but I tracked the ship it went by from the hour she sailed, and was anxious to inquire by every opportunity after her arrival; but the way here is to send letters from the office of the Secretary of State to the Admiralty, to go as soon as may be. Some little thing or other hinders the sailing of the ship, and the Admiralty do not consider, or perhaps do not know, of the importance of the Secretary of State's dispatches, the ship lies five or six weeks, and the dispatches answer to no purpose."[51]

This chapter contains much censure of administrators and administrative departments, and necessarily so since incompetence and lack of adaptability in both was at the root of many of the army's logistical problems. However, the historical context must be kept in mind. This was not an age noted for administrative competence, and if the army logistical administration was, as a whole, no better than administrations in general, it was also no worse. Given the impediments of patronage appointments, amateurism, and lack of initiative, compounded by the problems of commu-

[51] Diary of Thomas Hutchison, vol. 2, 44-45, entry of 8 May 1776. Quoted in Anderson, 87.

nications, five years was probably not an unreasonable gestation period for an efficient logistical administration. However, by 1781 the war was lost. Further, the war administration as a whole suffered from the lack of what Thomas Hutchison referred to as "one great director," a man to oversee and give vitality to the war administration—another Pitt. North was constitutionally unsuited to the task, and no one else in the administration had the necessary political stature.[52] One may doubt that the presence of a Pitt at Whitehall would have changed the outcome of the war, but there is little doubt that it could have improved the logistical situation of the army by enforcing greater cooperation between government departments. For instance, there is little question but that the Navy Board was better equipped than the Treasury to handle the task of collecting, inspecting, and shipping provisions for the army. The Treasury itself recognized this and requested in 1777 that that department take on the task.[53] The Navy Board refused, and without a "great director" to appeal to the refusal stuck until 1779. While the Treasury learned, the army suffered.

But for all the failures of the British logistical organization, it still remains a fact that the army in America was seldom in truly desperate circumstances. That being the case, it must be asked how much Clinton's inactivity was due to his supply situation. One is reminded of a bit of Churchilliana that records an exchange of messages between the Prime Minister and a British general having a hard time of it in World War II. The general's signal told of food and supplies running low, morale running lower still, and after more in the same vein concluded: "we are living under a volcano." Churchill's reply was brief: "Where else do you expect to live?" There is a temptation to apply Churchill's analysis to Clinton's situation, particu-

[52] Mackesy, 20-24.   [53] Syrett, 132-133.

larly in view of Professor Willcox's analysis of Clinton's personality as cautious and unsure.[54] If Clinton had been able to combine his own strategic sense and capacity for planning with the audacity of Cornwallis, or even Howe, Washington might have been brought to bay and the war won. But an analysis of Clinton's inactivity based on his character alone is inadequate. He was not justified in taking long chances: if his army was lost, so was the war. Undertaking extensive operations without adequate logistical support was to risk just that. From the time he took command until almost the middle of 1781, the army was only once in a sound logistical position, and, significantly, Clinton moved at that time against Charleston. That is not to say that lack of supplies was alone responsible for Clinton's inactivity. Willcox's analysis of his inner conflicts is too convincing to permit such a simplistic analysis. But it is clear that in the progressive dejection and disillusionment that Willcox describes, Clinton's consistently bad logistical position played a significant part. In his letters home, which reveal this disillusionment and his feeling that he was being abandoned and prepared as a scapegoat in a war which the government had already given up as lost, he consistently linked his provisions' situation with his other complaints. The provisions' crises of 1778 discouraged him, but when the deepest crisis of all finally ended in January 1779, he could still hope that in the future the situation would improve. But the promised reinforcements did not arrive on time and his provisions' situation, at least until early autumn, improved only from the impossible to the bad. In July he wrote to Eden: " 'Tis needless to complain of your neglect of us. With what you send us, when it arrives we

[54] Willcox, *Portrait of a General*, ch. XII; W. B. Willcox and F. Wyatt, "Sir Henry Clinton: A Psychological Exploration in History," *William and Mary Quarterly*, Third Series, XVI, January 1959; R. A. Bowler, "Sir Henry Clinton and Army Profiteering: A Neglected Aspect of the Clinton-Cornwallis Controversy," *William and Mary Quarterly*, Third Series, XXXI, No. 1, Jan 1974.

will do the best. We are told part of [the force with General Grant in the West Indies] returns to us. For what we get we shall be thankful, and as I must stay [as commander-in-chief] this campaign, I will work my utmost. But you must expect nothing from an army in fact above 20,000 less than S[ir] W[illiam] H[owe] had, and W[ashingto]n's very little diminished. Let who will command, if this cursed war goes on great alterations must be made in the manner of conducting it.

"The Rebel fleet is grown so insolent that they brave our coast, and our whole fleet must be assembled to protect us. I tremble for [the provisions' fleet] from Cork."[55]

In the following year when his complaints again reached a peak, logistics was a major focus. He wrote to Eden in the middle of August:

"What is the new contract of supply? Had not Mr. Wier exerted himself all was finished on the 7th of this month, no hint even of a Cork fleet. Why all this neglect? Perhaps you blame us for not returning the victuallers immediately to Cork; it cannot be, while expedition goes on, they must attend it; they have however been discharged from us these three months, & the Admiral does not send them home tho' we repeatedly apply. Well I will endeavor to forget we have missed an opportunity of attempting an important stroke, and in perfect good humour attend the Admiral, or at least send General officers to him for that purpose, to consult on future operations.

"For God's sake send us money, men, and provisions, or expect nothing but complaints. Send out another admiral or let me go home."[56]

Two weeks later he wrote again, expressing even greater dejection: "I have no money, no provisions, nor indeed any account of the sailing of the Cork fleet, nor admiral that I can have the least dependence on, no army. In short, I have

---

[55] CP, Clinton to Eden, 2 July 79.
[56] Newcastle Papers, NeC. 2,623, Clinton to [Eden], 14 Aug 80.

nothing left but the hope for better times and a little more attention."[57]

Much of Clinton's sense of neglect was ill-founded, but that concerning provisions was not. His continuously bad provisions' situation was very real and was due, not to neglect, but to the failure of the administration in Britain to develop an adequate logistical organization.

And insofar as it can be said that Clinton's inactivity was a result of the logistical situation, then logistics had another more subtle but not less serious effect. Bad provisions and shortages always endangered army morale, but so long as battles were being fought and victory a possibility, morale was usually high.[58] When these problems were combined with inactivity, the result could be disastrous. Clinton's conviction that he was being neglected seems to have affected the army both directly, in the sense that others shared in it, and indirectly in the sense that inactivity brought with it a loss of sense of purpose. This is the subtle message carried in the comments of Rodney and the other officers on the state of the army in the later years of the war related in Ch. V; they were describing an army in the process of disintegration. And in a war that has lost its purpose, it is easy for some to justify the sort of corruption that went on in the army service departments. That in turn had a further demoralizing effect on the rest of the army.

The above analysis, of course, is in large measure speculation. But any attempt to isolate the effect of one factor in a situation as complex as a war must necessarily be so. It is certainly not claimed as a conclusion of this study that logistical problems explain the loss of the Thirteen Colonies to Britain. That can be explained only in the context

[57] Clinton to [Eden], 1 Sept 80, Clinton, *American Rebellion*, 456.

[58] See, for instance, the humorous parody of the Lord's Prayer, composed by the soldiers on Rode Island (*supra* 106). And according to Sgt. Lamb the morale of the British army never faltered even under the appalling conditions it endured during Cornwallis' march across North Carolina (R. Lamb, *An Original and Authentic Journal*, 381.)

of a hundred years of British history. Nor can it be claimed that the failure of the British army in America during the war was the result of unsolved logistical problems. But it is clear that in any analysis of that failure, logistical problems must have a significant place.

APPENDIX

The following graph of the army's provisions' reserves from 1775 through 1781 has been compiled from commissary reports found in a large number of document collections. Most of the reports are in the T 1 and T 64 series in the Public Record Office. Many more came from the War Office records in the same repository, and from the Clinton and Mackenzie Papers in the William L. Clements Library. The letter books of Daniel Wier in the New-York Historical Society and the Historical Society of Pennsylvania were invaluable also.

The graph cannot pretend to complete accuracy. There are periods for which there are no returns at all and for other periods, as indicated in Ch. III, the returns are highly inaccurate. Further, the army not infrequently obtained considerable quantities of food from the countryside and records of this are often incomplete. The chart also records only the stocks of flour—or bread—and meat; when stocks of the two have differed significantly, I have taken the average. As a general rule the graph can be considered accurate to within no more than fifteen percent.

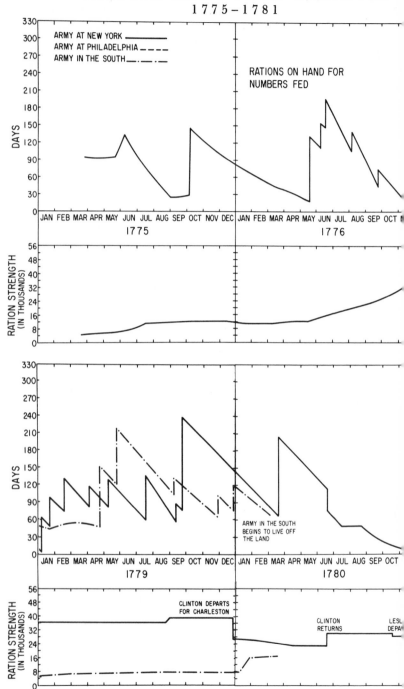

BRITISH ARMY FOOD RESERVES
1775–1781

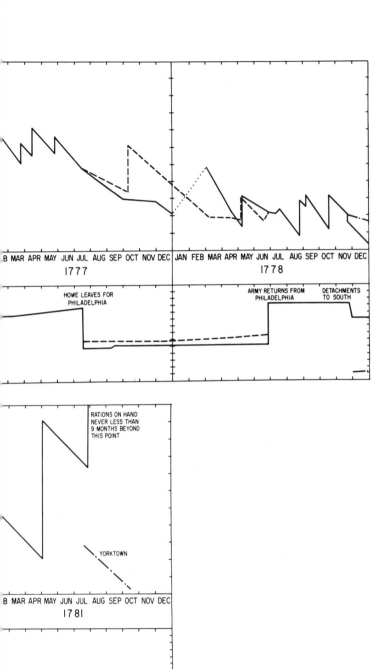

B MAR APR MAY JUN JUL AUG SEP OCT NOV DEC
1777
JAN FEB MAR APR MAY JUN JUL AUG SEP OCT NOV DEC
1778

HOWE LEAVES FOR
PHILADELPHIA

ARMY RETURNS FROM
PHILADELPHIA

DETACHMENTS
TO SOUTH

RATIONS ON HAND
NEVER LESS THAN
9 MONTHS BEYOND
THIS POINT

YORKTOWN

B MAR APR MAY JUN JUL AUG SEP OCT NOV DEC
1781

BIBLIOGRAPHY

1. PRIMARY SOURCES: MANUSCRIPTS.

A. Public Record Office

   (i) *Official Records.*

Colonial Office, Military Correspondence, 1783-1784.	CO 5/83-111
Colonial Office, Admiralty Letters.	CO 5/119-132
Colonial Office, Correspondence with the Treasury.	CO 5/145-153
Colonial Office, Promiscuous Correspondence, 1779-1784.	CO 5/182-184
Colonial Office, Military Entry Books, 1771-1782.	CO 5/235-240
Colonial Office, Dispatches to Commanding Officers.	CO 5/243-245
Colonial Office, Departmental Correspondence.	CO 5/254-262
Treasury, Miscellaneous Papers, 1774-1783.	T 1/510-595
Treasury Out Letters.	T 27/31-35
Treasury Board Minute Books.	T 29/44-53
Treasury Commission Books.	T 40/9-12
Commissary General in Canada to Treasury.	T 64/102-103
Treasury to Commissary General in Canada.	T 64/104
Treasury to Commander-in-Chief in America.	T 64/105-107
Commander-in-Chief in	

America to Treasury.	T 64/101, 108-110, 112, 113
Records of a Board of General Officers at New York.	T 64/111
Commissary General in America to Treasury.	T 64/114, 118, 120
Treasury to Commissary General in America.	T 64/119
Commander-in-Chief in Canada to Treasury.	T 64/115
Correspondence with Anthony Merry.	T 64/117
Treasury-Navy Board Correspondence.	T 64/200-201
War Office Commission Books.	WO 25/32-37, 91-95
Head Quarters Records, America.	WO 28/2-10
American Rebellion, Entry Books.	WO 36/1-4
Commissariat Accounts.	WO 60/11-32
State Papers, Domestic; Minutes of a parliamentary inquiry into the conduct of General Howe.	SP 37/18
Declared Accounts of Public Accountants.	AO 1
Commissariat Accounts, America.	AO 3/224
Diverse Accounts and Vouchers.	AO 3/118-122
Warrants and Commissions.	AO 15/61-67
Treasury to Commander-in-Chief and Commissary General in America.	AO 16/10
Navy Board Minutes.	ADM 106/2604-10
Commander-in-Chief in America to Admiralty.	ADM 1/484-490

(ii) *Other Collections.*

Chatham Papers.	PRO 30/8
Cornwallis Papers.	PRO 30/11
Documents of Unknown Ownership: Letters of Surgeon Richard Hope.	PRO 30/39/1
Carleton Papers.	PRO 30/55

B. British Museum

Add. Mss. 21,661-21,892, Haldimand Papers.

Add. Mss. 24,322, Miscellaneous Letters.

Add. Mss. 32,413, "Some account of the American War between Great Britain and her Colonies," in the form of a diary by Lt. William Digby, 53rd Regiment.

Add. Mss. 32,627, Journal of Alexander Chesney, 1772-1782.

Add. Mss. 33,030, Newcastle Papers.

Add. Mss. 34,416-34,417, Auckland Papers.

Add. Mss. 38,343, Liverpool Papers.

C. Somerset House

Probate Court of Canterbury, Records.

D. Scottish Record Office

King's Remembrancer's Office: Letters and Papers. Letters and papers relating to the activities of Major George Hay, Commissary for Captures in procuring provisions for the forces and dealing with captured Rebel property, 1780-1792.

Exemplification of the State of Account of Lt. Gen. James Robertson, Barrack Master General in North America, 1765-1776.

G.D. 21, Cunningham of Thortoun. Notebooks containing journal of Lt. (latterly captain) John Peebles of the 42d or Royal Highland Regiment during the War of Independence.

G.D. 24, Abercarrny Collection: Sec. 1, 458. Letters of Thomas Sterling, 1760-1787.

G.D. 26, Leven and Melville Mss. Letters of Major General William Leslie of the 17th Regiment.

G.D. 153, Gilchrist of Ospidale. Letters, accounts, etc., of Captain John Ross of Auchnacloich with the 71st Highlanders, 1776-1784.

E. Libraries and Historical Societies

William Salt Library, Stafford, Staffordshire.
  Papers of William Legge, 2d Earl of Dartmouth, 1731-1801.
University of Nottingham Library, Department of Manuscripts.
  Newcastle Mss. Collection of Henry Fiennes Clinton, 2d Duke.
    Sir Henry Clinton, Letters and Documents, 1775-1782.
    Papers of Maj. Gen. William Phillips, 1775-1780.
  Mellish Mss. Papers belonging to Charles Mellish (1737-1796).
    Letters from surgeon John Hayes, 1776-1782.
    Letters from Sir Henry Clinton, 1776-1781.
Liverpool Public Libraries.
  Tarleton Papers.
  Parker Family Papers. Letters from James Parker to Charles Stuart Esq.
Royal Artillery Institution, Woolwich.
  Lt. Gen. Sir William Howe, General Orders of the British Army in North America, September 1777 to February 1778.
  Letters and Papers of Brigadier General James Pattison, Mss. 7,9,11,57.
Historical Society of Pennsylvania.
  Correspondence of Daniel Wier, 1777.
William L. Clements Library, Ann Arbor, Michigan.
  Clinton Papers.
  Gage Papers.
  Germain Papers.
  Shelburne Papers.
  Mackenzie Papers.
  Orderly Books and Letters of Lt. Gen. Sir William Howe.
  Letters of James Stuart.

Library of the University of Michigan, Ann Arbor.
Northumberland Papers (Microfilm).
Library of the State University of New York at Buffalo.
British Army Headquarters Papers, America (Microfilm). These are the so-called "Carleton Papers." The originals are in the Public Record Office.
Lt. Gen. Sir William Howe, Narrative in a Committee of the House of Commons (Microfilm).
New-York Historical Society.
Papers Relating to Gen. William Dalrymple and his work as Quarter Master General.
Gates Papers.
Letter Book of Commissary General Daniel Wier, 1778-1780.
Commissary's Day Book, 1777-1779.
Quarter Master General's Account Book, 1777-1783.
Papers of Staats Morris Dyckman (Microfilm).
New York Public Library.
British Army in America.
Miscellaneous Mss., 1734-1815.
Journal, probably compiled by a member of the 47th Regiment of Foot, at Boston 1775-1776, and in Canada, 1776-1779.
Papers of Chief Justice William Smith.
West India Committee.
Minute Books, Vols. I and II, of the Committee of West India Planters and Merchants.
Ipswich and East Suffolk Record Office.
Albemarle Papers.

F. Private Collections

Baron Rayleigh, Berwick Place, Hatfield Peverel, Essex.
Papers of Francis Rush Clark.

2. PRIMARY SOURCES: PERIODICALS.

Court and City Register
Gentleman's Magazine
London Evening Post
Royal Kalendar
Universal British Dictionary

3. PRIMARY SOURCES: PRINTED.

Adair, D., and John A. Schutz (eds.). *Peter Oliver's Origin and Progress of the American Revolution*, San Marino, 1961.

Almon, J. (ed.). *Parliamentary Register*, London.

Anburey, T. *With Burgoyne from Quebec: An Account of the Life at Quebec and of the Famous Battle at Saratoga*, ed. S. Jackman, Toronto, 1963.

André, Major John. *Major André's Journal*, Tarrytown (N.Y.), 1930.

Baxter, J. P. (ed.). *The British Invasion from the North: The Campaigns of Generals Carleton and Burgoyne from Canada, 1776-1777, with the Journal of Lieutenant William Digby*, Albany, 1887.

Boulton, C. K. (ed.). *Letters of Hugh, Earl Percy, from Boston and New York, 1774-1776*, Boston, 1902.

Brown, M. L. (ed. & trans.). *Baroness von Riedesel and the American Revolution*, Chapel Hill (N.C.), 1965.

Buettner, J. C. *Narrative of Johann Carl Buettner in the American Revolution*, New York, n.d.

Burgoyne, Lt. Gen. J. *A State of the Expedition from Canada*, London, 1780.

A Supplement to A State of the Expedition from Canada: Containing General Burgoyne's Orders, London, 1780.

Carter, C. E. (ed.). *The Correspondence of General Thomas Gage with the Secretaries of State and with the War Office and the Treasury, 1763-1775*, New Haven, 1933, 2 vol.

Clinton, Sir Henry. *The American Rebellion: Sir Henry Clinton's Narrative of his Campaigns, 1775-1782, with an Appendix of Original Documents . . .*, ed. W. B. Willcox, New Haven, 1954.

DeFonblanque, E. B. *Political and Military Episodes in the Latter Half of the Eighteenth Century, Derived from the Life and Correspondence of the Rt. Hon. John Burgoyne, General, Statesman, Dramatist*, London, 1876.

Eddis, W. *Letters from America, Historical and Descrip-*

tive, Compromising Occurrences from 1769 to 1777 Inclusive, London, 1792.

Force, P. (ed.). *American Archives: Fourth Series, Containing a Documentary History of the English Colonies in North America from the King's Message to Parliament of March 7, 1774, to the Declaration of Independence by the United States,* Washington, 1837-1846, 6 vol.

Fortescue, Sir J. (ed.). *The Correspondence of King George the Third from 1760 to December 1783,* London, 1927-1928, 6 vol.

Hadden, Lt. J. M. *Journal Kept in Canada and Upon Burgoyne's Expedition in 1776 and 1777,* ed. H. Rogers, Albany, 1884.

Harcourt, E. W. (ed.). *Papers of Lt. Col. William Harcourt,* Oxford, 1880.

Historical Manuscripts Commission. *Report on the Manuscripts of the Earl of Dartmouth,* London, 1895.

Mss. of the Earl of Carlisle, London, 1897.

Report on the Manuscripts of the Late Reginald Hastings, Esq., of the Manor House, Ashby de la Zouche, London, 1928-1947, 4 vol.

Report on Manuscripts in Various Collections, London, 1901-1914, 8 vol.

Report on the Manuscripts of the Marquess of Lothian Preserved at Blickling Hall, Norfolk, London, 1905.

Report on American Manuscripts in the Royal Institution of Great Britain, London, 1904-1909, 4 vol.

Report on the Manuscripts of Mrs. Stopford-Sackville of Drayton House, Northamptonshire, London, 1904-1910, 2 vol.

Jones, T. *History of New York During the Revolutionary War, and of Leading Events in the Other Colonies at that Period,* ed. E. F. DeLancy, New York, 1879, 2 vol.

Journal of the House of Commons, XXXVII-XXXIX.

Lamb, R. *An Original and Authentic Journal of Occurrences During the Late American War,* Dublin, 1809.

Memoir of His Own Life, Dublin, 1811.

Lydenberg, H. M. (ed.). *Archibald Robertson, Lieutenant*

General Royal Engineers, His Diaries and Sketches in America, 1762-1780, New York, 1930.

Mackenzie, F. *Diary of Frederick Mackenzie, Giving a Daily Narrative of His Military Service as an Officer of the Regiment of Royal Welsh Fusiliers During the Years 1775-1781, in Massachusetts, Rhode Island, and New York*, ed. A. French, Cambridge, 1930, 2 vol.

New York City During the American Revolution: Being a Collection of Original Papers from the Manuscripts in the Possession of the Mercantile Library Association of New York City, New York, privately printed, 1861.

New-York Historical Society, *Collections*:

    1875—"Correspondence of Major General James Pattison."

    1881—"The Montressor Journals," ed. G. D. Scull.

    1882—"Lt. John Charles Philip von Kraft, Journal, 1776-1784," ed. & trans. T. H. Edsall.

    1883—"Letter Book of Captain A. McDonald, 1775-1779."

    1883-84—"Kemble Papers."

    1888—"General Orders Issued by Lt. Gen. Sir William Howe, 1775-1778."

    1916—"Minute Book of a Board of General Officers of the British Army in New York, 1781."

    1917—"Journal of Three Battalions of Loyalists Commanded by Brig. Gen. Oliver Delancy, 1776-1778."

New Complete Guide to all Persons Who Have Any Concern with the City of London, London, 1772.

O'Callahan, E. B. *The Orderly Book of Lieutenant General John Burgoyne*, Albany, 1860.

Pettengill, R. W. (ed.). *Letters from America of Hessian and Waldeck Officers*, Boston, 1964.

Postlethwaite, M. *Universal Dictionary of Trade and Commerce*, 4th ed., London, 1774, 2 vol.

Pulteney, Sir J. M. *Letters from America: Being the Letters of a Scots Officer, Sir James Murray, to his Home During the War of American Independence*, ed. E. Robson, Manchester, 1951.

Raymond, W. O. (ed.). *Winslow Papers, A.D. 1776-1826*, St. John (N.B.), 1901.

Ross, C. (ed.). *Correspondence of Charles First Marquis Cornwallis*, London, 1859, 3 vol.

Sabine, W.H.W. (ed.). *Historical Memories . . . of William Smith, Historian of the Province of New York, Member of the Governor's Council, and last Chief Justice of that Province Under the Crown*, New York, 1956-1958, 2 vol.

Searle, A. *The American Journal of Ambrose Searle, Secretary to Lord Howe, 1776-1778*, ed. E. H. Tatum, San Marino, 1940.

Simcoe, Lt. Col. J. G. *Simcoe's Military Journal: A History of a Partisan Corps Called the Queen's Rangers . . .*, New York, 1968.

Simes, Thomas. *Military Guide to Young Officers*, London, 1776, 2 vol.

Stedman, C. *The History of the Origin, Progress, and Termination of the American War*, London, 1794.

Stevens, B. F. (ed.). *Facsimiles of Manuscripts in European Archives Relating to America, 1773-1783*, London, 1889-1898, 25 vol.

Stone, W. L. (ed. & trans.). *The Journal of Captain Georg Pausch, Chief of the Hanau Artillery During the Burgoyne Campaign*, Albany, 1886.

Stone, W. L. (ed. & trans.). *Letters of Brunswick and Hessian Officers During the American Revolution*, Albany, 1891.

Stuart, Lt. General C. *Letters: New Records of the American Revolution: the Letters, Manuscripts and Documents Sent by Lt. General Sir Charles Stuart, to His Father, the Earl of Bute, 1775-1779, and Letters of General Howe, General Clinton, and Other Officers to Sir Charles Stuart, during the Revolution, 1779-1781*, London, privately printed, 1927.

Stuart-Wortley, the Hon. Mrs. E. (ed.). *A Prime Minister and His Son, from the Correspondence of the 3rd Earl of Bute and of Lt. General the Hon. Sir Charles Stuart, K.B.*, London, 1925.

Tarleton, B. *A History of the Campaigns of 1780 and 1781 in the Southern Provinces of North America*, Dublin, 1787.

Uhlendorf, B. A. (ed. & trans.). *The Revolution in America: Confidential Letters and Journals, 1776-1784, of Adjutant General Major Baurmeister of the Hessian Forces*, New Brunswick (N.J.), 1957.

Wilkins, W. H. *Some British Soldiers in America*, London, 1914.

Wyvill, C. *Political Papers, chiefly respecting the attempt of the county of York and other Considerable Districts . . . to effect a reformation of the Parliament of Great Britain*, London, 1794-1808.

4. SECONDARY SOURCES.

Abbott, Wilbur C. *New York in the American Revolution*, New York, 1929.

Albion, R. G. *Forests and Sea Power: The Timber Problem of the Royal Navy*, Cambridge, Mass., 1926.

Alden, J. R. *General Gage in America*, Baton Rouge, 1948.

Allen, G. W. *A Naval History of the American Revolution*, New York, 1962, 2 vol.

Anderson, T. S. *The Command of the Howe Brothers During the American Revolution*, New York, 1936.

Atkinson, C. T. "British Forces in North America, 1774-1781: Their Distribution and Strength," *Journal of the Society for Army Historical Research*, XVI, 1937; XX, 1941.

Baker, N. *Government and Contractors: The British Treasury and War Supplies 1775-83*, London, 1971.

Barck, O. T., Jr. *New York City During the War for Independence*, New York, 1931.

Bargar, B. D. *Lord Dartmouth and the American Revolution*, Columbia (S.C.), 1965.

Binney, J.E.D. *British Public Finance and Administration, 1774-1792*, Oxford, 1958.

Bailyn, B. *The Ideological Origins of the American Revolution*, Cambridge (Mass.), 1967.

Boatner, M. M. *Encyclopedia of the American Revolution*, New York, 1966.

Bowler, R. A. "Sir Henry Clinton and Army Profiteering: A Neglected Aspect of the Clinton-Cornwallis Controversy," *William and Mary Quarterly*, Third Series, XXXI, Jan 1974.

Burke, Sir J. B. *Burke's Genealogical and Heraldic History of the Landed Gentry*, London, 1937.

Burt, A. L. *The Old Province of Quebec*, Toronto, 1933.

Christie, I. R. *The End of North's Ministry, 1780-1782*, London, 1958.

    Wilkes, Wyvill and Reform: The Parliamentary Reform Movement in British Politics, 1760-1785, London, 1962.

Clark, D. M. *The Rise of the British Treasury*, New Haven, 1958.

Clark, Jane. "The Command of the Canadian Army for the Campaign of 1777," *Canadian Historical Review*, X, June 1929.

Clark, W. B. *George Washington's Navy*. Baton Rouge, 1960.

Clode, C. M. *The Military Forces of the Crown*, London, 1869, 2 vol.

Curtis, E. E. *The Organization of the British Army in the American Revolution*, New York, 1926.

Dabney, W. M. *After Saratoga: The Story of the Convention Army*, Albuquerque, 1954.

Davies, W. E. "Privateering around Long Island during the Revolution," *New York History*, XX, 1939.

Dickerson, O. M. *The Navigation Acts and the American Revolution*, Philadelphia, 1951.

Eelking, Max von. *The German Allied Troops in the North American War of Independence, 1776-1783*, trans. J. G. Robertson, Albany, 1893.

Ford, C. *A Peculiar Service*, Boston, 1965.

Ford, W. C. *British Officers Serving in the American Revolution, 1774-1783*, Brooklyn, 1897.

Fortescue, J. W. *History of the British Army*, London, 1899-1920, vol. III.

French, A. *The First Year of the Revolution*, Boston and New York, 1934.

Freeman, D. H. *George Washington*, New York, 1962, vols. 4, 5.

Gee, Olive. "The British War Office in the Later Years

of the American War of Independence," *Journal of Modern History*, XXVI, June 1954.

Glover, R. *Peninsular Preparation*, Cambridge, 1963.

Gruber, Ira D. *The Howe Brothers and the American Revolution*, New York, 1972.

Higgenbotham, D. "American Historians and the Military History of the American Revolution," *American Historical Review*, LXX, October 1964.

Hitsman, J. M. *Safeguarding Canada, 1763-1871*, Toronto, 1968.

Hufeland, O. *Westchester County During the American Revolution, 1775-1783*, New York, 1926.

Huston, J. A. *The Sinews of War: Army Logistics 1775-1953*, Washington, 1966.

Johnson, V. L. *The Administration of the American Commissariat during the Revolutionary War*, Philadelphia, 1941.

Johnston, H. P. *Observations on Judge Jones' Loyalist History of the American Revolution: How Far is it an Authority?*, New York, 1880.

Lanctot, G. *Canada and the American Revolution, 1774-1783*, trans. M. C. Cameron, Cambridge (Mass.), 1967.

Lossing, B. J. *Pictorial Field Book of the Revolution*, New York, 1850-1852, vol. II.

Lowell, E. J. *The Hessians and the Other German Auxiliaries of Great Britain in the Revolutionary War*, Port Washington (N.Y.), 1965.

Lundin, C. L. *Cockpit of the Revolution; The War of Independence in New Jersey*, Princeton, 1940.

Mackesy, P. *The War for America, 1775-1783*, London, 1964.

Mahan, A. T. *Major Operations of the Navies in the American War of Independence*, Boston, 1913.

Middleton, C. R. "A Reinforcement for North America, Summer 1757," *Bulletin of the Institute of Historical Research*, May 1968.

Namier, L. B. *England in the Age of the American Revolution*, London, 1930.

Namier, Sir L. and J. Brooke (eds.). *History of Parliament, 1754-90*, London, 1964.

Nelson, W. H. *The American Tory*, Oxford, 1961.

Ogburn, C. *The Marauders*, New York, 1956.

Palmer, R. R. *The Age of the Democratic Revolution*, Princeton, 1959.

Pargellis, S. M. *Lord Loudoun in North America*, New Haven, 1933.

Preston, R. A., S. F. Wise, and H. O. Werner. *Men in Arms*, 2nd ed., New York, 1962.

Risch, E. *Quarter-Master Support of the Army, 1775-1939*, Washington, Office of the Quarter Master General, 1962.

Robson, E. *The American Revolution in its Political and Military Aspects, 1763-83*, New York, 1966.

Scouller, R. E. *The Armies of Queen Anne*, Oxford, 1966.

Shy, J. *Toward Lexington: The Role of the British Army in the Coming of the American Revolution*, Princeton, 1965.

Smith, J. H. *Our Struggle for the Fourteenth Colony*, New York, 1907, 2 vol.

Smith, P. H. *Loyalists and Redcoats: A Study in British Revolutionary Policy*, Chapel Hill (N.C.), 1964.

Swiggett, H. *War Out of Niagara: Walter Butler and the Tory Rangers*, New York, 1933.

Syrett, D. *Shipping and the American War, 1775-83*, London, 1970.

Stryker, W. S. *The Battles of Trenton and Princeton*, New York, 1898.

Treacy, M. F. *Prelude to Yorktown: The Southern Campaign of Nathaniel Greene*, Chapel Hill (N.C.), 1963.

Trevelyan, G. O. *The American Revolution*, New York, 1905-1912, 4 vol.

Turner, E. S. *Gallant Gentlemen: A Portrait of the British Officer, 1600-1956*, London, 1956.

Tylden, Major G. *Horses and Saddlery: An Account of the Animals used by the British and Commonwealth Armies from the Seventeenth Century to the Present Day with a Description of the Equipment*, London, 1965.

Wallace, W. S. (ed.). *The Macmillan Dictionary of Canadian Biography*, 3rd ed., Toronto, 1963.

Ward, C. *The War of the American Revolution*, New York, 1952, 2 vol.

Webster, J. C. "Life of John Montressor," *Proceedings and Transactions of the Royal Society of Canada*, series 3, vol. 22, 1928.

Wickwire, F. B. *British Subministers and American Policy, 1763-83*, Princeton, 1966.

Wickwire, F. B. and M. Wickwire. *Cornwallis: The American Adventure*, Boston, 1970.

Willcox, W. B. *Portrait of a General: Sir Henry Clinton in the War of Independence*, New York, 1964.

"Why Did the British Lose the American Revolution?" *Michigan Alumnus Quarterly Review*, LXII, Summer 1956.

"British Strategy in America, 1778," *Journal of Modern History*, XIX, June 1947.

Willcox, W. B. and F. Wyatt. "Sir Henry Clinton: A Psychological Exploration in History," *William and Mary Quarterly*, Third series, XVI, January 1959.

Wise, S. F. *The Northern Indians in the American Revolution*, unpublished M.A. thesis, Queen's University (Kingston, Ontario), 1952.

Wolseley, Gen. Viscount. *The Soldier's Pocket-Book for Field Service*, London, 1886.

INDEX

accounting, 36, 38-40, 210, 214
Adam, William, 196
admiralty, 12, 109n, 243, 244
Allsopp, George, 213
Amherst, General Lord Jeffrey,
  12, 41
André, Major John, 73, 85-86, 181
Antigua, 54
Apthorpe, Thomas, 162-164
Arbuthnot, Admiral Marriot, 22,
  50, 130-131, 133-137
arms, *see* weapons
army, administrative structure of,
  12-13
army, American, 42, 84, 154, 223;
  in Canada, 214, 216-218, 222
army in Canada, organization of,
  212-214
Arnold, Benedict, 46, 137, 221, 224
artillery, 9, 35-36, 200, 246; with
  Burgoyne, 228-229. *See also*
  ordnance board
Association, Continental, 44
Association Movement, 208-209,
  211
Atkinson, Richard, 194n
audit office, 38, 175-176
Augusta, 90

baggage, 57-58, 229-230
Barclay, Captain, R.N., 44
barrackmaster department, 16,
  32-35, 149, 173-174
barracks, allotment of, 34
Barré, Colonel Isaac, M.P.,
  209-210

Barrington, Lord, 14n, 252
Barrow, Thomas, 164
batt and baggage, 171
Baume, Colonel, 227
Baurmeister, General, 73, 75, 85
bedding, 16, 149
beef, *see* meat
Bennington, battle of, 227
Bergen Neck, 78
bills of exchange, 17-18, 155-158,
  160, 163; profits on, 173
board of general officers, 167, 190,
  197-198
Boston, 14, 95, 158-159, 173-174;
  army at, 29, 147, 150; supply
  problems of, 41-46, 53-55, 60-61,
  95-96, 163; evacuation of, 43,
  62-63, 94, 107-108
Brandywine, battle of, 70
bread, 14, 28, 171; substandard,
  99-100
Brindley, James, 253
Bruen, Major Henry, 184-185
  191-199
Bunker Hill, battle of, 42, 60, 63,
  158
Burgoyne, General John, 49, 114,
  120, 208, 236; at Boston, 62-63;
  campaign of, 57, 214, 225-230,
  240-241, 243; in Canada, 213-218
Burke, Edmund, M.P., 209
Bute, Lord, 68
Butler, William, 100, 178-179,
  253-254
butter, 52, 92, 101, 252
Buzzard's Bay, 45

283

LIBRARY OF CONGRESS CATALOGING IN PUBLICATION DATA

Bowler, Arthur, 1930-
    Logistics and the failure of the British Army in America,
1775-1783.
    Bibliography: p.
    Includes index.
    1. United States—History—Revolution, 1775-1783—British
forces. 2. Great Britain. Army—Supplies and stores—History.
I. Title.
E267.B68   973.3'41   74-30492
ISBN 0-691-04630-1